Technically Together

Digital Formations

Steve Jones
General Editor

Vol. 28

PETER LANG
New York • Washington, D.C./Baltimore • Bern
Frankfurt am Main • Berlin • Brussels • Vienna • Oxford

Michele A. Willson

Technically Together

Rethinking Community within Techno-Society

PETER LANG
New York • Washington, D.C./Baltimore • Bern
Frankfurt am Main • Berlin • Brussels • Vienna • Oxford

Library of Congress Cataloging-in-Publication Data

Willson, Michele A.
Technically together: rethinking community within techno-society /
Michele A. Willson.
p. cm. — (Digital formations; v. 28)
Includes bibliographical references and index.
1. Information technology—Social aspects. 2. Internet—Social aspects.
3. Community—Philosophy. 4. Social interaction. I. Title. II. Series.
HM851.W555   303.48'33—dc22   2004022837
ISBN 0-8204-7613-7
ISSN 1526-3169

Bibliographic information published by **Die Deutsche Bibliothek**.
Die Deutsche Bibliothek lists this publication in the "Deutsche
Nationalbibliografie"; detailed bibliographic data is available
on the Internet at http://dnb.ddb.de/.

Cover design concept by Marika Auret
Cover art by Annette Iggulden, *Portrait of a Friend* (AG), 2002

© 2006 Peter Lang Publishing, Inc., New York
29 Broadway, New York, NY 10006
www.peterlangusa.com

Contents

Acknowledgments

As with any collective endeavor—which is ultimately what any book is—there are numerous contributions and debts that require acknowledgment. These fall across the spectrum of intellectual, practical, and emotional support.

Curtin University of Technology's Academic Study Leave program allowed me the time to finalize the manuscript. A Faculty of Media, Society, and Culture internal grant was also of assistance in this process.

Colleagues and students in Internet Studies have contributed in numerous ways to the development and refinement of ideas in this text. In particular, I would like to thank David Savat and Paul Genoni who have generously provided useful comments on chapter drafts. Craig Calhoun, Paul James, Michael Janover, and Steve Jones have also provided extensive feedback on an earlier version of this project. This feedback has been both provocative and influential, and I hope my responses in this text have been adequate.

The many people involved in Arena publications must also be mentioned. They have demonstrated, in words and in practice, a concern with community and social forms that is both insightful and engaging. This book would not have been the same without their influence.

Damon Zucca, editor Media and Communication, and the production team at Peter Lang provided prompt and helpful advice. Their assistance from afar has made the whole process significantly less daunting.

I would like to thank my mother, Annette Iggulden, for her overall support and for her permission to use the cover art image.

And, as they say, last but by no means least, thanks to my partner Tony, and our children Ben and Asha, for everything. Two small children and a manuscript are simultaneously a joy and a struggle! I couldn't have done it without their love and support.

Parts of the introduction, chapters two and four have incorporated and updated material previously published as Willson, M. (1997). Community in the abstract: A political and ethical dilemma? In David Holmes (Ed.), *Virtual politics: Identity and community in cyberspace.* London: Sage Publications.

Introduction

On each side of the political spectrum today we see a fear of social disintegration and a call for a revival of community. (Giddens, 1994a: 124)

In an age where people have more opportunity to be interconnected across space and time through technologically aided communication than during any other period in history, the (post)modern individual in contemporary Western society is paradoxically feeling increasingly isolated. New ways to understand and experience meaningful togetherness are being sought.[1] Nostalgia underpins some of this impetus. Re-presented memories of 1950s-style communities where moral, social, and public order flourished are contrasted with the depiction of present social forms as chaotic, morally impoverished, and narcissistic. However, there is also, theoretically at least, the desire to formulate more enriching ways of experiencing ourselves *in relation*, which escape the dangers of earlier, restrictive forms of community. The current (both theoretical and practical) interest in community can thus be seen as a search for a more inclusive, enriching way of life and as a reaction to the impersonal, alienating, and individuating effects of (post)modernity.

Community is one of those amorphous concepts that is easily and loosely employed while rarely defined or explained clearly.[2] It is commonly used to refer to a grouping of people with various attributes while also inferring that it is or contains something that is emotionally enriching and valuable. Despite the plethora of different understandings, it seems to me that the essence or fundamental component of any conception of community (recognizing the problems with many of these loaded terms) is an understanding of community as ways of being-together. Community has had a bad reputation; it has been understood as being repressive and conformist. However, it has also been associated with a valued sense of connection and belonging.

The dilemma faced by contemporary community theorists is how to formulate an ethically appropriate theory of community that avoids the excluding and conforming practices of the past, yet is able to recognize the ontologically important aspects of being-together. This dilemma entails balancing concerns for the freedom or autonomy of the individual and concern for social integration; or what I refer to rather awkwardly in this book as the differentiating/integrative dilemma.

Within Western techno-society, innovations in communication technologies create possibilities for new forms of sociality. Technologically mediated social practices have received a lot of attention, among scholars and public alike, in terms of the communal possibilities and constraints they afford. For example, virtual communities—or communities experienced through technological mediation over the Internet—are presented by some commentators as a form of postmodern community and as the answer to the search for a less exclusive or repressive experience of community. Writers such as Howard Rheingold and Mark Poster suggest that technological communities could provide the solution to the differentiating/integrative dilemma that community theorists are seeking. Likewise, writers such as Manuel Castells or Barry Wellman point to the advantages of mediated sociality for the "networked individual." While technological practices certainly offer social opportunities, I am uneasy about turning to the proclaimed liberatory and interconnective potential of these new relational forms for a vision of future ways of being-together. I am also uneasy about uncritically valorizing the so-called networked society. In view of society's reliance on technology to solve its problems, some skepticism toward and further examination of the claims surrounding technologically mediated social forms is required. For it seems plausible that this hunger for community evident in (post)modernity is in fact partly driven by the experience and implications of being an individual within a technologically organized and aided society.[3]

Broad recognition of the importance of considering interrelational or intersubjective activity *is* taking place.[4] The postmodern emphasis on the micro has too often meant that the focus has been placed solely on the individual, subject, or self. Relations with others (though concern over these relations is often the proclaimed rationale behind many postmodern approaches) have been either neglected or posited as a source or site of oppression. More recent work on community and networked relations could be seen as an attempt to redress this imbalance. Yet there is also recognition among community theorists of most orientations that a return to a traditional style of community is neither possible nor desirable. Hence the subtitle of this book: *Rethinking*

Community within Techno-Society. In this context, techno-society is being used as a shorthand term to refer to (predominantly Western) societies where the dominant modes of interaction and integration are increasingly technologically mediated. The title, *Technically Together*, is therefore part description and part question. It refers to the increasing ways in which being-together is technologically mediated, and it also questions the form, degree, and experience of this type of togetherness.

This book attempts a number of things. Its central premise is that the increasingly dominant practices of technological mediation and extension of social relations mean that we need to rethink our understandings and practices of community. Using communications technologies extends the capacity to connect with people through space and time, therefore enabling the continuation and extension of relations of community. Interpersonal interconnectivity is consequently heightened for both the individual and the community. Yet changing experiences of time, space, and the body, as a result of technological possibilities, impact on our ways of being-together altering individual subjectivity and intersubjective relations. These changing social relations require conceptualizing and discussing according to their positioning within and across various forms of community.

However, I also want to explore a number of contemporary writings on community to determine their understanding(s) of community and if and how they address technologically mediated social practices. The second half of the book is devoted to this task.

Throughout, questions are asked about the social and ethical ramifications of mediated social practices and the ways in which we understand these. Before progressing with these investigations, however, some background information and definitional concerns need to be addressed. For example, what is meant by *virtual communities*? If I argue that technologically extended social relations have ramifications for subjectivity and thus for community forms, then how is subjectivity to be understood? What do I mean when I refer to ontological categories, and to the ways in which different experiences of time, space, and embodiment are important to our ways of being-together? These issues are outlined briefly below.

Virtual Communities

At the very moment that there is talk about the loss of "real" community, many theorists, researchers, and practitioners—groups who don't typically "speak" to one another—all appear to share a common interest in the community enabled by the Internet. (Renninger & Shumar, 2002: 1)

In 1993 Howard Rheingold published a now-famous book entitled *The Virtual Community: Homesteading on the Electronic Frontier*. In it, he wrote of the liberating and inclusive potential of (virtual) communities realized through computer-networked interaction.[5] When linked to telecommunications networks, computer systems allow people to communicate with one another locally, nationally, and globally. Within these various networking systems, both community interaction and access to information can take place.

Virtual community is a term commonly used to describe communities that exist within bulletin boards, conference groups, MUDs, MOOs, and other interactive communication systems.[6] Increasingly, newer phenomena like MMOGs (massively multiple online games) and weblogs also fall within this category. Interaction is (still) predominantly textual, conducted through a keyboard. This is changing over time with the increasing sophistication of virtual reality technologies, the continual enhancement of graphic and video technologies, and the widening applications of digital technologies. However, while visual information remains largely limited to text-based description, and audile or other sensorial information is excluded from the interaction, the player or community member is able to depict her/himself in whatever shape, form, or gender s/he desires. The participants in any of these virtual communities interact, discuss problems, and offer support to those who are suffering personal crises and yet usually cannot *see* or *touch* the individuals with whom they interact; there is no physical person-to-person contact.

In 1993 Rheingold generally saw the future potential of these virtual communities optimistically, as a way in which democracy could be enhanced through increased citizen participation in the decision-making processes of government.[7] He likened interaction via the computer monitor to the re-creating of a public space where vigorous social discourse can take place. Within this public space, all who have access to the technological resources can participate. Rheingold argued that the interactions that take place through computers are *equalizing* (Rheingold, 1993: 62–63) in the sense that social and professional positions are invisible and do not enable the possessors of these privileges in the real world any such privileges or rights within the virtual community itself. Such communities, he argued, enable people to interact unencumbered by the prejudices they may experience in face-to-face encounters due to their embodied identities. Issues of race, age, gender, or disability are left behind, enabling freer, more equitable communities to develop. And while his later writings are more critically aware of the less utopian possibilities of virtual community engagement, his belief in these claims seems to still hold. [8]

Rheingold's portrayal of technological communities (and more recently of "smart mobs") creates the impression of new, possibly postmodern, modes of human interaction and of social forms. Mark Poster would seem to agree. Indeed, in 1995 Poster argued that we were entering what may end up being a new age: "the second media age" as he referred to it. This new age, he suggested, may have fundamental implications for a participant's subjectivity and her/his experiences of identity. The emergence of this new age is attributed to the possibilities enabled by new interactive communication technologies. Poster, along with many other Internet writers, argues that new interactive media enables a level of identity fluidity previously unknown. He writes that the new technologies are able to enhance social communication and community among those multiple fragmented identities that are symptomatic of the postmodern age. Such enhancement is seen as being transformative in the sense of opening up possibilities for new forms of community within techno-society.

This perception raises many questions. Are technological communities the vision of the future or simply a fantasy driven by the desire for a more enriching, interactive lifestyle? Does the *technological community* or the *network society* provide the answer for a more enriching social form that avoids the negative consequences of earlier forms of community? Or are these writings simply the hi-tech equivalent of the efforts of other community theorists concerned to strengthen or retrieve community forms? This book explores these questions—arguing that both technological and nontechnological community theorists are attempting to negotiate a balance between the accommodation of difference and togetherness. It also argues that both *types* of community theory fail to adequately consider the implications of the use of technology for understandings and experiences of community.

Community and Technology

As noted above, there is still much theoretical work to be done on the interplay of technology and community. This brings us to the core of this book and the problem with contemporary debates on community. Theorists, I argue, often ignore the issue of technologically mediated social practices (the first position), or else present technology simply as providing the means to achieve, supplement, or undermine desirable community forms (the second position).

The first position (nontechnological) fails to consider that the uses of technology to mediate social practices may warrant considered attention. This failure has more than immediate consequences. The current use of technology—particularly of communication/information technology—leads to the accentuation of a focus on the individual and to her/his compartmentalization. Indeed, as has already been suggested, some of this resurgence in interest into community forms could stem from the individuation that has resulted in part from the application of such technologies. A better understanding of community forms—and the coexistence and interrelationship of these different forms—within techno-society is thus crucial. Similarly, the implications of extending social relations across time and space through the use of technology require analysis.

The second position (technological) is primarily interested in the phenomenal possibilities that communication technology enables. This interest differs depending on how theorists understand the socio-technological relationship and how they understand technology itself. The positions can generally be characterized as follows: technology is seen variously as (1) a tool enabling the supplementation or destruction of existing communities; (2) providing the possibilities for new social forms; or (3) destroying/undermining the possibilities for community. These positions often fail to sufficiently consider the intersubjective implications of abstract social relations enacted through the technology. They do not adequately take into account the implications of changes in the ways in which ontological categories such as embodiment, time and space, and knowledge are experienced and practiced, and how these impact on both the forms and structures of community and on individual subjectivity.

Within Internet and new media studies, considerable attention is being placed on technologically meditated social forms and practices. There is also a growing pool of empirical data on these mediated forms to be drawn on. However, it seems to me that there is still much to be done in situating this work within a broader theoretical understanding of communities and ethical social relations and that there is valuable work being undertaken outside of these studies that could provide critical insight.

Subjectivity

Any discussion of technology and community requires consideration of issues of subjectivity. What is meant by the term *subjectivity* varies according to the theorist and theoretical school to which he or she belongs. For example, the structuralists (e.g., Levi-Strauss) emphasize the role of institutional and formal language structures in the shaping of subjectivity. The phenomenologists (e.g., Husserl, Merleau-Ponty) attribute the formation of a situated subjectivity to historical influences, experiences, and resultant social values and norms impacting on an embedded subject. And the poststructuralists (e.g., Foucault, Derrida) assert the importance of textual, spatial, visual, and discursive orderings.

All of these understandings of subjectivity are based on particular presuppositions about the subject and subject formation. The structuralists see the subject as a construct created through the structures and application of language. Language represents objects and ideas to us, thus portraying a specific understanding of the world and of ourselves. The phenomenologists understand the subject as socially and historically embedded; shaped by the phenomenal experiences encountered through life. The poststructuralists, on the other hand, broadly see the subject ("the self" would be a more appropriate term here) as decentered and multiple, implicated in and influenced through the application of knowledge, language, and images. The postmodern subject is represented as multiple and fluid, differing in subjectivity according to the influences and expectations enacted on the self. However, these are broad and by no means exhaustive outlines, and many theorists would exist in the margins and overlaps of several of these approaches.

Subjectivity, in the way in which I will use the term, refers to the ontological and phenomenal consequences of being an active social being within a particular body, a being who interacts and is interacted with, and who is positioned temporally and spatially. Therefore, a person's subjectivity is shaped by the historical, structural, and cultural/social settings into which s/he is born and lives: her/his embodied particularity; the identity that is attributed by these settings (indeed, some would say multiple identities attributed by a multilayered modern setting); and her/his intersubjective relations. This understanding emphasizes the agency, the sociality, the historicity and the particularity of the subject. It also highlights the socially embedded/constituted nature of the subject and her/his resultant subjectivity. This means that when considering the subjects of a community it is not possible to examine these subjects in isolation from the social environment in which they are positioned.

A Question of Form and Content

As stated, subjectivity and intersubjective relations are shaped through the interplay of societal, cultural, historical, and structural pressures. It is, in a way, an issue of form and content. The content can be the same, but if the form in which that content is manifested differs, the ways in which the content is experienced also differ. *Content*, in the way in which I will use it here, refers to the embedded particularities of social life. *Form* refers to the ways in which these particularities are structured, organized, and framed.[9]

Nikolas Rose (1996) writes that

> '[t]he self' is not that which is shaped by history, it is a particular historical plane of projection of specific projects and programmes that seek to govern humans through inciting them to reflect upon their conduct in a certain manner and act upon themselves through certain techniques.
>
> The human being, from this perspective, is less an entity, even an entity with a history, than the site of a multiplicity of practices or labours. ... The human being is that kind of creature whose ontology is historical; its history requires an investigation of the heterogeneous and localized intellectual and practical techniques that have comprised the 'instruments', as it were, through which being constitutes itself. (300)

I would concur that the human being, as outlined by Rose, is certainly influenced by the disciplines and techniques enacted on him/her. However, to depict the human being simply as a canvas on which work is undertaken is to remove all potential resistance, agency, and ontological importance from that being. Phenomenal considerations are of importance, but it is necessary to also acknowledge the effects that changes to deeper ontological categories have on subjectivity and social relations.

Therefore, the interplay of both form and content should be considered in studies such as those undertaken in this book. Any rigid delineation between phenomenal and ontological considerations is unhelpful—phenomenal influences are incorporated within and impact on considerations of ontology. This is where Paul James's understanding and use of the concept of ontology proves helpful. In *Nation Formation*, James (1996) explains the incorporation or recognition of phenomenal influences on ontological understandings:

> The concept [ontology] is used in the sense of the modes of being-in–the-world, the forms of culturally grounded conditions, historically constituted in the structures (recurrent practices) of human inter-relations. Thus the concept does not fall back upon a sense of the 'human essence' except in so far as the changing nature of being human is always taken to be historically

constituted. The concept is not confined to the sphere of selfhood except insofar as the self is always defined in interrelation with the 'other.' (xii)

This understanding is compatible with my understanding of subjectivity and the recognition of its historically situated and intersubjective nature and is used throughout the book.

Ontological Categories

This brings me to an explanation as to why ontological categories are significant when considering issues of intersubjectivity, technology, and community. I employ the term *ontological categories* to explain various ways of being. Changes in the ways these categories are lived and framed (content and form) result in different subjective and intersubjective relations. Technology is increasingly used to mediate relations within and across social relations, and this mediation is influential in the framing of different community forms. I am therefore interested in exploring the ramifications of altering the ways in which some ontological categories are experienced and understood.

The ontological categories that are particularly significant for this argument are knowledge, time and space, and embodiment. These categories are not distinct and unrelated—all feed into and affect each other—yet it is strategically helpful to treat them as distinct. I will discuss each in turn, in order to contextualize my central argument about the implications of technologically extended social relations for forms of community. The first category to be discussed is *knowledge* or, perhaps more usefully, *modes of social explanation*.

Modes of Social Explanation (Knowledge)

The phrase modes of social explanation is used to refer to the particular knowledge or explanatory schemas that explain the world, its various parts and its interconnections (e.g., cultural understandings, myths, intellectual practices). Knowledge schemas provide frameworks for interpreting and operating within the world in all societies. These frameworks also attribute meanings and interpretations to the other ontological categories mentioned. They explain how the particularities of bodies are to be understood and related to, and how the experiences of time and space are to be conceptualized. For example, Aboriginal people (prior to the European colonization of Australia) did not understand time as a linear chronological process; instead, time was understood within their lived explanatory framework as continuous, and geographically, physically, and socially embedded (Myers, 1986: 52).

Every historical period utilizes particular knowledge and organizational schemas to explain how the world is to be viewed and how social life and production is to be organized and sustained. These schemas, whether mythological, religious, technological, or scientific (or indeed a combination of these), help to shape an understanding of the world and its associated life practices. Organizational practices are also influential.[10] The description of late modern, Western capitalist system, for example, holds various conceptually descriptive representations of specific societal organizations and knowledge frameworks. *Late modern* or alternatively *postmodern* both describe particular organizational methods, explanatory schemas, and practices. Likewise, the term *Western* posits a particular orientation that is attributed in part because of geographical location but primarily because of the particular knowledge and organizational frameworks that traditionally derive from and are enacted in these regions. It is not necessary to outline these descriptions in detail; that has been undertaken in sufficient depth by many others elsewhere. It is enough for our discussion to point to the existence and coexistence of such schemas.

Foucault's writings argue that social institutions or disciplines—which produce, as he calls them, discourses—reflect but also work to shape social understandings and social practices. Institutional discourses create categories that prescribe understandings of normal behavior, outline that which is seen to be deviant or abnormal, and detail the procedures and practices for dealing with these various categories. In *Discipline and Punish*, Foucault outlines the unreflexive normalization processes that occur through the instigation and operation of these discourses, and their adoption by the subject into her/his behavioral framework. This normalization process is maximized through the application of strategies of power (particular ways of organizing people and places in time and space).

However, the above discussion is not meant to suggest that all knowledge schemas that have existed within particular historical periods are complementary or singularly focused in the same direction (e.g., promotion of individualism). The popularity or predominance of particular knowledge schemas can be identified at particular times. These trends mirror to some degree, and also in some degree lead to, the types of social relations and forms of community that are enacted. But such tendencies can also result in a dialectic. The dialectic created by the predominance of notions of individuality and autonomy results in an awareness of a lack of communality. This is where current interests in theorizing community could be situated.

Modes of Social Organization (Within Time and Space)

By referring to time and space as ontological categories, I am describing the ways in which understanding and experiencing time and space have implications for our ontological understandings of ourselves and of others.[11] All societies have their own particular time and space practices. In contemporary Western techno-society, social relations and communicative and informational practices are extended across increasingly larger areas of time and space. This has resulted in different understandings and experiences of time and space. The nation-state has been more easily conceptualized as a community as the development and utilization of transport technologies, of cartography, and of the print and electronic media have enabled the mental cognition of that space as an identifiable entity. The development of the capitalist system of production has necessitated the understanding of time as divisible, measurable, and linear.[12]

Part of Foucault's strategies of power process involves the positioning of people within a particular time and space so as to produce particular behavioral practice(s). Foucault's detailed examination of disciplinary surveillance practices instituted within areas of social life is instructive. In particular, his discussion of Jeremy Bentham's Panopticon demonstrates how the management and ordering of time and space in a particular fashion can lead to the production of certain economies of behavior and of particular subjects. While this particular strand of Foucault's work has come under attack because of his representation of docile bodies, this does not render the concern with, or examination of, the ordering of time and space irrelevant.[13] What is useful is the realization that the ways in which time and space are ordered, understood, and experienced have ramifications for the community, the persons within that community, and also the intersubjective relations among such persons.

Modes of Presence (Embodiment)

Embodiment refers to the fact that we live in bodies and relate through bodies. The fact of having bodies means that each of us is imbued with individual particularities as a consequence of our specific bodies. These particularities are such things as the color of our skin, our sex, our height, and so forth. However, the experience of being in a body and relating according to that body is also affected by the types of knowledge frameworks that are in place—these describe how that body and its relations are to be understood and thus experienced. And it is affected by how that body-in-interaction is placed within time and space. Gail Weiss (1999) prefers to describe this understanding as intercorporeality, drawing attention to the fact that we are socially embedded and that intersubjective relations are necessarily important. She writes,

> [t]o describe embodiment as intercorporeality is to emphasize that the experience of being embodied is never a private affair, but is always already mediated by our continual interactions with other human and nonhuman bodies. (Weiss, 1999: 5)

Some feminists and postmodernists argue that embodied identity is ascribed a particular place by the society's norms and values and that as such, ascriptions of gender, for example, are social constructs. These social ascriptions too have intermittently undergone change over time and across different societies. However, as noted above, there is also an added emphasis that embodiment carries with it specific experiences that are biologically determined and thus have particular influences on the subject (content). As Anne Balsamo (1996) explains in *Technologies of the Gendered Body*, there must be consideration for both the social construction of the body—that is, the way the society understands and constructs the body—and the physical experience of the body with all of its possibilities and limitations (23–24). Living within a body therefore carries with it its own particular biological constraints and considerations, as well as being imprinted with the socially constructed designation of where and how a particular body is situated within a culture. According to such designations, your body colors your perceptions of the rest of the world. You are born, you will age, and you will also die. Your body also has to be fed, washed, rested, and so forth. Yet how these processes are undertaken and understood also is mediated through social discourses and norms.

These ontological categories are discussed in more detail throughout the book. They provide a means, or conceptual language, through which to explore and to explain some of the implications of the increasing technological mediation of social practices. Technically mediated relations have consequences for our understandings and experiences of community and for our relations with the Other. These understandings need to be framed in an ethically appropriate manner.

Ethical Concerns

Any discussion of community and community relations inescapably raises the issue of how to conceptualize and negotiate these relations.

This brings to the forefront concerns over the ethical appropriateness of any theoretical construction. Concern for the Other must either be able to be accommodated or alternatively be justified in the current theoretical climate. When discussing community—particularly in light of its sometimes problematic historical manifestations[14]—such ethical issues are a central concern.

To achieve a politically and ethically appropriate theory, Stephen White (1991: 20) discusses two ethics that he believes need to be incorporated and given equal emphasis: a responsibility to act and a responsibility to Otherness. Any community theory needs to incorporate elements of both these responsibilities to be politically effective and ethically appropriate.

The theorists who are to be considered in the following pages vary in the emphasis they place on such considerations, which has implications for the political efficacy and ethical appropriateness of their theories. What is common to all these theorists is a concern about the isolation or individuation that predominates in contemporary Western society and the perceived need for a strengthening or recognition of connection with others. All grapple to varying degrees with the integrative/differentiating dilemma. However, their adherence to or concern with matters of practice are more problematic. The intersection of the phenomenal and the ontological is graphically demonstrated with the introduction of technological processes to mediate community forms.

Structure of the Book

The book is divided into two parts, consisting of three chapters each. The first part starts the process of constructing a theoretical framework for discussing community, technology, and social relations. Chapter One examines some general understandings of community. It notes the struggle that community theorists face when attempting to conceptualize a notion of community that is accommodating of individual difference while creating/recognizing integrative communal forms. The chapter also posits that any consideration of community necessitates an examination of community's subjective and structural elements. It derives three analytical categories by which to delineate structural forms: traditional, modern, and postmodern, according to the ways in which community mediates its social relations across time and space. Technology is introduced as being centrally involved in both the possibilities for and the predominance of extended community forms (such as modern and postmodern communities). The chapter also

considers the ways in which the subjective categories of community—
bonding, commonality, reciprocity and recognition, and identity—are
negotiated.

Chapter Two explores the possibilities and processes enacted by
the use of information and communications technologies in more detail.
It examines issues of interactivity within the various types and uses of
communication technologies. Interactivity is central when considering
the types of intersubjective relations that are practiced through the use
of technology, and for the subjective outcomes of such practices. Through
the discussion, it becomes clear that the claims made by many
proponents of such technologies as the Internet as to their liberatory
and communitarian potential are less than straightforward. The chapter
considers briefly the implications for social forms as a result of the
utilization and appropriation of technology to mediate and extend
sociality and integrative practices. It takes virtual communities as one
example of extended social forms and explores in more detail some of
the implications of extended or disembodied sociality. It then extends
the phenomenal considerations discussed so far a little further to
consider the types of processes—abstraction, extension and
compression, and instrumental rationalization—enacted through the
employment of these technologies and some of the ontological
considerations that result.

Chapter Three advances the argument that the intersubjective
relations between, and the subjectivities of, community members are
important in understanding community forms. It argues that as these
relations are realized within/across the specific ontological categories
of embodiment, knowledge, and time and space, their structuring has
ramifications for the types of intersubjective relations that are practiced
and experienced. Several types of intersubjective relations are identified
and are used to describe the types of relation held/practiced with the
Other. Technology is introduced as a way in which the extension of
community forms and the mediation of social forms have been enabled,
resulting in various intersubjective outcomes and possibilities.

Part Two of the book carries forward some of the concepts and
analytic distinctions discussed in the previous section and uses these
as a way to examine the works of three contemporary community
theorists.

Therefore, Chapter Four undertakes a critical analysis of the work
of Charles Taylor. Taylor is commonly grouped with other writers such
as Michael Sandel, Michael Walzer, and Alisdair MacIntyre (although
this list is far from exhaustive) into the loose description of
communitarian. Taylor's negotiation of the integrative/differentiating
dilemma is explored through his notion of authenticity (differentiating)

and of communicative relations (integrating). His understanding of intersubjectivity is examined, as are his discussions of the implications of technology. Consideration of his approach to the subjective considerations discussed in Chapter One is undertaken, as is his approach, if any, to structural questions.

Chapter Five discusses the work of French theorist Jean-Luc Nancy. In particular, it examines Nancy's most commonly cited work on community, *The Inoperative Community*, which explores an understanding of community that takes place in the space *between* singular beings—or more correctly, at the site or *limit* where singular beings meet. Nancy negotiates the integrative/differentiating dilemma through an approach that highlights the incomplete sharing of this *between*, and of the importance of literature (integrative), and the existence and activities of singular beings (differentiating).[15] Nancy's notion of subjectivity is also explored, and an attempt is made to draw out the implications of his (limited) statements about technology. From here his theoretical formulations are extended to see if they can accommodate my concerns vis-à-vis technology and community.

Chapter Six turns to a theorist who is interested in the possibilities for community enabled by technological potentialities. Mark Poster negotiates the integrative/differentiating dilemma through his understanding of the communicative and interactive possibilities of new technologies (integrative) and what he sees to be the new and multiple identity possibilities enabled by such interaction (differentiating). His notion of subjectivity is explored, as are his suppositions about the subjective implication of the use of communicative technologies.

Chapter Seven draws together the various threads of the book and explains if and how these community theorists can contribute to a further understanding of the interplay of community and technology. However, this chapter is also interested in highlighting some ethical concerns that become apparent as the book progresses. Relations with the Other are often seen as one of the most problematic outcomes of community formulation and of community practice. Contemporary community theoretical reformulations attempt to address this problematic through abstract processes—either theoretically or technologically. Finally, the conclusion raises some concerns as to the consequences of such abstract processes.

Our use of technology impacts on our experiences and understandings of time, space, and the body. It heightens our ability to connect with others in a manner increasingly unconstrained by temporal or spatial constraints. Yet it also accentuates the individual, who is *lifted out* of the social environment within which s/he is immersed. The increasing dominance of technologically extended social relations has implications for our understandings and experiences of community and community relations. The following pages begin an exploration of the nature and consequences of such implications and review the ability of some contemporary writers on community to adequately explain or accommodate these socio-technological relations. To begin such an undertaking, a conceptual framework needs to be constructed. It is to this task that the book now turns.

Notes

¹ The idea of community is experiencing a resurgence in interest among both theorists and the society at large. America has seen the growth of a Communitarian Network, which claims the community has suffered through the privileging of individual rights and concerns. There has been an increase in the rhetoric of community employed by politicians such as Bill Clinton and Tony Blair (see Willson, 1995). The Third Way is premised on the importance of community (Scanlon, 2000). And numerous texts point to the demise of community and a rise in individualist behavior (for example, Putnam's *Bowling Alone* or Bauman's *Community: Seeking Safety in an Insecure World*).

² Or at the very least, there are so many different understandings that the usefulness of the concept itself has been questioned. For example, see Bell and Newby (1979) for an overview of the many different sociological definitions of community.

³ This is not to take a technological determinist approach, inasmuch as I am not saying that technology alone produces specific, unavoidable practices or outlooks. Rather, I am arguing that the uses to which the technology is applied by the society/ culture; the modes of thought that are accentuated by technological applications; and the practices that are enabled or increased through the technological capabilities available all have ramifications for the experience of subjectivity.

⁴ This has been a recurrent theme through much of the work undertaken by feminist theorists. For example, see the works of Carol Gilligan or Iris Marion Young. This is also, though in a different form, seen in the work of Amitai Etzioni, who argues that the health of the community has suffered through the privileging of the individual in political and social life.

⁵ Since its publication, there have been a number of updates to this book. Such updates reflect the changing practices and demographics of virtual communities, as well as Rheingold's awareness of and engagement with more recent critical literature on the topic.

⁶ While virtual communities—in the sense of communities without propinquity—existed prior to the Internet and networked computers, the increasingly popular adoption of both the term and the practice of online gathering make them an important social form to be considered. The acronyms MUDs and MOOS have been adopted into virtual speak to refer to various virtual community forms, such as Multi-User Domains, etc.

⁷ He is certainly not alone in this vision. The notion of electronic town hall democracy is a common prediction (particularly among early writers) arising as a consequence of the technological possibilities of the Internet. See Rob Kitchin (1998) for some examples. While these claims have by no means disappeared, they are accompanied by more recent critical and less utopian assessments of the Internet's democratic potential.

⁸ Such arguments are extensive throughout writings about the Internet and cyberspace. For just a few examples, see the works of Howard Rheingold, Sherry Turkle, or the edited collections by Steven Jones. However, increasingly critical analyses of virtual communities and online subjectivity are also being published that question the degree of inclusivity and/or the openness of such interactive forms (see, for example, some of the work undertaken by Kolko, Nakamura, and Rodman on race).

⁹ I recognize that these are by no means straightforward or uncomplicated distinctions, and that it could be legitimately argued that content and form are simply positioned within a continuum of social forms. Nevertheless, I continue to employ them as useful analytical divisions.

¹⁰ This is an example of how the different ontological categories are not distinct and separate. Organizational practices involve the combination of being based on particular knowledge frameworks and they also result in bodies and practices being positioned within time and space in particular ways.

¹¹ See David Harvey (1990) for a detailed exploration of the changing ways in which time and space (for example, through the introduction and utilization of cartography) have been explored throughout modernity and postmodernity.

¹² See Harvey (1990) and Anderson (1991) or the edited collection by Friedland and Boden (1994b) for their discussions on the ways in which changes in the ways of experiencing, organizing, and representing time and space have altered conceptual understandings of such categories.

¹³ This is also despite Foucault's own modification of his position with relation to the subject and disciplinary practices in his later works.

¹⁴ Nazi Germany is one example held up to demonstrate the dangers of community.

¹⁵ While this statement is a somewhat inaccurate and clumsy reduction of Nancy's sophisticated analysis, the sentiment is largely accurate.

Part One

~~~

Establishing a Framework: Theorizing Community, Technology, and Intersubjectivity

The first part of this book brings together concepts and understandings that are frequently treated as theoretically disparate areas of analysis: community, technology, and intersubjectivity. Each of these concepts and understandings bring with it a rich and complex theoretical history. To make this daunting task somewhat more manageable, I have chosen to focus predominantly on contemporary understandings and theories (while also attempting not to completely ignore historical complexity). This focus on the contemporary—apart from its strategic motivations— is both consistent with and appropriate for addressing the primary concern of this book: rethinking community within techno-society.

However, to begin this task, a conceptual language must be developed and explained. This is the primary purpose of the first three chapters. These chapters establish a conceptual framework that is used analytically to examine various community writings and to explore the intersubjective implications of bringing together technology and community.

Zygmunt Bauman (1996) writes that

> [y]ou recognize any human condition by what it thinks it does not have but should have; by what it talks about obsessively since it desires it badly while being hopelessly short of the means of acquiring it. You could recognize the modern condition by its compulsive concern with order and transparency. You can recognize the postmodern one by its infatuation with community. (50)

Such a statement suggests that the postmodern world believes that it has lost community. This book asserts that community is not lost, rather that the ways in which we examine, understand, and negotiate being-together need to change. However, before such claims can be made, we need to understand what is meant by *community*.

Chapter One

~~~

The Concept of Community

Community has always been a rather murky political concept, not because it defies all definitions given, but because it seems to collect them. (Hiskes, 1982: 21)

The concept of community has been the concern of sociologists for more than two hundred years, yet a satisfactory definition of it in sociological terms appears as remote as ever....The subjective feelings that the term community conjures up thus frequently lead to a confusion about what it *is* (empirical description) and what the sociologist feels it *should be* (normative prescription). (Bell & Newby, 1979: 21)

Community is once again in vogue. Politicians, media personalities, and many academics are all, it seems, enamored with the possibilities of resuscitating or reinventing community. Whether it is to be achieved through legislative, technological, or social means, different forms and understandings of community are being proposed as a solution to many of the contemporary Western world's social and individual ailments. These different notions of community vary from vague rhetorical or philosophical labels to specific and rigorous outlines of what a community is and how it should behave.

Some of these notions of community are explored in this chapter, which employs an analytical framework to discuss different community forms. Some central elements of community are also extrapolated to provide a basis for further discussion and analysis of various community theories. This approach is taken for a number of reasons. Firstly, most discussions of community are undertaken in the singular as if community is an undifferentiated and universal phenomenon able to be encapsulated as such, whereas I will argue that community can be differentiated according to certain structural or framing considerations. Furthermore, as Hiskes's quotation above states, community is a somewhat amorphous concept, inasmuch as it changes in meaning depending on the circumstances, application, and understandings of the theorist. This means that a concise, all-embracing definition that would adequately cover all views of community is not possible: There are numerous understandings of both community and of the individuals that community encompasses. Indeed, "to assume that there is an essential set of criteria that defines community and social interaction is unnecessarily limiting" (Renninger & Shumar, 2002: 3). One of the ideas that I want to promote in this chapter is that community should not be seen as a static concept: that ways of being-together change; that they are experienced and understood differently at different times according to the ways in which they intersect with ontological categories; and that this experience is not singular—it is more complex than allowed for in much social analysis. But more on this later....

Hiskes (1982) raises the question of whether the concept of community is *descriptive* of a particular kind of social group, independent of ethical considerations, or whether it is a *normative* concept (22). From the research I have undertaken, it can be either or both of these, depending on the theorist. According to these various formulations, communities can be small or large; they can be described according to criteria such as place, language, culture, race, or on practice or profession. For example, for different writers, the nation-state is described as a community (located within common space); writers of science fiction are described as a community if sufficient interaction exists within the group (located around a similar interest); individuals who share a culture or language are also frequently described as a community. Commonplace usage of the term tends toward the descriptive, yet without denying an emotive component; to imply the condition of a group who are *bonded* together by some form of *commonality*, and who identify themselves as members of that group (it has an *identity* component).[1] It thus entails membership, a sense of responsibility, and *reciprocal* obligations.[2]

Before progressing with a more detailed examination of the concept, a couple of methodological issues must be discussed. First, an assertion about the importance of recognizing the value of commonality. People operate within a social framework that, although it may be experienced differently by different individuals, also carries numerous commonalities. These commonalities enable communication and reciprocal practices to be enacted. The existence of commonalities also enables generalizations to be made about uniformly experienced phenomena and socialized reactions.[3] Therefore, while assertions of difference are important, they should not be made without due recognition of, and allowances made for, the many commonalities that exist amongst people from within similar social environments. These commonalities can exist at all ontological levels, from the phenomenal and apparent to the deeply embedded and taken-for-granted. To recognize commonalities is to recognize areas or means by which people can come together and interact together.[4] Therefore, recognition of commonalities (as well as of differences) between people (in their subjective experiences and understandings) and their shared social frameworks is important for discussions of community.

Second, knowledge, embodiment, and time and space were presented in the introduction as ontological categories. To summarize briefly, ontological categories, in the manner in which I employ them, refer to particular aspects or ways of being in the world. These categories are always existent and interrelated, but they can take many different forms according to our changing experience of, or relation to, them. What I want to do here is examine and categorize communities according to the ways in which their social relations and other integrative practices[5] are structured across/through these ontological categories. Obviously, there are numerous other ways in which different forms of community could be examined. However, within the context of this book's overall objective, this method of categorization seems most useful. An ontological categories approach requires that, in addition to examining the subjective considerations of community, the structural (or framing) considerations of community within and across time and space are elaborated. I argue that, although the (subjective) characteristics discussed in the first half of this chapter are generally recognized as features or characteristics of community, these features are affected by their intersection with such structural considerations.[6] Structural considerations therefore form the basis of the second half of this chapter.

Subjective Considerations of Community

> In fact, all communities larger than primordial villages of face-to-face contact (and perhaps even these) are imagined. Communities are to be distinguished, not by their falsity/genuineness, but by the style in which they are imagined. (Anderson, 1991: 6)

As Anderson's innovative work *Imagined Communities* explained, imaginings play an important role in holding communities together across space and through time. The following discussion explores some of the ways in which these imaginings are important and also how they are made possible.

It is helpful at this point to turn to those common elements mentioned previously—*bonding, commonality, reciprocity,* and *identity*—as analytical tools for grappling with community while also recognizing that these elements are not distinct, unrelated, or uncontested.[7] Bonding is the most crucial of these elements, since it is the connection experienced among members that is integral to most understandings of community. Bonding is also one of the more valued—and feared—elements of community. Bonding can override or transcend the compartmentalization of the individual. It can also result in the suppression of difference and the exclusion of the Other. The other elements mentioned all actively work to create and assist in the bonding process and to structure and manage the interrelations of community. Commonplace usage appears a good place to start, since the concept is so often used (uncritically) in this way.

Bonding/Connection

For most theorists, community is understood as being more than a plurality of persons interacting or living together. The experience of membership, of sharing something in common—whether it is a role, an interest, or citizenship of a nation—gives a sense of unity to or connection among participants. Such connection or bonding is commonly reinforced through the operation of rituals and through the use of symbols that can be shared and identified with by all members. This sense of bonding or connection to a community can evoke such sentiment that in some cases, such as the community of the nation, people have been willing to sacrifice their lives to protect it (Anderson, 1991: 7).

Historically, Ferdinand Tönnies used the distinctions of *Gemeinschaft* and *Gesellschaft* to differentiate between two different types of social relation. *Gesellschaft* (translated as society) can be formed anywhere and among any group of persons motivated by "rational will," while *Gemeinschaft* (translated as community) requires a normative, emotive, and spiritual element (or "natural will") to bind its members together.

> The relationship itself, and also the resulting association, is conceived of either as real and organic life—this is the essential character of the *Gemeinschaft* (community)—or as imaginary and mechanical structure—this is the concept of *Gesellschaft* (society). (Tönnies, 1955: 37)

According to this understanding, community is a natural social relation where participants see themselves as parts of an interconnected whole. Society, on the other hand, is understood as a collection of individuals who interact through abstracted social forms with the express aim of furthering their own individual needs and goals; these individuals perceive themselves as located within a group but do not feel they are an essential part of a whole. Instead, society members understand themselves as autonomous units located within a particular environment from within which their own particular needs must be fulfilled. As Tönnies (1955) notes,

> [t]he theory of the Gesellschaft deals with the artificial construction of an aggregate of human beings which superficially resembles the Gemeinschaft in so far as the individuals peacefully live and dwell together. However, in the Gemeinschaft they remain essentially united in spite of all separating factors, whereas in the Gesellschaft they are essentially separated in spite of all uniting factors. (74)

The common understanding of this *Gemeinschaft/Gesellschaft* distinction attributes community with being intimate, organic, and rewarding, an attribute that it is doubtful ever existed in pure form. However, Werner Cahnman (1973) writes that "*Gemeinschaft* and *Gesellschaft* are not categorically opposed entities but contrasting aspects of a continuum of which they are merely extreme limiting points" (7). Elsewhere it is noted not only that these distinctions are ideal types rather than descriptions of existing social forms, but also that "no society could exist if one form or type existed to the exclusion of the other" (Loomis, 1955: xix). It is also necessary to recognize, as Anderson's work demonstrates, that there are less immediately obvious ways in which groups are held together. Even a society as understood by Tönnies would need some central values and modes of practice to be commonly held for that society to exist and function effectively.[8] However, such a differentiation of ideal types is helpful in its recognition that the emotive connotations of community are viewed as more valuable than a simple association. In other words, the nature of the connection among members of a community is imbued with considerable social and personal worth. The possibilities of a coexistence of forms is also useful for the later discussion on structures of community.

As has been mentioned, all communities, particularly the contemporary nation-state, incorporate or are bonded by an *imaginary* element (Anderson, 1991: 6). This, according to Anderson, explains the sense of belonging to and brotherhood with others of that community. Imagining entails a mental/cultural construction that binds people through generating a feeling of their belonging *together* even when the majority of the members of that community may never meet or know each other (Anderson, 1991: 6). This approach has been criticized for placing undue emphasis on a mode of thought that downplays the reality of the social and cultural situations in which community evolves and exists. Such criticism stresses that there are particularistic pressures or events—such as a shared history or shared disasters—that create both a feeling and practice of community.[9] While this may be the case (though Anderson's book is certainly historically embedded), Anderson's book highlights an important aspect of the bonding process: Bonding involves a perceptual, emotive dimension. This feeling or cognition of attachment could be likened to the attachment felt among kin, whereby it is the mental/conceptual understanding that blood and history are *shared* that leads to loyalty and feelings of connection among members.

However, this cognition is not the only prerequisite for community cohesion. Mental connection needs to be reinforced through shared interactive and integrative practices. These practices, and the media/ mediums through which they are enacted, provide a framework for imaginative processes to take place within time and space. Anderson (1991) points to the simultaneously shared practice of reading a national newspaper as one of the ways in which people were able to imagine or frame their conceptualization of themselves as belonging to a nation-state. The media of television and film also enable the extension of the imagination to understand the world as more accessible and conceptually manageable. And, as Holmes (2002: 5) notes,

> [I]n media societies where the geographic and kinship ties of the parish, local neighbourhood, or the industrial slum have virtually disappeared, individuals have historically become very heavily dependent on media of many kinds to acquire a sense of belonging and attachment to others.

The historical continuity of community forms also points to the necessity for institutions—whether formal or informal—within most understandings of community. These institutions ensure the mediation, reproduction, and communication of community norms and values. The importance placed on the role of institutions again depends on one's understanding of community—for example, Jean-Luc Nancy would not agree with the above statement. Nancy's argument, in contrast, is positioned at an extremely abstract or ontological (in the traditional philosophical sense of the term) position. He would argue that such assertions apply to totalitarian or totalizing structures. However, for most writers, such a requirement appears necessary.

Bonding is also represented as playing a practical purpose in the continuation and reproduction of a community. According to Rosabeth Moss Kanter (1972), three elements in understanding individual commitment to communities are identified: the cognitive, cathectic, and evaluative. All three elements indicate some level of commitment to a community; and those that demonstrate all three elements are likely to be the most successful communities. The first element—cognitive— involves the evaluation of the rewards and consequences of participating in a community; an assessment of the degree of personal sacrifice and investment takes place:

> When profits and costs are considered, participants find that the costs of leaving the system would be greater than the cost of remaining; 'profit,' in a net psychic sense, compels continued participation. (Kanter, 1972: 69)

It would seem fair to suggest that the greater the degree of personal investment in a community, the greater the depth of commitment to that community. This leads to the second element—cathectic—which refers to bonding of an emotional and affective nature created among members of that community. And the third element—evaluative— entails the acceptance and use of the community's values and standards by the individual member (Kanter, 1972: 68–70).

Kanter's understanding of community commitment appears to be premised on an atomistic understanding of the individual. She is trying to understand why people choose to belong to, and to participate in, particular social systems such as utopian communities or communes. Apart from the fact that she is talking about specific types of community, the idea of free association or an unrestricted choice of association takes literally the notion of complete individual autonomy. While some community involvements are certainly chosen by an individual, the notion of unconstrained choice undertaken by free-floating individuals is inherently problematic. As I argue in later chapters, such an understanding does not recognize the underlying structural framing of choices.

Therefore, discussions of bonding overlay, and are dependent on, the understanding of the subject that is held by the theorist. As Paul Morris (1996) notes, "It is important to note that *each and every theory of the individual necessarily entails some account of how individuals become, or should become, aggregated*" (226, italics in original). Thus:

> Beginning from the assumption of the existence and reality of the individual, who then, and only then, forges links between herself and other separate and discrete individuals, it becomes all but impossible to conceive of any sort of community at all. One plus one plus one plus one plus one just never seem to add up to more than a number! (226)

Instead, Morris, Nancy, Taylor, and others argue that any analysis must first recognize the socially constitutive nature of human life; that there is an ontological/essential connectedness among individuals or subjects that always and inescapably exists. However, I would also suggest that an awareness or perception of this connectedness needs to be held by self-reflexive people within contemporary society. Without such perception, social practices and institutions are less likely to demonstrate or encourage these interconnections. Instead we need to integrate our understanding of the possibilities for individual choice and individual action within an acknowledgment of, and a social practice that accommodates, the importance of this fundamental sociality. The current uses of and understandings of technology to extend and mediate social relations hold implications for such recognition, and are worthy of further contemplation.

Connectedness requires not only the experience of attachment to others or a sense of a mutual belonging, it also incorporates or is reinforced by certain expectations with regard to the reliability of member responses. Sociological studies have indicated that members' expectations of reliable behavioral and reciprocity responses from other community members are vital for the operation of support networks and feelings of responsibility toward that community.[10] Reciprocity and recognition are essential social processes.

Reciprocity and Recognition
Reciprocity reinforces the bonding process. One rarely feels long-term or significant attachment to a group unless this attachment is experienced as reciprocated (or returned) in some way. Reciprocity is a *process* that involves a mutual (usually asynchronous) exchange of something, whether it is a behavioral response, language, or material item. However, reciprocity need not be restricted to reciprocity of the same, as in an exchange of the same behavior or item. And an act of reciprocity is more than a simple act of exchange; there are other value attachments involved—symbolic, spiritual, or social. There are usually certain commonly understood codes of behavior that members are expected to follow if they are to be accepted by the group. Indeed, there are certain understood and accepted practices within any grouping that hold more meaning than may be immediately apparent. For example, someone may help a member of their community who is in a difficult situation with the implicit expectation that someone—if not the actual person they are helping, then someone else within that community— will help them if they get into a similar predicament. Within virtual communities, for example, such offering of assistance builds trust and forms part of the community-building behavior that is commented on by writers such as Peter Kollock (1999) or Steven Jones (1998a).

There is a human/social expectation of a return for any emotional or physical investment in an interaction. Community endows a level of security experienced with this expectation of reliable responses and the fulfillment of obligations. It therefore instills a sense of order and predictability that is reassuring to participants. From such predictability, members are able to ascertain to some extent—obviously not completely, since responses are reliant on individual human responses and therefore lack complete predictability—the likely outcome of their actions or anticipate the response from intended actions. Community continuity thus requires a history of reciprocal interactions and practices. A historically derived expectation of a reciprocal response or behavior widens an association into a relationship.

Community is fundamentally reliant on and constituted through communication processes. These communication processes, whether of a dialogical, written, or nonverbal form, provide the means by which social institutions and social relations are instigated and maintained. It is through communication processes that we recognize ourselves as social beings; it is our means of connection to others. For the theorists discussed later in this book—Taylor, Poster, and Nancy—it is communication in varying forms that provides the possibilities for and the sites of community. Communication is a reciprocal process in both its ongoing formulation and continual enactment.

The traditional exchange of gifts has been one form of instituting and reproducing community integration and connectedness. Marcel Mauss, in *The Gift: The Form and Reason for Exchange in Archaic Societies*, persuasively argues that complex social institutions are maintained within most if not all societies through elaborate rituals of gift exchange (Mauss, 1990). In particular, he recounts the ways in which tribal practices of gift-giving form part of an important cohesive social mechanism.

One of the ways in which modern societies enact reciprocity is through institutional forms such as the economic market. Pierre Bourdieu (1977) points to the capitalist appropriation of many rituals and gift-giving practices. While both the act of capitalist exchange and traditional gift-giving are understood as calculated (though the latter has less surety of outcome), Bourdieu argues that appropriation has removed much of the symbolic meaning inherent in traditional gift-giving practices and thus diminished their social value. Derrida (1995) too identifies the potential slippage that takes place between understandings and practices of gift-giving and of an economy. He notes that,

> [t]he moment of the gift, however generous it be, is infected with the slightest hint of calculation, the moment it takes account of knowledge [*connaissance*] or recognition [*reconnaissance*], it falls within the ambit of an economy: it exchanges, in short it gives counterfeit money, since it gives in exchange for payment. (112)

Thus, differentiation between market exchange and other forms of reciprocity may be unnecessary when considering forms of community. Instead, the focus might be more productively located with a recognition of the existence of integrative practices and processes (of which reciprocal exchange may form part). Where social forms are practiced across extended space, these practices and processes, of necessity, are more abstract or extended.

Reciprocity also implies recognition, since one can only reciprocate with another actor that one recognizes as such (as another actor). Recognition has been highlighted by identity theorists as playing an important role both within and between communities. It is also an important aspect of any communication process. However, the manner in which a person is recognized is also important—whether he or she is identified or recognized as the Same as the other member/s of the communication process, or seen as an Other who is different (and by inference, unrecognizable in some ways). Recognition therefore implies a shared level of mutual understanding that enables such exchanges to take place and to be understood. This process requires some commonality to exist among participants.

Commonality

> I feel a oneness with other Americans, a sense of common membership with people I have never met or heard of as individuals, with people who in direct interaction might repell or anger me. (Calhoun, 1991: 106)

Connectedness, reciprocity, and communication within a community are all brought about by members' perception that they share certain common characteristics with others in that community. This commonality enables members to empathize, and to gain some form of self-recognition and self-reassurance from others. It enables reciprocal practices to take place and to be understood within a specific context. Race, language, culture, place, religion, life experiences, class, or gender are all characteristics that can be commonly held, and they are used to identify communities (both by participants and by many theorists). Communities continue in the production, reinforcement, and management of other commonalities such as commonly held values, norms, ethics, and worldviews among their members.

Shared histories of events and ideas play a formative role in the shaping of norms, cultures, myths, and sentimental attachment arising from the sense of having suffered, triumphed or fought together. These shared myths and attachments bind participants together, for it is felt that those who hold such shared history and understandings are like oneself and are therefore familiar and understandable or nonthreatening.

The fate of death and finitude is shared by all. For Maurice Blanchot, true community is achieved only at times of crisis. For example, it is achieved among soldiers on the battlefield or when there is a birth or death. For Blanchot (1988) it is the *sharing* of such an intense experience that reinforces one's sense of finitude and yet at the same time one's connectedness to others. He writes: "This is what founds community. There could not be a community without the sharing of that first and last event which in everyone ceases to be able to be just that (birth, death)" (9).[11] He also argues that it is in the *sharing* that the experience is given meaning and recognition. Connolly would seem to agree with such sentiments. He writes: "Thus, in ways the radical individualist inadequately acknowledges, the very individuality of death connects us in life to others and to a future that continues without us after death" (Connolly, 1991: 19).

However, in modern Western society such connectedness is arguably diminished: Birth and death have largely been institutionalized and thus removed from the daily activity of everyday life. Now it is primarily through ceremonies such as funerals or christenings that connectedness is experienced, usually among close friends and family and not among a wider community. As this segregation of life and death from the community and the society accelerates, it further removes the recognition of the commonality of these events from us. It also therefore removes the potential to see the Other as in common with oneself; as someone who too shares such finitude. Technology and technological practices play a role in this diminished connection through associated rationalized activities and the abstraction from embodied contexts. However, technology also increases connection through the possibilities of exposing or communicating events, ideas, and images across time and space. Therefore, we are confronted with images of suffering, war, famine, and death in other parts of the country or other parts of the world in ways that expose our general humanity and finitude in innumerable ways. The real-time broadcasting of the terrorist attacks on the World Trade Center is a graphic example of this exposure. The seemingly paradoxical coexistence of distancing and of bringing-together will be explored in more detail in the following two chapters. However, for the moment, it should be noted that the bringing-together that takes place through technological means is experienced somewhat differently from the same experience when involved in face-to-face contexts.[12]

Commonality is implicit within Anderson's representation of experiences of simultaneity enacted through empty homogeneous time[13] by members of nation-states. Shared language, shared symbols, and shared rituals all play a role in such experiences.

> [T]here is a special kind of contemporaneous community which language alone suggests—above all in the form of poetry and songs. Take national anthems, for example, sung on national holidays. No matter how banal the words and mediocre the tunes, there is in this singing an experience of simultaneity. At precisely such moments, people wholly unknown to each other utter the same verses to the same melody. (Anderson, 1991: 145)

Experiences of simultaneity or commonality are integral to Anderson's conceptualization of imagining, and they reassert the importance of commonalities for bonding processes.

Communities have been criticized for their stereotypical, homogenizing tendencies and exclusive practices. It is often claimed that communities tend to emphasize a particular common characteristic or interest at the expense of other possibly heterogeneous interests held by their members. However, Cohen (1985) argues,

> the *commonality* which is found in community need not be a uniformity. It does not clone behaviour or ideas. It is a commonality of *forms* (ways of behaving) whose content (meanings) may vary considerably among its members. The triumph of community is to contain this variety that its inherent discordance does not subvert the apparent coherence which is expressed by its boundaries. (20)

Lynne Tirrell (1993) concurs that what is found, and is also desirable, in community is a harmony of similar interest, aims, or characteristics; not a homogeneity of these. This is really sidestepping the issue, for it would be impossible for everyone, as Cohen argues, to have exactly the same interests; each person holds his or her own specific interpretations as a result of individual experiences and community interaction. If the argument is that because there are not views that are exactly the same, the community is not as exclusive, then they are missing the point. What holds community together is the *perception* of commonality/similarity. Homogeneity may be too literally interpreted, and more specifically, seen in varying degrees in communities. Tyrell and Cohen thus do not adequately engage with the issue of the exclusivity of community—the implicit assumption being that exclusivity is a negative phenomenon. Yet it is possible and plausible to argue against this assessment. Exclusivity is not in itself negative, although it can certainly lead to negative outcomes. What is the primary issue of concern is rather the ways in which such exclusivity is conceptualized and practiced, and through such processes, the ways in which the relationship with the Other is managed. This is where the integrative-differentiating dilemma faced by the following community theorists can be positioned. These theorists are attempting to find ways of conceptualizing and practicing community that are able to accommodate differences in and between communities while simultaneously asserting commonalities or togetherness.

Another level of understanding of commonality can be seen in discourses about universal community, or the community of humankind. Habermas's (1981) notion of communicative action is one that foresees a universal community of rational discourse, where all those who wish to participate in rational discussion can do so freely. He claims this universal community is possible because of the existence of certain validity claims inherent in rational speech acts. These validity claims are *shared* by all human beings implicitly within and through the processes of communication.[14] Thus, for Habermas, it is the commonality of certain inherent presuppositions of communication that form the basis for a potential universal community of humankind. This means that for Habermas at least, communication is the key to overcoming integrative-differentiating dilemmas. However, I would argue that this approach, while helpful in pointing to both the importance of communication and of commonalities in communicative processes, is not able to deal sufficiently with the nuances of different forms of communication and other integrative practices when they are undertaken through different modes of presence or practice.

As the above discussion illustrates, the notion of commonality can be seen at various levels of perception—as extremely abstract universal qualities or in the form of concrete particular qualities. However, all perceptions of commonality—and it is necessary to emphasize that it is the *perception* or *recognition* itself of commonality on the part of participants that is the crucial ingredient—are important in the creation and self/group perception of identity.

Before progressing to a discussion of identity, however, another issue must be tackled. It has been suggested to me that commonality is not the only reason for people coming together or for community. Instead, it has been suggested that interdependence can also be another dimension or rationale for relationships.[16] In such a scenario, the participants might be connected through the fact of their differences. This seems to me to be a valid point and one worthy of further deliberation. However, it would also seem to me that such an assertion does not rule out the possibility of commonality—it simply alters the type of commonality that is being suggested. In such instances, perhaps it is a commonality of need or of outcome that forms part of the impetus for connection.

Identity

Identity is the sense we hold of ourselves; our perception of who we are and how we present ourselves to those around us. It is also the image that others hold of us that we see reflected in their behavior and attitudes toward us. As such, identity is intersubjective. It is also formed by the experiences, attitudes, and understandings to which we are exposed and that we incorporate into our understanding of ourselves in the world.

Most understandings of community present community identity as distinct from and yet contributing to the identities of the people who compose it, for an intricate interweaving of group and individual identities takes place. According to communitarian theorists, group identity reinforces and assists in creating individual identity. For example, in contemporary Western society, an individual who belongs to, and who identifies her/himself, as a Catholic or Protestant also perceives her/himself as an Australian and as a holder of numerous social and relationship positions—for example, wife, daughter, father, and so on. Or alternately, an individual can be said to belong to the virtual community of "Habbo Hotel,"[17] the local community of Richmond, an ethnic/cultural Asian community, a national community of Australia, and a global community of humankind simultaneously. Each membership demands various roles and actions from the member, but these may be dormant for most of the time. In other words, the contemporary community identity is not perceived as all-encompassing, but as a component or aspect of an overall individual identity. It is far more complex than ascribing a singular identity to each member of a community despite the member possessing the views, beliefs, and practices of that community. However, the community to which one belongs may be said to impute a certain perception or experience to the various other singular identities one possesses. Community norms and practices could be said to provide the social/ontological framework through which comprehension and orientation of individual and group experiences can be achieved.

However, community is also characterized as being understood and practiced as a totalizing identity that subsumes difference. Iris Marion Young writes that the ideal of community

> expresses a desire for the fusion of subjects with one another which in practice operates to exclude those with whom the group does not identify. The ideal of community denies and represses social difference, the fact that the polity

cannot be thought of as a unity in which all participants share a common experience and common values. (1990: 227)

Some of the claims about commonality were dealt with above. With regard to the claims about the totalizing nature of community identity, for now it is sufficient to note that this understanding appears to be premised on the particular understanding of community involved (and this can be encompassed to some extent in the structural characteristics, discussed below), and also on how the community relation is understood (i.e., is the community seen to be an entirety or can it exist in relation with other communities?).

If these elements — bonding, commonality, reciprocity and recognition, and identity — are all part of community as conceived and utilized in everyday language, does this mean that theoretical attempts to reformulate the concept of community wish to abandon or alter any of these elements? Or is it perhaps the way in which these elements are manifested that is of concern? How these issues are approached will be examined in Chapters Four, Five, and Six. Before addressing this issue, however, the argument about structures of community requires elaboration.

Structures of Community

As the above discussion illustrates, communities can take different forms across time and in space. Yet many theorists of community fail to consider in any meaningful or comprehensive manner the different types of interaction that take place within and between communities, the ways these different interactions are framed, or the effects of this framing on the interactions. Where differentiation of communities does take place, it is often centered on a single organizing principle. For example, Paul Morris (1996) concurs with the suggestion that there is more than one form of community. Yet despite undertaking a sophisticated analysis, he utilizes the simple dichotomy of "assent" and "descent" as a way of differentiating two *types* of community. Communities of descent fall into the same category as another commonly used grouping, communities of place, inasmuch as a member is understood as born into the community and incorporates that community's values, rituals, and identity. However, communities of descent need not be attached to a geographical space (as is the case in the usual understanding of communities of place). Instead, it is the participation in and the passing on of certain cultural, religious, and identity practices that constitutes and sustains these communities through and across time and space; Morris uses the example of the Jewish community. Communities of assent, on the other hand, seem to fall within the confines of a community of choice category. These are communities in which one makes a conscious decision to belong. Morris uses the example of Christianity, where members are understood as converted into, rather than born into, the community: It therefore can involve a missionary element where members assent to belonging and conforming to a particular understanding of community. Again, in this type of community there does not need to be an attachment to a particular geographic location or space. The important point for Morris is that communities are more diverse in type and practice than is allowed for in many theoretical discussions of community, and thus any adequate theory must be able to accommodate and recognize this diversity. This assertion is important, and Morris's distinctions are a useful beginning for the further development of a more complex community theory. However, this is only one part of the process. What is also needed is some way of understanding the different forms that these various communities—whether of assent or descent or any other type—take as they are structured differently through and across the various ontological categories.

For my purposes here, and without presuming to be comprehensive, it is analytically useful to appropriate a common distinction among traditional, modern, and postmodern forms of sociality. Recognition of ontological implications is partly encapsulated by the use of these terms. However, these distinctions are introduced reservedly, since they carry a great deal of conceptual baggage: For example, within social theory, these distinctions tend to be employed by theorists as overgeneralized categories of being or to designate particular historical epochs. There are a number of problems with such formulations, not least being the ways in which they tend to be depicted as mutually exclusive phenomena. For the moment, however, and in order to contextualize my preferred use of these terms, I would like to briefly examine the ways in which these distinctions are generally made.

Traditional communities are usually depicted as communities of place where choice of membership does not exist. People are understood as being born in a particular place and into a particular social position; this position becomes a point of reference for the continuing and complex designations of their social roles, expectations, and behavior. There is little public ambiguity surrounding how they are expected to behave, their obligations, or their anticipated life history. The boundaries between these forms of communities are understood as well-defined and fairly inflexible, although they are lived as variously constituted cultural boundaries rather than abstract lines on a map.[18] This form of community conforms to some degree with Tönnies's description of *Gemeinschaft*.

Modern communities are more generally depicted as being communities of choice (or alternately, as *Gesellschaft*). People have the phenomenal sense that they *could* move between communities freely if they so choose, or that they could belong to a multiplicity of communities simultaneously. There is a level of ambiguity about how they are expected to behave, their identity, and how they fit within their society. Boundaries are represented as more porous, enabling a freer, less ritualized movement among these communities and a more flexible membership.

Differentiation between traditional and modern communities is recurrent through the literature. However, a more recent addition to this schema—in the form of postmodern communities—is also important. Ignoring the inherent tensions in coupling together these two terms—*postmodern* and *community*—postmodern communities are presented as extending the degree of choice available to participants in both traditional and modern communities.[19] This extension of choice includes an increasingly flexible identity—through freedom from embodied or geographical identity—and an increase in the possibilities of multiple community memberships. There is considerable ambiguity or choice as to identity formation, expected behavior, and positioning within and between communities. Community boundaries are described as extremely flexible and more open than those of modern communities.

As is apparent from these descriptions, one of the main differentiations between types of communities is the degree and nature of individual *choice* (and thus, by inference, freedom) that community members experience as available to them. From there, other assumptions are made as to the nature and fluidity of identity, or the types of knowledge systems that are available and practiced. The emphasis placed on the degree of choice that individuals experience within these various forms of community (an emphasis, no doubt in part, influenced by the reputation of community as being coercive or restrictive for the individual) is inherently value-laden, with the underlying presumption being that all choice is good and the more choice available for the individual the better. This focus on the individual's freedom to make choices also contains some implicit (and sometimes quite explicit) assumptions about the individual and the relationship between the individual and the larger society. Yet this scenario often fails to accommodate the understanding that the individual is constituted within a societal framework—a secondary but complementary argument that is carried through this book. Indeed I would go further and agree with both Paul Morris and Jean-Luc Nancy (discussed later) that many of the problems that arise when considering community are a consequence of focusing on the individual or conversely on the community as the original point of analysis.[20] Such an approach fails to recognize either the socially embedded nature of persons or the individual differentiations that exist within community; or to consider that numerous forms of community can exist-in-relation simultaneously.

What *is* helpful about such categories—and partly why I have appropriated them here—is that they recognize that changes in the ways in which ontological categories are structured and experienced have some connection with the changing forms and relations of community. The degree of freedom noted in these differing forms of community is linked to (and largely enabled by) the ways in which a community is situated across time and space, and through bodies. I therefore want to (selectively) use these analytical distinctions as overlaying ontological frames of practice and meaning relevant to distinguishing different forms of community. This means incorporating recognition of the coexistence of and interaction among different community forms (despite any possible ontological contradictions that such coexistence might create) framed by a historically dominant mode of sociality. And rather than focus on the degree of individual choice, I want to focus instead on the ways in which these ontological categories—knowledge, time and space, and embodiment—are experienced, structured, and practiced through different community forms. This entails highlighting the primary forms or modes of interaction and integration (as situated in and across time and space), the ways in which embodiment is experienced and practiced, and the knowledge frameworks that are employed within these different forms of community. In particular, the first two categories (embodiment and time and space) receive special consideration, since they are central to the argument of my book. This process requires some simplification, generalization, and the isolation of complex social relations to derive particular characteristics. Yet such a theoretical maneuver is made with the caveat that these are purely analytical categories that would not exist in reality in such a simple or pure form.

My approach shifts the focus, to some extent, from the historically progressive emphases given by the previous descriptions.[21] It allows recognition of changing experiences of identity but draws attention away from a specific and value-laden conception of freedom or choice. It also allows the accompanying assertion that these community forms can and do exist in relation and that this in-relation has implications. Such implications will become apparent as the book progresses.

Therefore, I understand and employ these analytical distinctions of traditional, modern, and postmodern in the following manner. Traditional communities are to be understood as constituted and organized around face-to-face communicative relations and concrete embodied practices.[22] Notwithstanding connections and networks that can be quite extensive, the primary modalities of the experience and practice of social relations within these community forms necessarily operate across relatively small geographical locations. Relationships to time are thus experienced as coextensive, immersive, and continuous.

The modern community encompasses membership over larger geographical areas and thus has a different relationship to time. For example, as noted, Anderson (1991) explores how the imaginings of the nation-state as a community became possible when people were able to understand time as lived simultaneously and chronologically across the community. Such a community form is constituted and organized around more extended communicative relations and abstracted forms of embodiment. Relationships and other integrative practices are mediated through technological and institutional forms.

The postmodern community organizes itself through mediated and abstract integrative practices, where the primary form of interaction and communication is disembodied — detached from presence and mediated through technology.[23] Time becomes experienced as immediate and compressed, multiple and fragmented, yet easily accessible and traversable. Indeed it could be suggested that time becomes more individuated as activities and interactions are increasingly unconstrained by 'real space' temporality. In a sense, online time becomes your time — your information gathering and dissemination, and your social interaction, are largely unconstrained by the time constraints of your immediate environment (when programming, operating hours, and the realities of standard Eastern time constrain such activities in real space and real time).[24] Space becomes irrelevant, or perhaps more accurately, reconceived as detached from corporeality. (As an aside, I had some difficulty in deciding what term to use in describing interaction and experiences outside of cyberspace. *Real life* (RL) is problematic (despite its prolific use in the literature), as it places a distinction between embodied experience as being real and interaction via technology as not real. Participants in virtual communities would obviously wish to contest the unreality of their interaction, which may well play a very real part in their life. This term also fails to take into account the constructed or perceptual aspects of our interpretations of reality in embodied or real space. The descriptive *embodied space* indicates the realm of face-to-face contact alone, and therefore it is also problematic. It is also more unwieldy. In view of this, I decided that the term *real space*—while still not entirely appropriate—is more suitable.)

The members of these three forms of community are all bonded together, although each form experiences this process slightly differently. Traditional face-to-face communities, since they are constituted in terms of embodied presence, of necessity have quite small populations; everybody within the community either knows one another directly or knows of them. It would not be possible to interact within a predominantly face-to-face mode of practice if the population or membership became too large without the employment of disembodied practices.[25] Individual and group histories become common knowledge within the community. There is an intertwining and cross-sectioning of people's lives, bonding people closely together at various levels. The depth and degree of interconnectedness among members is therefore quite extensive and multiplex. Craig Calhoun (1991) refers to these types of communities as constituted through what he refers to as direct interpersonal relationships. Such relationships are understood as "typified by actual or potential face-to-face interaction" with the qualification that "even directly interpersonal relationships are not simply given materially but are constituted in communication and intersubjective understanding" (97).

Within modern communities, on the other hand, interactive and integrative practices are extended via the use of institutional and technological forms. This means that geographical space can be traversed in a way that diminishes the temporal and spatial constraints faced by traditional communities. Such a capacity means that community populations can be larger and more dispersed across space. Members can hold the perception or experience of being bonded together and all belonging to the same community (such as the nation-state)—without necessarily ever meeting one another. Such forms of extended community are, in many ways, less prescriptive with regard to the particularities or minutiae of members' everyday practices than is the case with embodied traditional communities, where the overlapping of individual lives and practices are coextensive.[26] The possibilities for multiple memberships are also enhanced as the constraints of time, space, and embodiment are extended. This means that there exist different ways of life, and different roles and obligations according to which communities one belongs to. It has been noted "that modern, especially urban, life was characterized by an increasing predominance of relatively attenuated, special-purpose relationships

over richer, more deeply committed and many stranded
1991: 105). It therefore can mean less intense conne
members or that the interconnective engagement b
specialized as communities become narrower in their ap
interest. In other words, it is arguably a thinner or more
form of bonding.

Within the postmodern community, geographical space is less of a
consideration, since the globe can be traversed almost instantaneously.
For example, a group of people can interact together through the
medium of a virtual chat room simultaneously, despite their actual
bodies being located in different towns in different countries (e.g.,
Beijing, Bristol, and Sydney). Such communities are therefore even less
constrained by space or time considerations than are modern
communities. The specialization/focus of each community becomes even
more intense, rendering community interaction to very specific
dimensional levels. Communities proliferate, each concentrating on
particular aims and interests. More specialization of community and
less commitment—people can move in and out of communities
whenever they desire—translates into potentially less individual risk
and less comprehensive bonding for participants. According to Bauman
(1996),

> [p]ostmodernity is the point at which modern untying (dis-embedding, dis-
> encumbering) of tied (embedded, situated) identities reaches its completion:
> *it is now all too easy to choose identity, but no longer possible to hold it.* At the
> moment of its ultimate triumph, the liberation succeeds in annihilating its
> object. The freer the choice, the less it feels like a choice. It lacks weight and
> solidity, as it can be revoked at short notice or without notice—and so binds
> no-one, including the chooser; it leaves no lasting trace, as it bestows neither
> rights nor responsibilities and as its consequences may be discarded or
> disavowed at will once they feel awkward or cease to satisfy. (50–51, italics in
> original)

There is certainly less physical risk for the individual, since the point
or locus of interaction undertaken within postmodern communities is
entirely disembodied. Within a virtual community people are able to
choose the level or degree of interaction they seek. They can choose
when to participate, they can choose their degree of involvement with
others—as long as those with whom they wish to be involved are
agreeable to this involvement.[27] Marriages take place, sexual
relationships are formed, and hierarchical, or administrative relations
created. Yet these relationships can be broken at any stage by the simple
withdrawal of the character/identity, leaving one to wonder at the level

...d depth of commitment or investment held within these relationships.
As Sherry Turkle (1995) commented:

> Women and men tell me that the rooms and mazes on MUDs are safer than
> city streets, virtual sex is safer than sex anywhere, MUD friendships are more
> intense than real ones, and when things don't work out *you can always leave*.
> (244, my emphasis)

People can also choose to be several characters within a community,
or several communities, at any one time. As such they flit between one
or another character and community continuously. This ability has led
observers to analogize the activities of character building and flitting
as the concrete depiction of postmodern theory, with its emphasis on
multiplicity and the navigating of surfaces (Turkle, 1995). This is not
completely different from the multiple memberships, social roles, and
thus identities, that people hold in modern society; however, the rate of
transition among these is not as instantaneous as in cyberspace. This
instantaneity accelerates the transformative skills needed to rapidly
assimilate into each character and may indeed have ramifications for a
person's experience and means of relating to the world and to others.

Therefore, to return to Morris's differentiation between communities
of assent and descent, I would like to point out that these community
types could take traditional, modern, and postmodern forms. However,
I also want to stress that in contemporary society it would be possible
to find people belonging to a traditional form of community, in the sense
in which the term is employed here (where the primary mode of
communication and integration is constituted through the face-to-face),
who also belong to and participate in modern and postmodern forms
of community.[28] It is also necessary to reaffirm that where these forms
exist simultaneously, they are not unaffected by such coexistence. For
example, where universal communities such as Christianity had been
operational in the past, before the possibilities of electronic technological
extension, they relied on travel and on mediation through written and
spoken forms to construct and maintain a sense of cohesion and
identity.[29] This mode of integration had consequences in terms of how
the subjective characteristics noted in the earlier discussion were
experienced. In contemporary society, however, we also find
postmodern forms of these communities being enacted through the
Internet and supplementing or interpolating traditional Christian
communities.

Barry Wellman has done extensive research on the use of
technologically mediated communication in his work on networks, and
he notes the ways in which technology is used to supplement—but also,

in the process, to transform—certain social understandings and practices. For example, technologically mediated interactions via the telephone currently coexist with or supplement traditional (face-to-face) social practices. The capacity to extend communication across space institutes practices that would not have been required or possible in past relationships that were constituted purely through the face-to-face. The coexistence of different modes of sociality has ramifications for the understandings and experiences of those participating in these communities. As Arthur Vidich (1980) explains,

> new styles do not completely replace old ones, but simply become accretions to them. Innovations in styles of life thus increase the complexity of traditional modes of behaviour because older styles can coexist and merge with new ones. (113)

This coexistence of different forms of community and some of the consequences and possibilities of their interrelations will be explored over coming chapters.

At this point, however, the question must be asked as to what makes the "forms of community" approach presented here different from any other community schema. What is it that I want to take from this chapter and carry forward through the rest of the book? I am not proposing a specific model of community as *the* definitive form. Instead I have suggested that we need ways of understanding and talking about different forms of being-together as a consequence of varying ontological influences and structures. Discussion of the subjective elements of community provides a language or focus for the following discussions of community across different theoretical backgrounds. These subjective elements are experienced differently or result in differing practices according to the forms of community within which they are incorporated. Recognition of different forms of community thereby allows the analysis to incorporate or recognize the coexistence of varying forms of community at any one historical point in time, and enables a more nuanced and complex understanding of social life to be attained. Recognition of a socially embedded and socially constituted individual is an important reason for asserting the coexistence of various forms of community. The assertion being made in this chapter is not that modern communities replace traditional communities, nor that postmodern communities replace these other forms of community—it is that these forms of community coexist in various ways. There may be a social dominance of one particular form of community during any particular historical period; however, even if this dominance was of a postmodern form, this would not detach the individual entirely from the influences of her or his embedded and embodied community relations. Recognition of different forms of community also allows an acknowledgment of the importance for social forms of changes in the ways in which we experience the ontological categories of time and space, knowledge, and embodiment. This recognition is central to any discussion about the implications for community and sociality of using communications technologies.

Therefore it seems appropriate to turn to the issue of technology and the ramifications of its use for social relations and integrative practices. This material is the subject of the following chapter.

Notes

[1] Corlett (1989) describes these forms of community as "community with unity."

[2] For the record, it should also be noted that there are ongoing debates about whether community must be attached to a particular geographical place, or whether other spaces, such as cyberspace, can be seen as places for these purposes, or indeed, whether place is important for community at all. Understanding of place and space form part of my argument about ontological categories. Thus, place is seen to occupy a different status from the other community elements.

[3] One of the important motivations behind the theoretical conceptualization of the existence of multiple selves is the desire to avoid formulating a universal subject and subjectivity. The imagery of a subject can result in a possible understanding that enforces homogeneity and suppresses difference. The idea of decentered multiple selves is therefore enlisted to allow for the multiplicity of different forces and pressures that a person encounters and the difference between the result in that person and in others who are also exposed to these forces. Such an assertion is important; however, the nature of theoretical activity is such that generalizations and assumptions are largely unavoidable. What is essential, therefore, is for the theorist to be aware of the dangers inherent in her/his activity and to make allowances for these. It is not enough simply to assert multiplicity at the beginning of any endeavor and then to avoid acknowledgment of one's own assumptions and generalizations. Or alternately, to focus on procedure as a way of avoiding these mistakes when in fact, even such approaches are unable to filter out the subjective choice of procedures or interpretation undertaken by the theorist.

[4] To fail to acknowledge these is to commit the same mistakes as the advocates of difference. In some ways this commonality/ difference debate results in a similar dilemma from that faced by community theorists. The similarity rests in terms of theorists acknowledging and working with integrative community forms while also allowing for the recognition and existence of individual differences.

[5] Integrative practices refer to those routine practices that are understood and enacted by all members of a community. These practices hold a community together through shared understanding and expectations.

[6] The next step in the argument is to assert that it is through technological practices that the structural implications of the positioning of community relations across time and space become as extensive as they are in contemporary Western communities.

[7] Much of the work undertaken by Nancy, and others, is an attempt to move beyond these components, which are seen as restrictive and exclusive. Therefore issues such as commonality are moved beyond the possession of certain common characteristics held by certain groups of people, to become an understanding whereby singular beings' commonality is more that of being in common. See Chapter Five on Nancy for further discussion.

[8] Timothy Luke (1996), when discussing the standard differentiation between tradition and modernity that he aligns with *Gemeinschaft* versus *Gesellschaft*, writes that even the operation of *Gesellschaft* cannot happen in a vacuum. "It inevitably requires a fixed set of conventions, a stable set of rules which regulate cultural and social life, or perhaps something pulled from an old hat, namely, 'traditions'" (111).

[9] See James (1992).

[10] For example, see Walker, Wasserman, and Wellman (1993).

[11] This would seem to emphasize more than a mental connection except in the sense of recognizing oneself in the Other. According to this understanding, it is actual physical circumstances that play a role in creating community.

[12] This is not to assert that desensitization does not take place in the face-to-face, just that the nature and experience of abstracted exposure is more compartmentalized than is generally the case in immersive face-to-face contexts. The impact of the World Trade Center example mentioned above—where viewers in Australia received images and information through the media of print, television, radio, and the Internet—was manifested emotionally and physically in a number of ways through the general population. Yet the sense of unreality, confusion, and separateness was heightened (and altered) by the event's transmission/location at-a-distance.

[13] Anderson (1991) uses this term to describe a modern understanding of time as chronological, and empty—waiting to be filled with events and happenings.

[14] This is premised upon a certain understanding of a detached rational subject who is able to objectively distance him/herself from the three spheres of reality: the social world, inner nature, and external nature (Habermas, 1981).

[15] I would like to thank Craig Calhoun for raising this issue.

[16] Habbo Hotel is the name of a virtual community on the Internet.

[17] See Harvey (1990), Anderson (1991), or James (1996) for discussions about the implications of changing representations and experiences of time and space. (For map references, see Anderson, 1991: 170–178.)

[18] For example, *postmodern community* is a term used by Mark Poster and Howard Rheingold.

[19] This is a similar point to that made by sociologist Amitai Etzioni and the Communitarian Network, although with different expression and theoretical approach.

[20] Progressive in two senses: firstly that, as in other descriptions of epochal development (for example, agrarian, industrial, and postindustrial), earlier forms of community disappear as they evolve into or make way for the newer forms of community; and secondly, that as the movement 'forward' takes place, more choice and—by inference—more freedom is positively achieved.

[21] Here, for the purposes of the book and its emphasis on modern and postmodern communities, I have bundled together a number of different forms of community under the appellation *traditional*.

[22] These differentiations correspond quite closely with Paul James's notion of the face-to-face, the agency-extended, and the disembodied-extended forms of social integration (see James [1996] for further explanation of these concepts). However, I am uncomfortable with the notion of agency-extended as being distinct from

disembodied. I would instead prefer to accentuate the difference between the modern and the postmodern as the acceleration of (already existent) disembodied interactive processes and the location of these within a technologically mediated format/medium.

[23] Such customization, however, also heightens subject individuation. Benedict Anderson wrote of the importance of newspapers for uniting nations and for citizens' conceptualization of synchronous and simultaneous (shared) national time. With the Internet and the possibilities of transcending the temporal constraints of your nation, there develops a disjuncture between the time that you live in your embodied world (though this is increasingly unconstrained by time due to the processes of globalization) and the time you can experience and access at whim individually online.

[24] All forms of community use disembodied practices to some degree. My argument is that it is the dominance of particular integrative forms that leads to a differentiation between these various community forms and their subjective implications. See James (1996) for discussion of different uses and degrees of disembodied or abstract practices.

[25] Except perhaps when such forms of community are generally understood as monitored by a greater omniscient deity.

[26] In the few cases where mutual agreement has not been involved, there has been tremendous discussion around the issue. For example, virtual rape has provoked significant debate about the impact of a textual act of violence. See Julian Dibbell (1998) for his discussion of this issue.

[27] This emphasis on the simultaneous coexistence of different forms or levels of social organization is strongly influenced by and draws on the work of Geoff Sharp, Paul James, and other *Arena* writers.

[28] See Anderson (1991): "In a pre-print age, the reality of the imagined religious community depended profoundly on countless, ceaseless travels" (54)—in effect, the physical mediation or traversing of time and space.

Chapter Two

~~~

Technology and Sociality

Technology, it has been claimed, has contributed to the fragmentation and alienation of the postmodern individual. Indeed, some theorists argue that the contemporary person consists of a multiplicity of selves as a result of the increasing use of technological means of communication and representation. Technological processes certainly extend ever further into individuals' everyday lives, practices, and social relations. Technology alters work practices by enabling physical separation from the office environment. As communication is increasingly undertaken via technology and abstracted from the face-to-face, social practices undergo change. And by enabling more immediate, and some say more equitable, political participation and access to information, political practices are altered.[1] Technological possibilities widen exposure to other cultures; and accelerate the demystification of life processes through the expansion of scientific research. Technologically derived visual representation is altering our sense of the real. Indeed, it has been argued that "[w]e have modified our environment so radically that we must now modify ourselves in order to exist in this new environment" (Weiner, cited in Barrett, 1978: 210).

This chapter concentrates on the ramifications of information and communications technologies for subjectivity and social relations, and thus, implicitly, for forms of community.[2] By *information and communications technologies* I am referring to technologies that are used to mediate or communicate information to and among people. This includes the broadcast media (such as television or radio), telephones, facsimile, and computers that are linked through telecommunications systems. These technologies all abstract from the body inasmuch as the information or communication practices are not embedded within a face-to-face setting. Instead the information or communication is extended across space and time in varying degrees, allowing it to transcend spatial and temporal constraints. These communication processes are increasingly employed as globalization processes accelerate and technological innovations continue to make communication more accessible. For simplicity, I use the term *communications technology* to cover both information and communications technologies; as will be apparent in the following section, the merging or convergence of both these (previously separate) technologies and the processes that they enact means they increasingly refer to one and the same thing.

As has been noted by numerous social commentators, the introduction of personal computers, the development of the Internet and the World Wide Web, and the increasing possibilities of multimedia have introduced a new dimension to technological communication processes. I am not going to relate a history of the development of the Internet or other communication technologies, nor am I going to describe in detail their physical mechanics. There is more than enough literature available in these areas. It is sufficient for our purposes here to note that these technologies have been adopted enthusiastically among the general population. For example, use of the Internet in the Western world has increased exponentially since its inception. This increase has led to proclamations of a new era or a period of development requiring new understandings of social relations.

> Telephone, radio, film, television, the computer and now their integration as "multimedia" reconfigure words, sounds and images so as to cultivate new versions of individuality. If modern society may be said to foster an individual who is rational, autonomous, centered, and stable [...], then perhaps a postmodern society is emerging which nurtures forms of identity different from, even opposite to, those of modernity. (Poster, 1995: 24)

At the very least, most people would agree with Paul James (1993) when he says:

> While there continue to be relations grounded in face-to-face association—that is, in relations of continuity and reciprocal interdependence conducted by people living in the same locale—they are increasingly being overlaid and dominated by more abstract and globalized processes. These processes are contributing to the fragmentation of the face to face. (33)

The use of and increasing reliance on technologies to mediate human practices means that questions need to be asked about their impact (if any) on social forms. The following pages examine some of the writings on technology and sociality.

The chapter is divided into four sections. The first section examines issues of interactivity with the various types and applications of communication technologies. It becomes clear by the end of the discussion that the claims made about technologies, such as the Internet, as to their emancipatory and communitarian potential, are less than straightforward. The second section considers briefly the social implications of the utilization and appropriation of technology to mediate and extend sociality and integrative practices. In the previous chapter, technology was described as being centrally involved in both the possibilities for and the predominance of extended community forms (such as modern and postmodern communities). For example, postmodern communities were presented as forms of community that are enacted through a disembodied — and extended — mode of practice. This extended mode of practice is facilitated by the use of technology. Discussions of these forms of community, therefore, fall easily within the rubric of analyses of technology and social practices. The third section takes the phenomenon of virtual communities as an example of postmodern social forms and explores in more detail some of the implications of extended and disembodied sociality. The last section takes the phenomenal considerations discussed further to consider the types of processes enacted through the employment of these technologies and some of the ontological considerations that result.

A Closer Look at Interactivity and Information/Communications Technology

Communication technology is involved in the process of extending or mediating community relations across time and space. Yet technology, even communications technology itself, is not homogenous. Different possibilities are enabled through different technologies, and also different ways in which these technologies mediate communication among the people who use them.

This section investigates some of the ways in which mediation, communication, and extension takes place. The presupposition contained within most writings on the subject of the Internet and other interactive communications technologies is that because these technologies are more *interactive* in their use, they are somehow better and more suited to enhancing community forms than previously (technologically) possible. However, the delineations between the surveillance and administrative, and between the communicative and interactive, elements of these technologies are not as straightforward as some writers would have us believe. These different elements have different subjective and intersubjective effects, as will become more apparent in the following chapter. For the moment, a closer look at issues of directionality and interactivity is called for.

We can separate technological applications into collection and broadcast (unidirectional) and interactive communications (bi- or multidirectional). There is of course significant overlap between these areas. Unidirectional refers to those system technologies and databases used by the public and private sectors to gather and record information, and the broadcast media that transmit information and images outward.[3] Multidirectional refers to technologies such as the Internet that enable interactive communication and information exchange between users.

Databases are used to accumulate, combine, and in the process, create information on all facets of life, including people's personal lives. They are primarily unidirectional in that they derive information from a subject—objectifying the subject through this process, since the subject/ object has no recourse to respond or contribute in any self-directed manner. This administrative process also creates information and devises action according to the (gathered and created) information— resulting in outcomes affecting those at whom action is directed.

Database systems are becoming increasingly interconnected and sophisticated, taking on the form of global information systems capable of infinite analysis, profiling, and information combinations. This interconnection has implications for the subjectivity of social actors through the creation of a technologized panopticon.[4] The Western individual increasingly experiences her/his life as monitored by technology: being caught on speed camera; being captured on video while shopping; having work efficiency monitored through technological surveillance techniques; or taking out a loan, which is recorded, linked with other financial transactions and purchasing practices, and combined with demographic statistics. This continuous but often unverifiable surveillance has implications—as Foucault noted in *Discipline and Punish*—for the instigation of normalization practices.[5] This process is accentuated by the subject's own perception of the depth and pervasive nature of her/his visibility. Databases extend the gaze through disciplinary space, enabling a more pervasive, widespread surveillance of each and every subject than would be achievable without technological assistance. The subject of surveillance is universalized in that s/he is reduced to one file among many, but also individuated through being personally identifiable, trapped within time and space by the continual visibility enabled through the database/s. Data can be invoked at any time through a simple command tapped into a computer terminal. This has the potential to compartmentalize the individual, separating her/him from others through the isolating qualities of the disciplinary gaze.

Databases are perceived as a means to assist the surveyor. The surveyor is usually an institution of some description, viewing those outside of (or working within) its system. Intonations of George Orwell's "Big Brother" — or many "little brothers" — are ominously invoked. The technology is oriented toward attaining control through information storage, analysis, and manipulation. Within the data field, information itself becomes an entity. Detached from its referent subject, it can be moved, rearranged, and transformed. The subject from whom the information has been derived often has little or no recourse as to the form, content, or outcomes of this process. S/he becomes purely an object for observation and manipulation.

Broadcast media also works in a largely unidirectional manner. However, there are also differences that have ramifications for the subjective impact of each of these technologies. Television, film, and radio broadcast information and images outward (whereas databases primarily collect information inward) to a passive audience.[6] This process universalizes through its standardized and undifferentiated form, and, objectifies the audience through its lack of interactivity. It portrays events, occasions, and situations in a manner that is removed from/at a distance from the audience, positioning them as voyeurs.[7] This is particularly apparent with televised talk shows that broadcast an individual's most intimate personal details to a national or international audience. It is also a vital component in the proliferation of television reality shows, such as the various editions of the television show *Big Brother*, where the viewer watches essentially mundane life practices taking place within an orchestrated setting. As with databases, the audience has no direct recourse as to the form, outcome, or content of this process apart from withdrawal, rejection, or individually controlling the manner in which the broadcast information is received.[8] They may have indirect control through commercial considerations that require broadcast producers to attract and maintain audiences (although minority groups have less visibility or influence in such considerations). Although interactivity is forecast as "just around the corner" with the introduction of digital television, it is not generally possible to interact directly within or through the medium itself.

Like databases, the Internet similarly enables information to be viewed, moved, transformed, and manipulated. It is employed in a variety of practices: information collection and publication, academic and social interchange, entertainment and gaming, the dissemination of a wide variety of views, and the undertaking of financial transactions. The Internet is also largely unimpeded by nation-state boundaries, and it is increasingly accessible on a global scale.[9] In comparison to system databases or broadcast media, however, the Internet is frequently depicted by social commentators as a liberating technology that is able to transcend inequities based on biological, social, political, and cultural differences. It is also imputed to enhance individual agency. Allucquere Rosanne Stone (2000) writes about the difference between interaction in cyberspace when contrasted with exposure to or involvement in cinematic space:

> Interaction is the physical concretization of a desire to escape the flatness and merge into the created system. It is the sense in which the 'spectator' is more than a participant, but becomes both participant in and creator of the simulation. In brief, it is the sense of unlimited power which the dis/embodied simulation produces, and the different ways in which socialization has led those always-embodied participants confronted with the sign of unlimited power to respond. (521)

This description highlights the subject-empowering and creative possibilities attributed to interactive technology. Participants are seen as active agents who contribute not only to activities within cyberspace, but who are also able to influence the form and site of the interactive location. This is very different from the perceived consequences of unidirectional technologies.

The Internet is a diverse, decentered communications system with unlimited input—inasmuch as anybody who is connected with a network can participate in the system—resulting in seemingly uncontrolled and unpredictable development. This is viewed by some institutions as potentially threatening, leading to media coverage of illegal, deviant or socially destructive activities taking place over the Internet and attempts by politicians to grapple with this issue through discussions of censorship and guidelines.[10] Yet these institutions also seek a greater utilization of the technology, devising ways through which Internet users can (un)wittingly contribute information about themselves or their practices, and thus to their own surveillance. Howard Rheingold raises the conceivable scenario of those who are information poor, or have limited access to the technology, being offered "free time" in exchange for the relinquishing of some personal privacy or control over private information (Rheingold, 1993: 293–294). An alternate scenario raised by Andrew Shapiro conceives of privacy becoming a valuable commodity that people have to pay for online (Shapiro, 1997). Technological constructs—intelligent agents—are increasing in both ability and number. These agents can create profiles and records on individuals' activities online. For example, one type of agent, cookies, enable information to be recorded about an individual's Internet practices: which sites are accessed, how long sites are used, and so forth.

In this situation, the Internet also operates as a database. Other communicative technologies—especially as they become more entwined with Internet technologies—also survey and accumulate information about the user. For example, satellite technology means that mobile telephones can be used to track and record a user's movements and activities (Keegan, 2000).

In the case of databases and the Internet, the perception of difference appears to be largely a matter of emphasis. Like the databases, the Internet universalizes, inasmuch as all activity is granted the same status. The individual may well be able to have a voice through her/his own home page, blog, or participation in a discussion; however, s/he is one voice amongst a vast sea of voices and thus the assurance of being heard or engaged in communication is far from absolute. Individual difference is, in some senses, negated, as the communication becomes homogeneous in form (due to the constraints of the technologies). Internet technologies are both unidirectional and multidirectional in form and in application.

Despite their interconnective capacity, any interaction through multidirectional technologies physically isolates because of the singular nature of entry into the interaction: via the technology of a keyboard, cellular phone, and so on. To return to an earlier example, mobile phones, while connecting an individual to another across space, simultaneously distance the individual from those with whom s/he is concretely and proximately situated. Paradoxically, therefore, these technologies psychically disconnect the individual to some extent from the embodied interactions surrounding her/him, to enable participation with others in a virtual space. Although it may not presently individualize through the operation of the gaze to the same extent as through databases, interaction through interactive technologies such as the Internet still heightens the solitary or individualistic nature of this form of activity.

I mention these possibilities, as well as the technologies' current capabilities, to highlight the similarities among database use, parts of the Internet, and other communication technologies, and therefore the arbitrary designation of *controlling* or *liberating* to these technologies. Obviously, it is not the technologies themselves that are either of these, but rather the social and cultural uses for which the technologies are employed and the consequent subjective effects that result. For example, in 2000, it was noted how it would not be long before global-positioning technology—"enabling information geared to where you are to be sent to you (or keep tabs on errant teenagers)" (Keegan, 2000: 1–2)—would be commonplace. The technology is indeed now commonplace, but unremarkable in its own right: It is the functions that it performs—or more importantly, the ways in which the technology is understood or imagined as a surveillance tool—that are worth noting. Digital technology also enables the mobile phone to be used as a camera and for video-conferencing to take place. Thus a widened interactive *and* an increased surveillance capacity are both enacted within the same technology. The emphasis on interactive potentiality often fails to incorporate consideration of the potential surveillance activities of these technologies and therefore fails to acknowledge social implications such as those noted above.

The importance of this discussion for my argument is now obvious. When used in an interactive manner, the Internet and other communication technologies enable the extension of relationships and other interactive possibilities. The way in which this takes place results in particular forms of interaction and of subjectivity. And the Internet (and increasingly other communication technologies) also operate as databases with specific subjective effects. These two possibilities coexist within the same technology/ies and therefore cannot be considered in isolation. Many of the current analyses of the interactive possibilities of communication technologies are limited by this oversight.

Analysis of communication technologies, because of their central role in extending and monitoring an essential aspect of human relationships—communication—becomes increasingly important when considering their implications for social forms. Changing social forms that are brought about, at least in part, through changes as a result of the use of communications technologies and the constraints and possibilities that are associated with this use are the focus of the next section.

Technology and Changing Social Forms

Changes in the ways in which we access, understand, and communicate within the world as a result of using communication technologies have led to changes in the forms and practices of social relationships. As Craig Calhoun notes, communication technologies have played an important role in the constitution of extended communities (or, in my terms, modern and postmodern communities), both in terms of the spatial extension of relationships, and in terms of providing an integrative and cohesive means for transmitting shared customs and social traditions across time and space (Calhoun, 1991: 110).

The technological extension of relationships and social practices across space enables people to physically relocate without completely disengaging from prior relationships. The spatial and temporal extension of relationships is strengthened by the development and utilization of those technologies that simulate, or give the user more of a sense of, the face-to-face. Therefore, for example, the telephone that brings the communicator's voice seemingly into one's presence or immediate geographical location appears more immediate than communication received through the postal system. Likewise, synchronous and asynchronous computer communication (for example, e-mail or Internet relay chat systems [IRC]) also appears more immediate, enhancing the sense of a continuing relationship. Such immediate forms of communication across space have been vital for the development of globalization processes, the mobilization of labor that this requires, and the extension and continuation of relationships that become necessary if labor is not to become extremely alienated and unproductive.

However, the question as to whether conducting a relationship through technological means has altered the nature or form of that relationship has been the subject of heated debate. Discussion of studies undertaken on the use of the telephone is illustrative. For example, research has highlighted the manner in which individuals appropriated the use of the telephone to enhance their personal relationships.

> [A]lthough the telephone was intended as a business tool, it became even more important in personal usage and had far-reaching effects not only on organizational forms such as the branch office, but also on rural life, on families, on teenagers, and on parents. (Kiesler & Hinds, 1993: 120)

While the technology was used to continue contacts and relationships with others, the form of communication itself altered the manner of communication as well as the way in which social relations were viewed and conducted. Access to another could be immediate— as long as they answered the phone—without having to physically relocate oneself to within the same space as the other. This allowed more individualized behavior; one could seek contact with others as one's needs dictated. Answering machines and the practice of screening calls meant that it was possible to know who was ringing and to exercise individual choice about whether to speak to the caller. Caller ID technology extended this capacity.[11]

New or modified forms of conversing and behaving have developed to cater to the particularities of each technology. Using the example of the telephone, it has been noted by commentators that the removal of presence from the communicative process, apart from that aspect of presence (the voice) involved in the carrying of speech, has allowed some communicators to feel less constrained or inhibited in their conversations. According to Lenk, research on telephone conversations "indicates that these are not a weak version of face-to-face discussions. Contrary to expectations the telephone released unsuspected power of speech from the constraints imposed by face-to-face conversations" (Lenk, 1982: 293). This is a similar claim to those that are currently made about communication through a newer technology—the Internet. Communication through IRCs or e-mail, for example, use different formats from those of verbal, face-to-face interchange. These mediated communications are subject to their own particular codes of conduct or rules of communication. For example, studies have noted how online there is a reduction of linguistic indicators, a brevity of language form, and copious abbreviations and modifications of the language itself (Werry, 1996). Yet according to at least one analyst, this is undertaken in an attempt to replicate or simulate the casualness and informality of communicating in a face-to-face mode (Werry, 1996: 61).

Replication is not ontologically the same as the actuality of face-to-face discourse—as the 'released from constraints' comment above makes quite apparent. There is something that is *different* about mediated and extended communication. While communication technologies—because of their mediating nature—do, at one level, remove some constraints from the experience of a communicative act, on another level they alter that communication in numerous ways. This is partly because of the parameters of the particular technology employed. It is partly because of the individuating (and in some ways, disconnecting or abstracting) aspects of extended communication that remove the speaker from experiencing fully the direct consequences of such an act.[12] And it is partly because of the *lifting out* of that communication from the immediate and immersive environment within which it originated, to be received in another space. Through this process, the communication itself becomes thinner.

Claude Fischer (1992) conducted an extensive social history study of early telephone usage in America. He notes the initial, varied views of commentators as to the types of social relations that are fostered by the mediating technology of the telephone. The claims sound very similar to those being made about the Internet today, ranging from the utopian—creating or assisting closer social relations through overcoming distance and creating community—to the dystopian— inculcating "inauthentic" relations and undermining or impoverishing social life. However, Fischer (1992) concludes that "[i]n more general terms, Americans apparently used home telephones to widen and deepen existing social patterns rather than to alter them" (262). And that,

As well as using it to make practical life easier, Americans—notably women—
used the telephone to chat more often with neighbours, friends, and relatives;
to save a walk when a call might do; to stay in touch more easily with people
who lived an inconvenient distance away. (263)

Fischer suggests then that the communicative possibilities of the
telephone expanded sociability through its ability to compress space
and time—it was often the most convenient and efficient means of
contact. It also altered some social practices; for example, phoning ahead
before dropping in for a visit (Fischer, 1992: 239).

It has also been suggested that the general accessibility of varying
means of communication, and the increasing flow of information
available to individuals, have altered social structures. For example, it
has been claimed that the telephone "did more than enable people to
communicate over long distances: it threatened existing class relations
by extending the boundary of who may speak to whom; it also altered
modes of courtship and possibilities of romance" (Poster, 1990: 5).

Access to knowledge has always dictated position and power in
society. Joshua Meyrowitz's studies on information/communications
technologies reveal the ways in which the introduction of technology
alters the accessibility of information.[13] Others have similarly
commented that,

[t]he durability and portability of information [enabled by technology] affects
not only the distribution of information but also the distribution of social
relationships—who knows whom—and the form and quality of these social
relationships. (Kiesler & Hinds, 1993: 118)

With the increasing use of communications technology in both the
procurement and manipulation of information as well as the extension
of relationships across time and space, this comment becomes all the
more relevant. The technological extension of relationships, social
practices, and information processes across time and space has also
resulted in changes to the dominant ways—or modes of practice—
through which we organize our societies. In contemporary Western
society, face-to-face practices are less central to the experience of
everyday life than they were, say, one hundred years ago. Telephones,
computers, facsimiles, and bureaucratic institutions all mediate or
extend practices and routines that previously would have been
conducted predominantly face-to-face. As Calhoun (1986) notes, "[n]ew
computer and communications technologies affect social integration
primarily by shifting the balance between relationships that are directly
interpersonal and those that are mediated" (332).

A growing number of studies are being undertaken that investigate the changing dominance of mediated social forms, and the ramifications for both mediated and directly interpersonal interchange. Work on the network society stresses that the individualized behavior noted above is accentuated as a result of the "affordances" of communications technologies (Wellman, 2001: 228). Manuel Castells, Barry Wellman, and others have described, in some detail, what they perceive to be a change in social structure; the growing importance of networks, in part, as a consequence of the possibilities of mediating technologies. For Wellman (and his colleagues), there has been a "transformation of community from solidary groups to individualized networks" (Wellman, 2001: 228), indicating changes in intersubjective relations and practices.

The DiMaggio et al. (2001) article, "Social Implications of the Internet," charts some of the divergent views held about the impact of the Internet. These divergences can be explained, in part, by the time during which the particular views were held and by the changing demographics and practices of Internet users. The writers note,

> The research literature is limited, and many questions remain. But there is a pattern: Early writings projected utopian hopes onto the new technology, eliciting a dystopian response. Research on each [of the study's chosen] topic yields two conclusions. First, the Internet's impact is more limited than either the utopian or dystopian visions suggest. Second, the nature of that impact will vary depending upon how economic actors, government regulation, and users collectively organize the evolving Internet technology. (DiMaggio, Hargitti, Neuman, & Robinson, 2001: 310)

Di Maggio et al. (2001:316) also note that "an increasing body of literature suggests that the Internet enhances social ties defined in many ways, often by reinforcing existing behaviour patterns." This is similar to Fischer's findings about the ways that the uses of the telephone impacted upon sociality. While this is important and worth noting, the "definition" of social ties itself is also of interest and worthy of further exploration.

At this point it is helpful to consider in more detail the phenomenal implications of technologically extended relations and social forms. Virtual communities are ideal for this analysis, since they are formulated and enacted entirely within a technologically disembodied realm.

The Phenomenal Possibilities of Technology: Virtual Communities in More Detail

As noted in the introduction, the label *virtual communities* is most commonly applied to those community forms that are enacted entirely online.[14] These communities are depicted as being free of the physical, spatial, or temporal constraints faced by real space communities. Therefore, virtual communities are presented by many social commentators as being inherently liberating and equalizing. For example, Mike Featherstone (2000) suggests that the engagement with these communities and the use of other technologies such as virtual reality could be ideal for the aged, who may not be physically mobile (609–618). The use of SMS (Short Message Service) through the screens of mobile telephones has been of great—and unforeseen—benefit for increasing the communication possibilities for the deaf (Adams, 2000: 3).These benefits fall comfortably within, and thus reinforce, the rhetoric and ideal of technology as progressive; freeing humans from physical constraints.

Other outcomes and possibilities that arise as a consequence of overriding these constraints are also commonly noted. Geographical space is compressed—insofar as the physical location of the participant's body is transcended through the extension of any interaction in cyberspace—into a readily traversable medium. Virtual communities are seen as a way of overcoming the inherent isolation of contemporary life, where people do not know their neighbors; are not involved in their local township decisions; and possibly work from home. This understanding overlooks the physically isolated nature of the form of interaction, where it is only the extension of the mind of each participant and of the communicative form that enables mutual interaction.[15] However, virtual communities are increasingly understood as also supplementing or intersecting with real space communities, drawing attention to the need to theorize the intersection of different forms of community and/or to understand the implications of a dominant mode of social relations.[16] Questions need to be asked—and this book goes some way toward addressing these questions—about the ways that mediated social forms differ.

Participants in virtual communities can indeed (virtually) escape their embodied identities through the removal of visual or audile cues, and thereby escape overt discrimination directed toward their particular embodied selves For example, race, gender, age, and physical disability are often visually indiscernible on the Internet. Any basis for enacting discrimination on the basis of the visual identification of embodied characteristics is thus removed, freeing access to participation and nominally granting each participant equal status within the network. However, new developments are constantly being introduced that attempt to imbue online communication with embodied characteristics: to make the interaction as close as possible to that of the face-to-face. For example, with video technology, the possibilities for disembodied engagement are diminished. There is also a growing literature pointing to the underlying framing of online interactions and the ways that the structuring of online communities can indicate inherent cultural and embodied biases.[17] I am drawn to question too why the removal of embodied characteristics, which are the focus of discrimination but also an essential part of each person, is viewed so positively. The removal of these characteristics simply overrides the basis of discrimination, rather than effectively dealing with the discrimination itself. Participants are thus rendered as 'the same' rather than allowing for the accommodation of differences that may be viewed as threatening or uncomfortable. This is an extension of the Cartesian devaluing of the body: the leaving behind of the body allowing people to *see* one's true self (the mind). Yet, as has already been indicated, such a separation is inherently problematic because of its failure to recognize the importance of embodied particularity for experiences of subjectivity, identity, and intersubjective relationships.

The leaving behind of the body is seen to carry other liberating potentials. In *Life on the Screen*, Sherry Turkle discusses how we can experiment with various projections—both masculine and feminine— of ourselves through cyberspace in what she depicts as a nonthreatening (physical) environment. Mark Poster (1997) concurs, writing that "one may experience directly the opposite gender by assuming it and enacting it in conversations" (223). It *is* possible for a man or woman to portray him/herself within a virtual community as a member of the opposite sex. Such a portrayal may lead to a gendered interactive experience inasmuch as the character may find her/himself encountering gender-directed behavior from other characters. For example, female characters in chat rooms are often harassed as a consequence of their representation as female. Obviously, developments such as the increasing use of video technology mentioned above will have some impact on these scenarios (although it is possible that such visual tools may not be adopted within certain realms of interactivity, this seems unlikely). For the moment, however, a technologically mediated enactment, whether textual or graphical (using avatars), while possibly experientially liberating and insightful, cannot be equated with the actuality of physically living that particular gendered form. Living within a particular body carries specific biological and experiential particularities, which have certain consequences for subjectivity.[18] This is quite apart from (although it can be related to) the social constructions of gender.

The perception of anonymity is presented as another plus by proponents of virtual community. Liberated from the normative gaze of both institutions and society, identity cannot be verified and attached to the embodied user, and behavior is not constrained by real space norms and values. The degree of anonymity actually achieved is questionable, and will prove increasingly so as more effective means of accumulating information on network users are devised.[19] Additionally, the chaos within some communities—as a consequence of anonymity being equated with a lack of accountability—has led some communities to impose the use of stable participant identification. On the WELL,[20] for example, participants are obliged to link all presentations of self with an unchanging referent user-ID, thus enabling identities to be verified (Rheingold, 1993). The need for a kind of order within community interaction has therefore led some communities to sacrifice the liberatory aspects of anonymity in favor of order and accountability. The recording and archiving of interactions also creates a historical trace of a character, decreasing the ability of a character to interact anonymously, unidentified by past behaviors or statements.

Therefore normative guidelines do exist within these communities, and the gaze—although in a different form—does apply. Marc Smith writes that, as in real space communities, virtual communities must invoke and maintain the commitment of members, monitor and sanction behavior, and carry out the production and distribution of essential resources (Smith, 1992). There are specific rules, within each community, that participants must agree to follow in order to maintain participatory rights. Many of these rules are either fashioned by the participants themselves or, more frequently, by the person/s who originally constructed the community space. For example, in many conference groups, the host has control over the discussion topics and over the rules of behavior permitted, to the extent of being able to ban certain topics or certain users if desired.[21] This potential for autocratic control raises questions about claims made by proponents as to the democratic potential of these communities.

The question of ethics, or a notion of the common good, existing within virtual communities (or even within the notion of virtual communities themselves) is related to the above discussion of normative guidelines. Communitarian theorists, such as Sandel, Taylor, and MacIntyre, have focused on the importance of a certain notion of the common good for communities.[22] These theorists examine the incorporation of socially developed ethics and norms within institutional arrangements, and within the practices of communities. Those advocating the merits of virtual communities would see the good life being achieved through the opportunities of flexible, disembodied identities unconstrained by geographical time and space, and no longer dependent on meaningful others.[23] Therefore it is the *forms* of participation that result in meaningful experiences for participants. The focus on multiplicity and choice places more emphasis on procedural measures where it is the ability to choose identities and location that is celebrated, rather than explicating the nature of the good life itself.

However, virtual communities must also be understood as multiple and heterogeneous, making it impossible here to delineate the qualities or understandings of each within one encompassing generalization. As DiMaggio et al. (2001: 317) note,

> "Online communities" come in very different shapes and sizes, ranging from virtual communities that connect geographically distant people with no prior acquaintance who share similar interests, to settings that facilitate interactions among friendship networks or family members, to community networks that focus on issues relevant to a geographically defined neighbourhood.

Any discussion of virtual community must therefore recognize at least two different levels of analysis: an analysis of the potentialities of the technology that enable virtual communities to exist in their present form(s); and an analysis of the specific characteristics of each virtual community. The first focuses on the capabilities and means of all communities existent within virtual space, enabling generalizations to be made about these. The second focuses on the specificity of each virtual community with its own particular norms and regulations. Any analysis must incorporate recognition of these (related) aspects.

Where communities are constituted and maintained predominantly within a disembodied, extended mode of practice, it is suggested that this has specific consequences for intersubjective relations and for the subjectivity of participants. Multiple characters can participate relatively freely in virtual communities, seemingly unhindered by relations of dependence or connectedness, apart from those chosen by the participant. This is problematic for a number of reasons, but particularly for its privileging of a seemingly autonomous, independent subject/ identity. Interaction is abstracted away from more concrete and embodied particularities, within an environment shaped by the actors themselves. A loosening of connections may appear liberating. However, such an understanding devalues many of the positive and ontologically important aspects of these relations. It also appears contradictory to elevate the enriching aspects of virtual communities while at the same time devaluing or ignoring relations such as those that exist between parent and child, and other relations of dependence or interconnection, that many theorists would see as fundamental for any community. This would seem to suggest a superficial understanding of a community where interaction appears one-dimensional and largely utilitarian.

What is described in such utopian forms is the ability to *play* with identity and to promote both communication and information collection. While there are indeed liberating, equalizing, and relationship-enhancing qualities that are experienced by participants, these are not uncomplicated or without consequence. I would suggest that the dissolution or fragmentation of the subject, and the instantaneous, transient nature of all communication, potentially disconnects or abstracts the individual from physical action and a sense of social and personal responsibility to others offline. A fairly superficial example can be drawn from Turkle's book *Life on the Screen*. Turkle describes a virtual community participant who was actively involved in the political machinations of his cybersociety but who was also completely apathetic and disengaged from the political situation surrounding him in his offline life (or embodied location) to the extent that he was not interested in participating in a local senate election (242). While virtual communities may be interactive, they do not require either physical commitment — apart from attendance at a keyboard — or any moral, political, or social extension outside of the network. Of those who use the Internet and virtual communities, it is only a small percentage of users who actively participate within their community. The rest of the users operate from a voyeuristic or viewer position similar to that practiced through television viewing.[24]

However, in the edited collection *The Internet in Everyday Life* (Wellman & Haythornthwaite, 2002), a debate about the consequences of online interaction and its impact on civic engagement suggests that it is not the online nature of social activity that is of concern. Instead, almost obviously, various authors suggest that those individuals who are politically active will use the Internet to enhance their political activism, rather than to avoid it, and those who are not politically involved are unlikely to become so because of Internet possibilities, thereby drawing attention to the various ways in which the virtual communities are perceived and practiced. These discussions also highlight different (participant and theorist) perceptions about the social-technological relationship. In the Turkle example noted above, the individual views the virtual community as a new social space that can be completely absorbing. Others view the virtual community and the technology as a means to achieve certain goals and outcomes.

Claims for virtual communities being *the* desirable postmodern community form require more critical attention. The ways in which technological media are used is a continuing progression of the segregation and separation of life practices into various realms. This separation has consequences for our understanding of ourselves and our social relations.

Contemporary Western society has seen, for example, the separation and confinement of birth, death, illness, and education from the community, placing these within institutional spaces (Giddens, 1991).

Now community is potentially being separated from physical interaction via the disembodiment enabled through virtuality, and relegated to operating within the confines of a technological network. Such a process involves a separation of mind and body, and a separation of the body from social interaction. Physically embodied interaction is, on one level, arguably more complex than virtual interaction (as presently experienced). However, a user's corporeal experience of his or her virtual interaction is also undeniable (but different from those experienced face-to-face). Online, since other peripheral distractions are filtered out by the reliance on technology constrained descriptions, interaction becomes intensely focused. Attention is placed solely on the act of communication as perceived through the visual interpretation of information (largely text) presented on the computer screen.[25] Such a concentrated focus leads to claims by observers that relations on the Internet are more intense than those that take place in real space.

What also requires further critical attention is the relation, if any, between virtual experiences and those of real space. This issue has implications for the form and practices of virtual communities, as well as the ways in which we understand them. It also extends the question of how viable or adequate these communities are in answering the hunger of techno-society for more enriching experiences of togetherness, or indeed, finding concrete ways of achieving these. While, as noted, empirical data is being gathered that aims to re-embed studies of the Internet and online social practice within the broader context of everyday life, much of the literature is descriptive and takes the individuals' experiences and perceptions as phenomenally or ontologically uncomplicated. In other words, such analyses fail to consider or to articulate the possibilities that the subjectivity of the individuals themselves may have been affected by or might affect their use of mediating technologies; or that the position from which they articulate their perceptions and experiences may have been altered by the processes of technological mediation themselves.

This possibility leads us to extend the analysis of technological processes a little further. I have already explored some of the consequences of the phenomenal actualization of technological processes. Now let us consider some of the underlying ontological implications of such processes. This involves consideration of the ways in which the ontological categories of knowledge, time and space, and embodiment are impacted on or influenced by the employment of technological processes.

Ontological Implications and Processes

A common approach to technological issues is to argue that technology is a tool that can be used to enhance the prospects for certain types of communities. Advocates of the tool argument understand technology as simply overcoming constraints, whether these are of a biological, temporal, or spatial nature. Technological processes are therefore represented as extending, enhancing, or transcending natural processes. Howard Rheingold is one proponent; he sees computer networks as a tool for enabling the development of communities that he argues are *as* enriching and *more* liberating than those of the face-to-face community. Many activists, local communities, and other communication technology users approach these technologies from a tool perspective; as simply expanding the repertoire of instruments they have at hand to achieve particular objectives.

Mark Poster argues that rather than a tool, interaction through technological forms such as the Internet is similar to interacting within a geographical place or social space—he uses Germany as an example—and therefore that the communication incorporates many of the characteristics, traditions, and identities attached to place.[26] Those interacting within these places are influenced by their involvement in and exposure to this space/place. Indeed, Poster (1997) argues that it is not helpful to ask about the effects of the Internet, since:

> [t]echnologically determined effects derive from a broad set of assumptions in which what is technological is a configuration of materials which affect other materials; and the relation between the technology and human beings is external, that is, where human beings are understood to manipulate the materials for ends that they impose upon the technology from a preconstituted position of subjectivity. But what the Internet technology imposes is a dematerialization of communication and, in many of its aspects, a transformation of the subject position of the individual who engages within it. (215)[27]

This argument problematizes assumptions evident in many of the empirical studies noted above. While such studies can determine the subject's perception about social lives and social practices, they are not adequately able to reflect on the possibility of transformed subject positions.

Martin Heidegger (1977) similarly argues against viewing technology purely as a tool. Instead of trying to understand technology itself, he argues that we should seek to understand the processes and understandings that are indicated by our use of technology. He writes,

> the essence of technology is by no means anything technological. Thus we shall never experience our relationship to the essence of technology so long as we merely conceive and push forward the technological, put up with it, or evade it. Everywhere we remain unfree and chained to technology, whether we passionately affirm or deny it. But we are delivered over to it in the worst possible way when we regard it as something neutral; for this conception of it, to which today we particularly like to do homage, makes us utterly blind to the essence of technology. (4)

And other writers highlight the ways in which particular technologies are culturally constructed and culturally employed. Andrew Feenberg, for example, notes,

> As a social object, technology ought to be subject to interpretation like any other cultural artefact, but it is generally excluded from humanistic study. We are assured that its essence lies in a technically explainable function rather than a hermeneutically interpretable meaning. (1995: 8)

In this book, I question whether the use of communications technology (and the increasing dominance of this use within techno-society) to extend social forms influences subjective and intersubjective relations, and thus has implications for the experiences and forms of community. This is to understand technology neither purely as a tool, as neutral, nor as inescapably determining. It is, also, to sidestep questions about the socio-technical relationship when framed as questions about technological or social determinism, constructivism, and so forth. Instead, these implications or outcomes are presented here as a result of a number of processes, derived from the various uses of technology, that impact on the ways in which we experience and understand ontological categories such as knowledge, time and space, and embodiment. Marshall McLuhan (1967) wrote:

> Ours is a brand new world of allatonceness. "Time" has ceased, "space" has vanished. We now live in a global village ... a simultaneous happening. (63)

The remainder of this chapter explores whether this pronouncement of McLuhan's is indeed the case, and what the implications are for community and intersubjective relations when ontological categories are transformed. Throughout, my working hypothesis is that technology is used to *extend* relationships and integrative practices across time and space, *compressing* these categories in the process. In this process, it *abstracts* the user and her/his practices from embodied interaction, and it has the potential to *instrumentalize* relationships and integrative practices.

Extension/Compression (of Time and Space)

> Advances in technology have impacted on the perceived space-time relationship through the creation of phenomenological [global] space. The ability to make phone calls to other countries is now an accepted fact of life and this has contributed to the development of a global telephone culture which negates distance. Similarly the television provides an 'eye to the world', and simulates a global space within the flat screen. (Ostwald, 1997: 130)

The extension and mediation of relationships and practices compresses the experience and conceptualization of both time and space, making both ontological categories appear more manageable and more easily traversed. The use of technology has been inseparably involved with this transversality, the crossing of expanses of space and time with increased facility, and the resulting mediation and extension of community relations. Regardless of whatever other social developments and changes may have taken place, it would not have been possible to experience time and space in the ways that are currently possible without the development of transport and communications technologies. Developments in technology have enhanced the mobility of people, leading to changes in life practices and routines that were previously unimaginable. The industrial revolution led to the rapid growth of cities as people left the country in search of work that had been created as a result of technological development. In contemporary Australia, a worker in Canberra can fly home to Melbourne in 45 minutes, enabling her/him to keep in steady physical contact with family and friends despite the 900 or so kilometers separating work from home. Elsewhere, colleagues in London, New York, and Sydney can conduct transactions and make joint decisions in a matter of minutes despite the fact that each person is physically situated in a different part of the globe.

Consideration of the implications of condensing time and space through technology—whereby information, people, and communication can traverse large distances almost instantaneously—becomes increasingly important. These changes have ramifications for community and social interaction. Mobility of labor, and the use of information systems, have brought the Other closer so that s/he is no longer outside our boundaries but situated within, forcing the reexamination of questions of identity. Media images of Ethiopia, Somalia, or Bosnia bring the world into our living-rooms. The conceptualization of the global system becomes more manageable.

As time and space have become more easily traversed, our ways of understanding time and the places that we live in have been affected. One of the interesting consequences or outcomes of the popular adoption of cyberspace—technologically created space—is the way in which this new conception of space has created terminological difficulties and problematized experiences and descriptions of place. For example, I have referred to the real world or real space to describe aspects of life that are not conducted within the virtual or techno-realm. However, as noted earlier, this distinction is not intended to infer that the technologically mediated or the virtual are any less real in terms of their consequences for social life. Different practices of time and space lead to different understandings and experiences of these categories.

The connection between the practice of writing (technology as practice) and changed experiences of time and space has been noted by numerous commentators. For Benedict Anderson, there is an identifiable relationship between the introduction of writing and a changed conception of time; between the social use of a technology and the social experience of an ontological category. Through writing and literature it became possible to envisage/imagine situations and people possibly unbeknownst to oneself, acting in different places simultaneously. The notion of historical linear time became more tangibly and concretely imaginable. This "imagining" was expanded with the introduction of mass printing processes and the corresponding increase in literacy. Time and space could be suspended on paper, or at least, more easily negotiated. Giddens (1994b) notes how writing enabled the coding of information; in the process "reconstructing space and time." He comments,

> [b]ecause writing "records," it permits a reappropriation of past time and a novel "cutting into" the future; and it allows a control of space, making possible the coordination of objects, events, and human actions well beyond what could be achieved in oral cultures. (Giddens, 1994b: xi)

Writing enabled the development of administrative institutions; notes and records could be made and stored for later reference. It also enabled distance to be overcome and time to be transformed by bringing a sense or representation of a face-to-face relation into the communicator's presence. As Mark Nunes (1997) points out, "From Derrida's standpoint, writing serves as a means of calling forth presence, of making the subject 'here' without being here" (168).

The increasing application of communications technologies in ever-expanding circles of social life continues this process of invoking presence across distances. For example, the Internet and other computer-linked systems (e.g., intranet systems) extend the possibilities for the recording of and referral to communications; fixing them beyond and yet also within a single communicative period. These systems also enable synchronous communication, whereby I can type a message on my computer and it will appear almost instantaneously on another's screen in another geographical location. Likewise, I can telephone friends and share in their joys and disappointments through instantaneous voice communication. However, the types of relationship that exist when the subject is "here without being here" are different in form and expression from a face-to-face relationship. This idea will be examined in more detail in the following chapter.

With technologically mediated communication and increasingly abstract interaction, the creation of transcendental possibilities, or the development of new spaces, has been asserted. Stone (2000) writes:

> It is interesting that at just about the time the last of the untouched 'real-world' anthropological field sites are disappearing, a new and unexpected kind of 'field' is opening up—incontrovertibly social spaces in which people still meet face-to-face, but under new definitions of both 'meet' and 'face'. These new spaces instantiate the collapse of the boundaries between the social and technological, biology and machine, natural and artificial that are part of the postmodern imaginary. (506)

Therefore, according to commentators such as Stone, not only do time and space come to be experienced or understood differently when these categories are compressed or extended; for many, cyber-communication practices also lead to the creation and incorporation of new forms of time and space. Whether one agrees with this assessment or not, there is little doubt that the ways in which we experience and understand time and space have changed dramatically. The different forms of community—traditional, modern, and postmodern—discussed in the previous chapter are all constituted according to these different conceptions of time and space and their experiences of embodiment/presence.[28]

Paul Virilio has commented extensively on the effects of using technology for experiences of time and space. Virilio (1993) argues that we are currently witnessing the loss of the phenomenon of departure. With the increasing use of communication technologies, he argues, everything becomes situated within present time—accessible within the now—and experienced as a simultaneous happening. As he explains,

> the interface in real time definitely replaces the interval that had formerly constructed and organized the history and geography of our societies, leading

> to an obvious culture of paradox, in which everything arrives without there
> being any need either to travel or to leave in the slightest physical sense. (10)

Nevertheless, I would argue that we have not yet realized a fully postmodern form of society whereby all practices are disembodied, detached, or simultaneous. Although Virilio's observations are worth noting, they fail to recognize the coexistence of different experiences of time and space. Instead, disembodied practices coexist with embodied; immersive time with linear. However, it must also be acknowledged that,

> [m]odernity has, however, brought enormous and increasing changes in the
> tensions between the immediacy of here and now, our physical location in
> space and time, and the sorts of experiences, actions, events and whole worlds
> in which we can partake at a distance. Our experience of here and now has
> increasingly lost its immediate spatiotemporal referents and has become tied
> to and contingent on actors and actions at a distance. (Friedland & Boden,
> 1994a: 6)

While Friedland and Boden overstate the degree of embodiment or embodied practices prior to modernity (disembodied practices also took place then, though in different ways), they still highlight the changing experiences of time and space—in part through the adoption of various technologies—and the ontological consequences of such changes.

Abstraction (from Materiality, Including Bodies)
Friedland and Boden (1994a: 7) also make the point that language was "the first of many human inventions designed to manage space and time." One of the ways that language was used in oral cultures was to transmit stories and myths about the past to succeeding generations. Language is an abstract process inasmuch as it relies on shared understandings of symbols and abstract references to convey meanings. However, in oral cultures, language required embodied presence for its presentation and reception. It also enabled the presenter to use additional forms of communication—gestures, intonation, and so forth—to assist with the conveyance of meaning. As Boden and Molotch (1994: 259) note, "Co-presence is 'thick' with meaning." This requirement of co-presence was eliminated with the introduction of another (more) abstract process: writing. The use of writing to mediate relations changed both communicative possibilities and social practices.

Jack Goody (1986) asserts that writing enabled people to perceive themselves as detached from objects and experiences. Writing and literacy created a distancing; a separation of subject and object and a new way of envisaging, creating, and also theorizing one's own identity.

It also allowed the presenter of ideas or messages to reflect on these ideas and messages by enabling her/him to look over, ponder, and alter the content of written ideas. For Goody, the movement from an oral to a literate culture therefore provided the means for people to undertake more abstract cognitive processes. As Gerry Gill (1984) writes:

> abstract thought, critique, the various modes of mediative and systematic reflection that the medium of writing makes possible, have always allowed varying degrees of standing outside or abstraction from the given cultural framework. (82).

Though it is problematic to assume that it is possible to stand outside of a given cultural framework, the reflexive possibilities enabled by the distancing achieved through writing (with the fixing of the text in time and space, and the removal of presence) cannot be ignored. Goody argues that individualism becomes possible because individual achievements, tasks, and so forth are able to be recorded and later examined by anyone regardless of whether the individual to whom the record referred was personally known. This differed from preliterate society, where oral communication swallowed up individual achievement and incorporated it into a body of transmitted custom.[29]

The computer-networked transformation of information and communication possibilities similarly contains the potential to alter the way in which we think and relate to the world and to each other. Technologically mediated communication, at one level, accentuates the distancing or detachment experienced through writing. This distancing is even more extensive as a result of its prolific employment—as an increasingly relied-on form of communication—although the process, at another level, simultaneously decreases the perception of distance through the immediacy of communicative responses that are enabled. As a consequence, some mediation is experienced as intensely immersive and therefore, paradoxically, less detached. These seemingly contradictory experiences are worthy of further investigation.

In his own idiosyncratic way, Marshall McLuhan would agree with the argument that technology alters social forms through alterations in cognitive processes. He argues that writing abstracts thoughts from actions, leading to fragmentation and increased specialization (McLuhan, 1962: 22). In their book *The Global Village*, Marshall McLuhan and Bruce Powers argue that the effects of electronic technology are as dramatic as the social and individual transformations that they believe followed the development and implementation of the phonetic alphabet. "It [visual space] is a space perceived by the eyes when separated or abstracted from all other senses" (McLuhan & Powers, 1989: 45), whereas,

> [a]coustic space structure [that which is experienced in oral cultures and
> increasingly, McLuhan and Powers argue, in technological society] is the
> natural space of nature-in-the-raw inhabited by non-literate people. It is like
> the 'mind's ear' or acoustic imagination that dominates the thinking of pre-
> literate and post-literate humans alike. (45)

According to their analysis, visual space enables detachment and
objectivity, while acoustic space is involved and subjective. They write
about pre-literate and post-literate individuals operating within acoustic
space: "Thus they have no detached point of view. They are wholly
with the object. They go emphatically into it" (1989: 45). There is certainly
something about their recognition of the immersive nature of some
experiences of communication technology that resonates with
contemporary experiences. As noted earlier, some argue that online
communication within virtual communities is more focused as a result
of a reduction in the breadth and diversity of sensory input. However,
immersion within a communicative space through technology is
different from immersion within an embodied context, as is noted (later
in Chapter Three) by Blanchot. McLuhan's argument is that
overemphasizing one sense, disproportionate to the other senses, has
implications for the way in which we think and act (McLuhan, 1962:
265). For McLuhan, electronic technology is spontaneous and instantly
experienced. He attributes this form of technology with the capacity to
unite the people en masse, into almost tribalistic groupings where rituals
and emotional involvement are predominant.

> The electronic society ... does not have solid goals, objectives, or private
> identity. In it, man does not so much transform the land as he metamorphosizes
> himself into abstract information for the convenience of others....Loss of
> individualism invites once again the comfort of tribal loyalties. (McLuhan &
> Powers, 1989: 98)

> It was the funeral of President Kennedy that most strongly proved the power
> of television to invest an occasion with the character of corporate participation.
> It involved an entire population in a ritual process. (125)

However, when he is referring to technology, McLuhan is primarily
describing broadcast media, a unidirectional technology, which
emphasizes sound and rapidly changing images. His analysis does not
take into account the current modes of individuated interaction taking
place through communication technologies, such as in virtual
communities. Here participants are actively engaged in forms of
interaction via a keyboard and computer screen. This interaction is
detached in the same sense as writing except that here it can be either
synchronous or asynchronous communication processes that are taking

place. Interaction is removed from the body through its enactment textually, is seen visually, can be reflexively altered, and also can be recorded. Interaction via the Internet is also more individuated in its subjective outcome than broadcast media. This is because of the form and multidirectional process of Internet communication. Mobile telephones carry similar individualist tensions. Even their use in instigating "flash mobs" (seemingly spontaneous physical gatherings of strangers brought together through text commands received on phone screens, through blogs or other electronic media) is instantiated in different and more individual ways than through mass reception of a simultaneous broadcast.

Despite their concentration on broadcast media, McLuhan and Powers (1989) anticipate the effects on the individual of a global electronic village where time and space have been conquered:

> Without the countervailing balance of natural and physical laws, the new video-related media will make man implode upon himself. As he sits in the informational control room, whether at home or at work, receiving data at enormous speeds—imagistic, sound or tactile—from all areas of the world, the results could be dangerously inflating and schizophrenic. His body will remain in one place but his mind will float out into the electronic void, being everywhere at once in the data bank.
>
> Discarnate man is as weightless as an astronaut but can move much faster. He loses his sense of private identity because electronic perceptions are not related to place. (97)

We have yet to reach the stage where interaction via communications technology is experienced in the form forecast by McLuhan and Powers. However, I would argue that instead of losing one's "sense of private identity" as is hypothesized, in actuality the user of information and communications technology heightens his or her sense of private identity through physical distancing from others and the resultant compartmentalization that takes place. This process is explored in more detail in the next chapter.

Another difficulty with McLuhan and Powers's approach is that it assumes a passive subject who is unable to reject, modify, or control the medium or its effects (Poster, 1995). The approach is technologically determinist inasmuch as the technology is depicted as creating the effects, detracting from the understanding that it is the uses to which the technology is employed and the ways in which it is employed that create the effects.

Within the pages of the Australian journal *Arena*, an ongoing debate has centered on the subjectivity of the (post-) modern individual in a world dominated by practices of technology and science.[30] The *Arena* argument is that technology abstracts from and appropriates human social interaction and functions to the extent that human relations become increasingly impoverished of meaning for their participants. Phenomenally, much of human behavior, its interactions, and integrative practices are endowed with ritualistic or particularistic meaning for participants. When these practices are mediated or replaced by technology, human interaction is emptied out of these meanings and symbols, becoming more means-end oriented. Geoff Sharp (1993) uses the example of *in vitro* fertilization as an illustration of this argument. According to Sharp, to replace the practice of conceiving a child within a relationship with the practice of conception of a child by accessing *in vitro* techniques on demand undermines a socially and culturally significant process.[31] Sharp's argument is explored further below.

This *Arena* approach bears some similarities to the argument proposed by Albert Borgmann. Borgmann (1984) maintains that the introduction of technology to manage a task transforms that task, negating its social and cultural implications. He uses the example of heating systems, comparing the work, cooperation, and ritualized behavior involved in maintaining a fire for heating and cooking, with a central heating system. The first entails different people carrying out different tasks—for example, splitting the wood, collecting the kindling, stoking the fire—while working together as a unit or team, and the second involves the flick of a switch at the very most...and at the least, the system has been programmed to run itself after the initial program has been implemented.

Though these are appropriate observations, they also become open to criticisms of nostalgia and stasis. While I would not wish to reinforce the mantra of the inevitability of technological progress, to criticize the substitution or mediation of human practices with technological techniques on the basis of the undermining of ritual or cultural meaning appears limited—there does not seem to be adequate explanation or consideration for the ways in which humans invest all new mediation with their own particular symbolic or cultural meanings.[32]

What does need to be emphasized and appears to lack sufficient development in Borgmann, and to some extent in Sharp, is the way in which different forms of mediation across space and time alter the nature of the interaction. While technological mediation extends and expands the capacity for interconnectivity, it simultaneously enhances the individuation and compartmentalization of the individual. Therefore, while the individual can connect/interact with more people more frequently than in the past, s/he is also more (physically) isolated through the very form of the interaction itself. Increased individuation also results with the use of technology for enacting or mediating social practices, since there is less of a need for activities to be managed through group or communal efforts, as Borgmann noted. Therefore, as the need to engage with others becomes increasingly restricted to social interaction alone, the other activities and practices that are part of contemporary life become more and more compartmentalized and individuated.

However, the *Arena* perspective, in a sophisticated turn of theory, also emphasizes that there are different *levels of constitutive abstraction*. This emphasis goes beyond the approach undertaken by Borgmann. The term, levels of constitutive abstraction, is employed to describe the existence of varying degrees or relations of abstraction from presence, enacted within society concomitantly. For example, communication enacted through the use of a computer terminal is more abstract in form—more removed from presence—than communication that is enacted through letter writing, and even more abstract than face-to-face communication. The extent or degree of abstraction undertaken has implications for the ways in which the subject perceives him/herself and also the form by which s/he interacts with others. This understanding recognizes that the individual is always interacting across a number of different levels of abstraction, with some of these working in contradiction to one another. The *Arena* perspective is therefore able to accommodate arguments that technology has implications for social forms and intersubjective relationships, but it also incorporates recognition that such abstracted or extended forms coexist with those forms that are constituted predominantly in the face-to-face (although these 'earlier' forms are not unaffected by such coexistence). Within contemporary society, *Arena* argues, integrative practices are predominantly constituted through processes of extension and abstraction.[33]

Traditional, modern, and postmodern communities operate according to differing dominant levels of abstraction. Yet while there are undoubtedly differences between the levels or degrees of abstract processes that are dominant within each form of community, finding a language that is able to adequately encapsulate such abstract processes, their differences, and also apparent contradictions is extremely difficult. Traditional communities are enacted through predominantly face-to-face practices. As such these practices are most commonly linked or enacted through concrete embodied items and relations. Reciprocal practices, even when extended or abstracted outside of the face-to-face (when traditional forms of community were the dominant social form), were located in the exchange of concrete items that were handled directly in face-to-face exchanges. Modern communities stretch across larger areas of space, time, and persons, and therefore enact abstract or extended practices in a more generalized way. They are framed by the use of such abstract or representative items as newspapers that are produced and circulated through more extended processes such as the economic market. Postmodern communities display the most abstract processes—integrative processes that are disembodied. For example, exchanges are enacted through the mediation of symbolic or representative items. Online credit is an interesting illustration of this process. The purchase of an item online—with only a visual reproduction of the item—is undertaken through the entering of a credit account number. Even though concrete processes are enacted with the physical entering of such a number, these processes are merely the surface engagement of what is a more complex and abstract process. Through the entering of a credit number, the purchaser knows that s/he is accessing money—money that is physically realizable but abstractly represented as figures on a statement. S/he knows that certain processes will take place—for example, that the vendor will contact the bank and a transfer of money will take place from her or his account to the vendor's account, and that the item will be packaged and mailed through the postal system—and that s/he will receive the item in a predefined amount of time. Yet most of these processes take place at a distance or removed from the purchaser—to anyone not familiar with such processes, it would seem like the purchaser simply entered a stream of numbers into a machine, and then an item arrived; the connection between the two actions, or the complex processes that took place in between these two events, would not be apparent.

While abstraction processes do not inherently or necessarily involve the use of technology—they can take place as a result of the most concrete and 'un-technological' social practices—the growing utilization of technologies in contemporary social processes renders these abstract practices commonplace. For example, the earlier credit card illustration would have been incomprehensible to a person living at a time when barter was the sole means of commodity exchange. It similarly would have been difficult for a person who used coins made of metals (that were worth the value of the coin that they were signifying) to understand that a plastic card could take the place of coins. Part of this confusion would be a result of exposure to technologies that were, at that time, a long way from development, but it would also be as a result of certain conceptual moves and material processes that need to be made to accommodate such developments. [34]

These conceptual moves related to the material abstraction of social processes are also relevant to understanding the technological enactment of instrumentally rational processes, including the instrumentalization of relations with the Other.

Instrumentalization/Rationalization

> But in the contemporary period, the technological controls appear to be the very embodiment of Reason for the benefit of all social groups and interests — to such an extent that all contradiction seems irrational and all counteraction impossible. (Marcuse, 1968: 22)

> If man is challenged, ordered, to do this [exploit energies of nature], then does not man himself belong even more originally than nature within the standing-reserve?...Yet precisely because man is challenged more originally than are the energies of nature, i.e., into the process of ordering, he never is transformed into mere standing-reserve. Since man drives technology forward, he takes part in ordering as a way of revealing. But the unconcealment itself, within which ordering unfolds, is never a human handiwork, any more than is the realm through which man is already passing every time he as a subject relates to an object. (Heidegger, 1977: 18)

As mentioned earlier, Martin Heidegger believed that we should be concerned not with the question of technology itself, but rather with understanding its essence: technology as a manifestation of the underpinning worldviews and metaphysics of modernity. By turning to examine technology, we can gain insight into these underpinnings. According to his essay "The Question Concerning Technology," when we examine issues concerning the essence of technology, it becomes apparent that technology is more than a tool, and that its development and utilization have consequences and potentials that are ontologically important. For Heidegger, the essence of technology is ambiguous — it contains incredible potential for danger as well as the positive possibilities of revealing a new/truer essence of what it is to be human.[35]

However, most of Heidegger's attention — and it is this that concerns us here — is focused on the ways in which the use or implementation of technology is tied up with certain thought processes and a specific worldview. For Heidegger, using technology both reflects and affects the ways in which we view nature and ourselves.[36] To put it baldly — and probably badly — technology demonstrates an instrumental approach to the world; to see everything in terms of what it can do for us, and can do most effectively, rather than to see it in its own specificity. It is to turn everything into "standing-reserve." Heidegger (1977) writes:

> The revealing that rules in modern technology is a challenging [*Herausfordern*], which puts to nature the unreasonable demand that it supply energy that can be extracted and stored as such ....The earth now reveals itself as a coal mining district, the soil as a mineral deposit. (14)[37]

Thus for Heidegger, instrumentalization leads not only to objectification, but also to the undermining or potential elimination of existence. Even if we do not accept the full force of his argument, it is plausible to suggest that the use of technology to mediate social forms is in turn to understand these social forms as standing-reserve— objectified and also on hand to be able to satisfy individual social needs on demand. This suggestion reinforces the earlier argument proposed about the increasing instrumentalization and objectification of the Other as a consequence of technological mediation. The postmodern community—as the most technologically mediated community form— comes to be practiced and understood as the most rational, means-end efficient manner for individuals to manage their community relations.

Rationality is a dominant theme within debates around the intersection of society and technology. I am referring here to a specific form of rationality: that which Habermas refers to as instrumental rationality. As such, discussions about technique by Jacques Ellul, Lewis Mumford, or William Barrett become important in terms of describing the implications of technologies on the subjectivity of the individual. According to Jacques Ellul, technique does not refer solely to technology as device, rather, it is a particular mind-set that emphasizes the most efficient manner or procedure used to achieve an end. Technique is therefore explained as a procedural approach that can be taught, or as Ellul (1964) explains:

> Technique refers to any complex of standardized means for attaining a predetermined result. Thus, it converts spontaneous and unreflective behaviour into behaviour that is deliberate and rationalized. (vi)

Ellul argues that this reliance on technique leads to solutions for all problems being sought automatically from within the technological arena. Technology (as device) is employed since it is often understood as the most effective and thus efficient way of achieving a certain end. Technology (as device) is therefore an extension of rationalized behavior; it is utilized wherever it is deemed to be appropriate. Thus technological solutions are sought to remedy problems derived from the use of other technologies. An illustrative example can be seen in the methods by which people attempt to deal with information overload. As Tim Jordan (1999) notes, there is a spiral of technopower that develops. People turn to technological solutions to solve the problems introduced by the use of technology. He writes:

> [First]...information overload is an automatic result of entering cyberspace; the world of information is the world of too much information. Second, problems of information overload are normally dealt with by introducing

new technological tools that both manage information and place further technological distance between the user and information. Third, the new technological tools simply return users, after varying lengths of time, to the first step because new forms of information overload emerge. (128)

The continuing societal emphasis on means-end utilitarianism and instrumental rationalization—with its privileging of science and technology—has affected not only the way in which people see themselves, but also the authority and expectations they invest in such techniques and disciplines. This outcome is similar to the one described above by Heidegger (although arrived at through a different approach). Heidegger points to the enframing that has taken place with the turn-towards and utilization of technology—an enframing that reveals everything as standing-reserve and as a potential resource.

The possession of and control over information also become important here. Knowledge and information enhance the potential for control, and thus increased efficiencies. The perception is that the more information one can attain, the more efficient (better?) the society becomes. Habermas's (1981) colonization of the lifeworld thesis describes the manner in which instrumental rationalization—with its controlling and totalizing tendencies—appropriates ever more of those symbolic and mystic areas of social relations that orientate our norms and values. Habermas discusses the loss of meaning in society as being a consequence of the *lifeworld* being gradually appropriated by the *system*.[38]

It is Habermas's argument that within modernity, the traditional and cultural interpretations and meanings that structure the symbolic lifeworld have gradually been demystified and appropriated by the system via the use of technical (instrumental) rationality. This explains some of the alienation and cynicism displayed within current society. While we may disagree with aspects of Habermas's analysis, it is indisputable that the application of science and technology to enact, enhance, or control social processes has raised social and philosophical dilemmas as to the meaning and value of these processes. IVF technologies, genetic manipulation, and cloning have all resulted in the reassessing of the question of human existence. In a similar, though less philosophically challenging manner, the use of technologies to extend human relations and communication across time and space raises questions as to the value and meanings of certain social norms and practices. It could be argued that greater individual freedom has been the result of such practices, but also greater 'unfreedom.'

Superficially, technology looks like the pure servant of freedom: By increasing our powers it multiplies our opportunities to be free. But in attaining those powers we could very well lose the direct and organic sense of our relatedness to nature that humankind once knew; or, in Heidegger's words, we could attain mastery over beings, but lose the sense of Being itself. (Barrett, 1978: xix)

The pervasiveness of instrumental rationality and means-end utilitarianism is evident in all areas of social life, including in the form, content, and processes of constituting and maintaining relationships. Indeed, in his argument for network sociality as a new and pervasive social form, Andreas Wittel suggests that, increasingly, "personal relationships are *perceived* as becoming more important" (2001: 54). Wittel argues that these relationships are viewed as important because they are understood as economically valuable; an enactment of the adage "it is not what you know, but whom you know that matters," except that network sociality also views the *numbers* of people known as similarly important.

As technology has increasingly enabled the bridging of time and space, this has allowed the individual greater autonomy as to the relationships s/he chooses to maintain. It also means that these relationships can be slotted into the busy individual's life with as little disruption as possible. For example, technology has enhanced the possibility of twenty-four-hour access to social interaction. Of course, these technological developments and social practices arise largely as a result of the expansion of capitalism. Yet the processes enacted and the possibilities enabled by technology play an important role here too. Not only does the compartmentalization of the individual through technological practices and mediated relationships lead to him or her actively seeking out ways to reconnect, or strengthen bonds with others, but technology makes these connections with others seem less constrained by limiting factors such as time and space. And it is as Ellul noted: Technology is sought to solve the problem of compartmentalization and disconnection that is partly a consequence of extended and abstracted relations brought about by the use of technology. Yet the form and depth of such relationships on demand certainly requires examination. They have ramifications for the shape and expression of existent, and new, social forms and subjectivity.

These technological processes of abstraction, extension and compression, and instrumental rationalization intersect with the ontological categories of time and space, the body, and knowledge, altering the form in which they are experienced and understood. This intersection has consequences for subjectivities and intersubjective relations. Use of communication technologies affects community forms through these processes—of rationalization, abstraction, and compression/extension—and the ontological outcomes that result.

Heidegger makes the important point that it is not the content or specifics of particular technologies that should concern us; it is the processes that result as a consequence of (or are indicated by) technological thinking and practices that warrant further attention. This chapter has attempted to broaden the analysis of such processes through bringing together discussion of the *capacities* of communication technologies with discussion of the *processes* that arise as a consequence of their utilization.

It is now time to extend this analysis further to consider the intersubjective and subjective implications of these processes for forms and practices of community. This is the subject of the next chapter.

Notes

[1] Globally, there are increased opportunities for direct (via technological communication systems) political pressure and participation. For example, there is much debate about the introduction and possibilities of cyberdemocracy. However, the fact of digital divides (whichever way these are conceptualized) means that these claims are only applicable to some people—others face decreased possibilities for participation and information acquisition.

[2] This is not to negate the effects of the other forms of technology; it is simply a strategic move to create a manageable project.

[3] For more elaboration of the political and cultural implications of the broadcast media, see McCoy (1993) and Holmes (1997b).

[4] See Foucault (1977), Poster (1990), and Lyon (1994) for further elaboration on the effects and potential of the Panopticon (based on Jeremy Bentham's prison model). Poster refers to this phenomenon as a Superpanopticon. However, he does not emphasize the role of the gaze, or visibility, in the application and self-imposition of a subject's normalization processes. Databases enable an extension of that visibility into abstracted space, enabling a more pervasive and intrusive gaze than that achievable without technological extension.

[5] The power of normalization refers to the process by which a subject self-imposes or internalizes particular norms and behaviors to conform to a self-perceived (but socially constructed) understanding of normality. See Foucault (1977).

[6] Passive only in the sense that they cannot contribute in the information process back to the producers—the only recourse they have is in the manner they choose to accept, reject, or view the material. See Poster (1995) for his discussion of the broadcast media.

[7] Although some writers argue the immersive nature of broadcast media and note the close attachments that individual viewers experience to characters on-screen. See Thompson's (1995: 219) notion of mediated quasi-interaction, which he describes as non-dialogical, non-reciprocal "intimacy at a distance."

[8] Increasingly we are seeing attempts being made by the traditional broadcast media to incorporate audience interaction into their productions. For example, *Big Brother* allows the audience to decide on the outcomes of the show (i.e., who gets voted out of the house).

⁹ This is not to be drawn into the debate as to the universality, or otherwise, of access and participation on the Internet.

¹⁰ For example, President Clinton's attempted bill—the Communications Decency Act—was intended to monitor and censor objectionable material being broadcast over the Internet.

¹¹ Rice asserts that there is little difference in the function of "pre-electronic" practices such as the use of the social calling card to manage social encounters (Rice, 2002: 127). This may be true; however, the practices facilitated by technology discussed here are not necessarily being claimed as different in function. Instead it is the form of the practice that is of interest. These practices instantiate particular and individual practices of time and space within an everyday routinized context.

¹² It is much easier, for example, to deliver bad news to somebody whom you feel you are letting down via the phone or through e-mail than face-to-face. This is partly because you do not have to deal with the full expression of the other's disappointment, and partly because you can escape more easily from the situation (because you have a more immediate way of terminating discussion, through hanging up or using asynchronous discussion, than a more extended walking-away-from). Such escape heightens the compartmentalizing of relationships, which, it is argued here, is increasingly taking place. See also Boden and Molotch (1994) for more on the differences between face-to-face and mediated relationships.

¹³ This is despite the fact that those in the strongest positions of power continue to control or have greatest access to these technologies, and those in the weakest positions have the least access.

¹⁴ Virtual communities are disembodied communities or those communities that are conducted through an abstracted or disembodied form. Textually oriented groups have also been described as virtual communities. See Stone (2000) and Connery (1997).

¹⁵ It is worth noting that these virtual community participants often feel the need to reinforce/complement their disembodied relations with other more embodied or sensorial contacts. For example, participants on the WELL—a virtual community on the Internet—have regular face-to-face picnics and social gatherings (Rheingold, 1993).

¹⁶ See the various works by Barry Wellman and colleagues investigating the interrelationship of virtual and real space communities.

¹⁷ For example, see Kolko, Nakamura, and Rodman (2000).

¹⁸ See Balsamo (1996).

¹⁹ See Lessig (1999) for his discussion of the increasing regulation of cyberspace designed to meet the needs of commercial operations.

²⁰ This is the name of an early virtual community.

²¹ This is a fairly drastic step and usually requires certain consultation with others before action is taken (Smith, 1992: 29).

²² These will be touched on to some degree in Chapter Four.

²³ This notion of the good life is quite antithetical to understandings like MacIntyre's. MacIntyre—along with numerous other critics of postmodernist writings—argues that what is missing in contemporary life are common understandings and ethics that provide guidelines, cohesion, and meaning for our society. Without an intersubjective notion of the good life, he argues, we have turned to procedures as a way to determine everyday practices and lifestyles (MacIntyre, 1981). This procedural approach results in an increasing social reliance on instrumentally rational processes, and correspondingly, on technological assistance.

²⁴ Statistics show that 50 percent of postings on the WELL were contributed by only 1 percent of users (Smith, 1992: 96). Most users do not, therefore, actively participate in the construction of community (see also DiMaggio et al., 2001: 318).

[25] Now graphics and sound are being gradually incorporated.

[26] These arguments will be examined more closely in Chapter Six. However, it is necessary to mention at this point that an understanding such as Rheingold's fails to consider the subjective and intersubjective implications of mediation through, and use of, technology on the individual and the community. Poster, it will be argued, fails to develop these subjective implications adequately.

[27] While I would agree that the subject should not be considered as operating from a "preconstituted position of subjectivity," I do not agree with Poster's assertion about the inappropriateness of examining effects. While technology does reflect, accentuate, and reproduce the processes of modernity, it must also be understood as directly implicated in the production of these processes and effects.

[28] As stated, they are affected by their intersection with other forms of community and also the dominant modes of time and space operational within the society in any particular historical period.

[29] See McLuhan (1962: 27–37) for further explanation. The inclusion of writing in discussions of technology may perhaps seem a little liberal in interpretation. It can be seen, however, later in this discussion, that writing can easily fall within the rubric of technique and the rationality that is incorporated within it. This is where overlap and interconnections can be seen.

[30] As Geoff Sharp (1993) explains, his focus is on "the radical difference between interactive engagement, entailing as it does mutual presence, and the technologically extended forms of the social which dispense with presence and with direct interaction as well" (225). As such, even the pen (writing instrument) acts as a technological extension.

[31] Geoff Sharp (1993) also argues that writing and the printing process were the beginnings of technology—or in his schema, technological extended forms of the social. He writes that they "are associated with a distinctive form of identity and social being and that their proliferation in the present period contributes to that condition which is variously referred to as late modernity or, in line with my own preference, post modernity" (221).

[32] It should be noted that the *Arena* position takes a far more complex approach than simply positing the end of rituals to changes resultant upon mediated social practices. See Sharp (1993) for a more detailed discussion.

[33] See Sharp (1985).

[34] Here, the *Arena* argument brings us closer to a way of theorizing such changing modes of practice. Sharp (1993) talks about the abstract practices used by intellectuals and the increasing incorporation of these practices within everyday life. The intellectual is required to remove her or himself intellectually from the phenomenon that s/he is examining in order to critically engage with that phenomenon.

[35] See in particular *The Question Concerning Technology and Other Essays* (1977), page 33 onward. "The essence of technology is in a lofty sense ambiguous. Such ambiguity points to the mystery of all revealing, i.e., of truth. On the one hand, Enframing challenges forth into the frenzy of ordering that blocks every view into the coming-to-pass of revealing and so radically endangers the relation to the essence of truth. On the other hand, Enframing comes to pass for its part in the granting that lets man endure—as yet unexperienced, but perhaps more experienced in the future— that he may be the one who is needed and used for the safekeeping of the coming to presence of truth. Thus does the arising of the saving power appear" (Heidegger, 1977: 33).

[36] "Technology is therefore no mere means. Technology is a way of revealing" (1977: 12).

[37] See Heidegger (1977: 14–16) for more discussion on standing-reserve.

[38] The *lifeworld* is described as the sphere of symbolic intersubjective relations. It is characterized as representing the intersubjective, normative, and ethical practices that orient the social practices and relations in any society. The *system* describes the structures and institutions through which society operates (the state and the capitalist market). The operation and development of science, technology, and "impartial reason/instrumental rationality" characterize the system. See Habermas (1981).

Chapter Three

~~~

Intersubjectivity, Technology, and Community

In the previous chapters, it was argued that the ways in which social relations are understood and experienced across time and space have ramifications for the types and forms of community that are enacted. It was also argued that technological usage has contributed to the increasing dominance of extended social forms and social practices. Despite the varying and numerous understandings of the concept, community necessarily describes ways of being-together: It involves interactions between, and the coalescing of, groups of people. Thus, any discussion of community concerns both the subjects of a community and also the relations between those subjects. Norms, values, and attitudes are socially constituted and transmitted through communication processes and integrative practices. Attitudes and approaches with regard to relationships with the Other are also displayed. A study of communication processes allows suppositions to be drawn about the nature of the relationships between participants. This is particularly relevant in any discussion of community. And since technology is increasingly employed to mediate or extend communication processes, it too becomes relevant within any analysis of community.

The community theorists considered in the second half of this book all emphasize the importance of communication in one form or another as being central to practices of community. Yet the ways in which these theorists consider and position issues of communication differ. For example, for Charles Taylor, communication is understood as dialogue of a verbal nature supplemented by nonverbal communication such as dress or body language; whereas for Jean-Luc Nancy, communication in the form of literature and writing reveals community. These understandings or emphases on the type and importance of communication are premised on particular understandings of subjectivity, intersubjective relations, and interactions.

This chapter explores the implications of changes in the structuring of ontological categories for intersubjective relations and thus for community. Technology is centrally involved with these structural changes; through the material processes of abstraction, extension, and rationalization, technology enables the stretching of community across time and space, changes the experience of embodiment, and alters our understandings of being-in-the-world, including our understandings of being-together. As relations are mediated or become more abstracted from concrete embodied interactive forms, I argue, that they become thinner and potentially more instrumental, thus undermining the possibilities and spaces for mutuality. Mutuality is understood and used here as relations, communication, and other integrative practices enacted by those who recognize and interact with each other as equal, ethical participants. These statements will be developed throughout the chapter.

Again, as in the introduction, the importance of the theoretical consideration of both form and content (in the way that I have used the terms) must be asserted. As such, the following pages will explore different types of intersubjective relations and the implications these hold for relations with the Other, and they will also examine the implications of extending communication and intersubjective relations through and across different ontological forms of knowledge, time and space, and embodiment.

A further point with regard to methodology must be made. While this chapter will consider the implications of changes to the form or structure of ontological categories, I also want to ensure the inclusion of more phenomenal considerations. This means that elements of a Foucauldian approach—at least in regard to consideration of the ordering of humans within space and time—are useful. This is not to take a poststructuralist position on questions of order, but, as in previous chapters, to acknowledge the descriptive power of such an approach.

This chapter is divided into three sections. The first revisits the discussion of ontological categories begun in the introduction. The notion that the forms in which these categories are experienced are constitutive of subjectivity and that they result in the enactment of different intersubjective relations is discussed. The second section develops a conceptual language to describe and understand different forms or practices of intersubjective relations. The third section brings elements of section one and section two together to consider the implications of different framings of interactive and integrative practices for intersubjectivity. From here some assertions are made as to the predominance of particular intersubjective relations in particular forms of community.

Ontological Categories Revisited

In the introduction, it was noted that changes in ontological categories have ramifications for community forms and social relations. The categories of knowledge, time and space, and embodiment were highlighted in particular, as relevant to the analysis undertaken within this book. It was also noted that these categories were in no way to be considered as distinct and unrelated in practice, but that it was simpler for the purposes here to treat them as analytically separate (while acknowledging the practical existence of their interrelation). Chapter Two explored some of the processes that are instituted through the use of technologies to mediate and extend social relations and integrative practices. These processes intersect with ontological categories, altering subjectivities and intersubjective relations.

The purpose of returning to an examination of ontological categories is to reassert how changes in the ways in which these categories are experienced influences subjectivity and the different community forms that are realized (and therefore, necessarily, the forms of intersubjectivity). I have argued that the technological extension and mediation of integrative practices has consequences for the form in which the various categories are experienced. This claim is elaborated here in more detail. From this point it will be possible to draw some correlations between the following discussion about types of intersubjective relations and the framing of ontological experiences.

Modes of Social Explanation (Knowledge)

As mentioned earlier, knowledge schemas provide explanations and frameworks through which society understands and negotiates its daily life. Mythology, theology, and philosophy, for example, are all modes of explanation or knowledge. These modes are initiated and enacted by people when attempting to understand and navigate through their lives—their roles, positions, relations, and expectations. But these frameworks are not constructed or adopted from out of a vacuum, untouched by social events and practices enacted around them; a complex interchange takes place in which practices and ideas feed mutually into one another. Nikolas Rose (1996) argues:

> The history of our relation to ourselves should not be posed in terms of ideas, but of *technologies*: the intellectual and practical instruments and devices

enjoined upon human beings to shape and guide their ways of 'being human.'
(300)

Conversely, I have stated that it is not so simple to separate technologies and devices (techniques) from ideas; they are intertwined. Technologies, in the sense that Rose employs the term, are outcomes of and also sources for ideas.[1] It is a chicken-and-egg argument to argue for the primacy or importance of one over the other. What I want to do is point not only to the interconnected ways in which knowledge schemas are constructed out of particular phenomenal situations but also to how they create and change situations. Therefore, these schemas can be understood in part as a reflection of the society or community within which they are produced, and also as being partly responsible for particular configurations and organizations of social forms. Rose also argues that understandings and suppositions drawn about particular or contemporary subjectivities are themselves subject to and arise out of particular understandings or discourses of what it means to be human: "Any way of describing ourselves and others—as persons, selves, individuals, personalities, characters, gendered bodies... is a *resultant* of the processes under study" (Rose, 1996: 299). For example, as social relations are increasingly mediated or able to be extended further across time and space, knowledge schemas reflect, explain, and situate such changes in ways that enable them to be adopted and understood by social actors. However, these schemas also play a role in the possibilities of this extension in the first place.

It is part of the argument in this book that as community relations in general become more abstracted and mediated across time and space, away from direct and embodied interaction and integration through the employment of technological mediums, that subjectivity and intersubjective relations are affected. For example, as explained in Chapter One, in modern (and even more noticeably in postmodern) communities there is the perception of increased individual freedom and increased choice as actions and relations are experienced as being less constrained by particular space and time limits. This is largely a consequence of the possibilities enabled by the development of certain technologies. Yet as the perception of individual freedom is increased, conversely the emphasis on or awareness of complex social interconnectedness is diminished.

As noted in Chapter Two, the development and utilization of technology itself is part of specific knowledge schemas.[2] For example, instrumentally rational processes—that were shown to be part of the impetus for the development and use of technology—originate out of specific knowledge schemas. For the moment, however, it is more than simply interesting to note that many of the schemas that are currently in place (and predominant) are those that assert individuality and autonomy. This has a significant bearing on the nature of community and broader social relations in the present.

One understanding underlying contemporary Western society is the notion of self-construction. Charles Taylor refers to an "ethic of authenticity," Geoff Sharp and the *Arena* group write of the "ideology of autonomy," while others such as Ulrich Beck talk of the necessity of constructing one's own biography. While each theoretical position differs in some ways, all emphasize that choices are imposed on the individual; and on that individual desiring choice, unlimited choice. Certainly, with the questioning of grand narratives and the positing of other alternatives (and how much of this has to do with the increased flexibility and mobility enabled by technological developments?), individuals are being required to make choices about every aspect of their lives. Sharp notes that, in contemporary Western societies, people "experience themselves as the makers of their own individual lives as well as of their collective historical existence" (Sharp, 1993: 223). And Beck and Beck-Gernsheim (1996) comment that:

> [t]he decisive feature of these modern regulations or guidelines is that, far more than earlier, individuals must, in part, supply them for themselves, import them into their biographies through their own actions....For modern social advantages one has to *do* something, to make an active effort. One has to win, know how to assert oneself in the competition for limited resources— and not only once, but day after day.
>
> The normal biography thus becomes the 'elective biography', the 'reflexive biography', the 'do-it-yourself biography.' (25)

Individuals are thus described by some commentators as being required to consciously and actively construct themselves from a multiplicity of choices, without the guidance of unquestioned social values, traditions, or truths. While this description is disputed by others,[3] the perception of self-construction is certainly widely held in Western society and it reflects most individuals' active experience of life. For example, most people in Australia would see themselves largely as the makers of their own destiny, and they would understand their life as consisting of a series of choices, the determination of which could "make or break" them.

On one level, however, the degree or extent of agency available/ attributable to the self or subject is debatable. The subject operates within a framework in which s/he has been socialized. S/he understands the world through the explanatory schemas and guidelines that operate within (and preceding) her/his time period. According to Foucault, practices of the self are not something the individual invents, but "patterns that he finds in his culture and which are proposed, suggested and imposed on him by his culture, his society and his social group" (Foucault, 1988: 11). This means that even though, at another level, there is certainly the experience or perception of being an unconstrained individual who is consciously responsible for fashioning her/himself and the direction of her/his life, this experience takes place within certain constraining and enframing structures. To assert otherwise is to fail to recognize and acknowledge the embedded and enframed nature of the social relations within which one is already immersed. Although the framing and experience of these relations have changed to some degree historically, this is not to assert that newer forms lack framing and structure themselves. It is simply that they differ. Therefore, in contemporary Western society, there is definitely choice available to the individual (as there was in earlier times), but the framing and types of such choices are different from previous ones.

However, having made such a qualification, it must be acknowledged that social life has become less constrained in some ways. Part of this lessening of constraints can be attributed, as has been mentioned, to the possibilities enabled by technology. It is also necessary to point to the fact that as social relations are increasingly mediated through 'individually activated' technological means, that a greater emphasis is placed on the individual and his/her individual choices and desires. The contemporary (networked) individual can choose quite purposively—and indeed is required to choose in such a way—whom s/he wants to keep in contact with, and whom s/he wishes to exclude and ignore, to a degree not possible previously. For example, answering machines, mobile phones, and online access are all frequently oriented toward the individual's maintenance and also management of her/his social contacts.[4] Phone calls and phone numbers can be screened, and answered selectively. Contact can be initiated and maintained with others on the other side of the world, whilst the neighbors next door can be ignored (or contact not initiated). Surveillance and data collection practices also heighten an awareness of individual action and accountability. Knowledge schemas that promote individual autonomy and self-realization fit neatly into and perpetuate such practices.

What does all this say for understandings of community and communal relations? The emphasis on the idea of autonomy focuses on self or individual choices—of course this can and does mean choices to participate in a particular community, but the origin of that choice is centered on what appears best for that individual. Much of the discourse surrounding the network society evinces many of these notions. As space and time become more readily and easily traversed, understandings and practices of globalization feed into concepts like the nation-state and the notion of individual autonomy, leading increasingly to the perception that community memberships can be easily chosen or discarded (and perhaps devaluing community membership in the process?). The uncritical promotion of virtual communities or the networked individual likewise encourages this individualistic orientation. Indeed, it is arguable that even the imagined possibilities for such disembodied modes of interaction and integration reflect or serve to accentuate instrumental and individualistic understandings toward the community and toward the Other. These understandings are replicated in the prevalent modes of social organization.

Modes of Social Organization (Within Time and Space)

Modes of social organization refers to the ways in which people collectively order and manage their lives. The observance and practice of routines, traditions, or cultural norms are some of the many ways through which societies coordinate and manage themselves. These strategies involve designing, coordinating, and experiencing activity and production within and across time and space in particular ways.

Space and time are lived phenomena across which social relations and integrative practices are enacted and ordered. Where different organizations, experiences, and understanding of time and space exist, they are linked to different forms of social relations and to differing forms of subjectivity. As discussed in the previous chapter, numerous social commentators have noted the increasing compression of time and space and the implications this holds for subjectivity and social forms. For example, David Harvey (1990) talks of the rationalization of time and the compression of space and time, while Anthony Giddens talks of different ways of experiencing and organizing time and space, or "time-space distanciation."[5] It is part of the argument in this book that the compression/extension of time and space has ramifications for the forms of community that are possible. For example, modern or postmodern forms of community could not *be* without the existence of some capacities for extending social relations and integrative practices across time and space. These community relations also incorporate different understandings of these categories.

Modes of understanding have been involved in, applied to, and derived from the social experiences of such time and space extension/ compression. Modes of organization have also necessarily been involved as ways of coordinating changing lifestyles, populations, and practices become necessary. Charles Taylor (1991) notes that in contemporary Western society,

> [m]obility is in a sense forced on us. Old ties are broken down. At the same time, city dwelling is transformed by the immense concentrations of populations of the modern metropolis. By its very nature, this involves more impersonal and casual contact, in place of the more intense, face-to-face relations in earlier times. All this cannot but generate a culture in which the outlook of social atomism becomes more and more entrenched. (59)

Social relations and integrative practices have necessarily had to evolve and change to accommodate circumstances, developing and adapting the technologies—both in terms of physical devices and of social practices—necessary to facilitate these processes. For example, the interconnective capacities of communication technologies are eagerly adopted as a means of supplementing and/or creating social connectedness within an environment of social atomism. Yet, as discussed in Chapter Two and explored below, there are phenomenal and ontological consequences of technologically mediated social practices to be taken into account.

Historically, Michel Foucault notes how different techniques of power were introduced to manage and coordinate growing urban populations in order to produce more effective and efficient subjects. Anthony Giddens describes a similar phenomenon in his account of the growth of bureaucratic structures and the associated increase in surveillance strategies in the workplace, the home, and within the state. And Benedict Anderson (1991) reveals how techniques and technology become entwined in the pursuit of a coherent and unified nation-state:

> No one has found a better metaphor for this frame of mind than the great Indonesian novelist Pramoedya Ananta Toer, who entitled the final volume of his tetralogy on the colonial period *Rumah Kaca*—the Glass House. It is an image, as powerful as Bentham's Panopticon, of total surveyability. For the colonial state did not merely aspire to create, under its control, a human landscape of perfect visibility; the condition of this 'visibility' was that everyone, everything, had (as it were) a serial number. This style of imagining did not come out of thin air. It was the product of the technologies of navigation, astronomy, horology, surveying, photography and print, to say nothing of the deep driving power of capitalism. (184–185)

Therefore, changes in the ways in which time and space are lived and organized have ramifications for intersubjective relations and subjectivity in at least two ways. Firstly, as community relations, communications, and social practices are extended in time and across space they are mediated, whether institutionally, or through technological means; and secondly, these relations, communications, and practices are subjected to organizing and surveillance processes.

The first change, the living of increasingly extended relations—as will be discussed in the following section of this chapter—results in more instrumental, thinner, and increasingly abstract experiences of intersubjectivity. Anderson, Harvey, and Calhoun, among an increasing number of social commentators, point to the development of technologies such as the printing press and transport technologies as enabling the production and maintenance of extended communities. Such technologies are necessary for the extension and mediation of community relations and for integrative practices to be employed where communities are primarily constituted outside of the face-to-face. Yet extension has implications for the depth of associations enacted. Relations are thinned as they are stretched across time and space, becoming less dimensional as they become increasingly specialized in focus, and are more instrumental as a consequence. This claim is further elaborated in the following section of this chapter.

The second change, the organizing and surveillance of relations and practices, also leads to particular subjective, and thus intersubjective, outcomes. As was mentioned in the introduction, Foucault's discussion of disciplinary power and disciplinary space is instructive in terms of describing the effects of situating and organizing subjects across space and time. This mode or technique of power was utilized to coordinate and effectively manage (and to encourage the self-management of) the population and its systems of production across space and time. These techniques are part of the operation and reproduction of systems necessary for the functioning of larger imaginary communities such as the nation-state. Foucault notes that the increased use of extended abstract surveillance, or disciplinary space, leads to a more universalized but individuated subject—a subject who is self-monitoring.[6] As noted in Chapter Two, the use of interconnected communication technologies for surveillance and administrative processes has increased the scale of disciplinary space, extending and heightening the effect of surveillance on the individual.[7]

A merging of both communication and surveillance intents often takes place. Architecture plays a part here, with its management and ordering of space. It organizes space so as to open some areas for communal or social activity, and it closes some areas to individual activity alone. It can enable the separation and segregation of some from others, or the merging of those some with others. Gated communities are a very obvious example of the ways in which architecture and technology work together to enable some groups of people to live and socialize together, while simultaneously excluding all others external to the group from entry and participation. With the growth of online communities, virtual architecture, and interactive technological communications, new ways of organizing space and time (and relations with the Other) have become evident. Virtual communities, for example, have their own gates; there are certain preconditions for entry and for (continued) membership. These communities are also being celebrated as new public spheres that are opening possibilities for democratic and open communication, and for new modes of sociality.[8]

> They [electronic virtual communities] are part of a range of innovative solutions to the drive for sociality—a drive that can be frequently thwarted by the geographical and cultural realities of cities increasingly structured according to the needs of powerful economic interests rather than in ways that encourage and facilitate habitation and social interaction in the urban context. (Stone, 2000: 523)

These interactive forms have implications for the ways in which we understand and experience time and space. As Merleau-Ponty wrote:

> For us to be able to conceive space, it is in the first place necessary that we should have been thrust unto it by our body and that it should have provided us with the first model of those transpositions, equivalents and identifications which make space into an objective system and allow our experience to be one of objects, opening out onto and "in itself." (Merleau-Ponty in Kennedy, 2000: 18)

With virtual (postmodern) communities, however, it is not the body that is thrust into space, it is the awareness of and participation in an interaction that is conducted apart or detached from the body.[9] Yet whether this is because virtuality is an extension of an embodied experience of spaces, or because its conceptual framework depends on particular understandings of space, participants do tend to think of their interaction as located within a particular spatial location. And while this is a space that is detached from physical bodies, it is experienced emotionally and psychically through bodies. Such reconfiguring or reconceptualizing of the relationship between embodied and disembodied spaces requires new ways of understanding issues and experiences of embodiment. This is the third theme.

Mode of Presence (Embodiment)

> Bodies, bodies everywhere. Philosophy, feminist thought, cultural studies, science studies, all seem to have rediscovered bodies. In part this may be because we have to do some reflection upon being embodied in relation to

the various new technologies that we are encountering in the twenty-first century. (Ihde, 2002: xi)

According to Hubert Dreyfus (drawing heavily on Merleau-Ponty), there are three aspects of embodiment. First, there is the biological and phenomenal aspect of being-in-a-body with all of its physical capabilities and constraints. This leads to the second aspect, where these capabilities and constraints frame the ways in which we view and approach the world (for example, whether we view a mountain as passable or not depends on our physical capacities). This is to understand the subject as self-world relational—people understand the world according to how their physical bodies engage with/in the world. It also entails the development and refinement of skills for negotiating the physical world. The third aspect is the application and utilization of skills acquired for/ in the negotiation and understandings of the cultural world that the subject is embedded within. Dreyfus uses an example of a letterbox, arguing that these boxes "afford" mailing letters and that this is an "affordance that comes from experiences with mail boxes and the acquisition of letter-mailing skills. The cultural world is thus also correlative with our body; this time with our acquired cultural skills" (Dreyfus, 1996). The analysis seems adequate until we introduce questions about the social implications of varying experiences of embodiment brought about through the utilization of technology. If we extend Dreyfus's discussion, then it might be possible to understand technology as simply a tool that extends physical capabilities. In this context, embodiment is viewed according to the physical and cultural possibilities enabled by the technology and the skills acquired through its utilization. Yet I have argued that technology is to be understood as more than simply an extension of human capabilities; more than a tool. While skills acquisition is important, it is the subjective and intersubjective affect derived through, but also evidenced within, the enactment of these skills to which I want to draw closer attention.
Stone writes that

[i]n technosociality, the social world of virtual culture, technics is nature. When exploration, rationalization, remaking and control mean the same thing, then nature, technics and the structure of meaning have become indistinguishable. The technosocial subject is able successfully to navigate through this treacherous new world. S/he is constituted as part of the evolution of communications technology and of the human organism, in a time in which technology and organism are collapsing, imploding, into each other. (Stone, 2000: 523)

This statement follows Dreyfus's and Merleau-Ponty's point about the self-world relational aspect of embodiment; as allowing for the ability to navigate through a world according to personal capabilities and competences. However, it does not extend the analysis sufficiently to enable discussion of intersubjective relations as a consequence of these experiences of embodiment. Consideration of such issues is important for understanding the types of intersubjective relations enacted within different forms of community.

In Chapter One, I introduced three analytical forms of community for discussion. These forms—traditional, modern, and postmodern— all display different dominant modes of integration and communication. I want to argue that the ways in which the body and being-in-a-body have been experienced has changed as these dominant modes of social relations have become abstracted and extended across time and space. Knowledge schemas have also participated in and reflected these changes. It is arguable, and indeed is argued by some theorists discussed in the previous chapter, that the increasing ability to engage in a disembodied manner enables a reflexivity that was not practiced in earlier, embodied, aural (pre-literate) societies. In such societies, all interactive and integrative practices were either taking place in a face-to-face context, or were represented in the exchange of concrete items that were encoded with specific (shared) social meanings.[10] The argument made by these writers is that the development of written culture enabled a corresponding development in individual and social reflexivity and detachment to take place.[11] Written communication certainly enabled the extension and mediation of an individual's personal communications to take place across time and space, detached from the body of the communicator. This was different from the earlier movement of symbolically encoded items which, while they certainly extended communication and integrative practices across a particular time and space, were constrained by the necessity of moving among those who understood such encoding, and also more importantly, were not able to convey the intentions and expressions of individual actors in a way that is possible in written communication. This ability to extend individual communications across space and time heightens the individual focus of the communication, lifting it out of the communal or social setting. I am not asserting that communication is not culturally loaded or socially encoded; all communication and integrative practices arise within a cultural and social environment that inscribes meaning to these practices. However, extended or mediated communication is lifted out to the extent that the utterance or communication is not received in the same social setting within which the communicator is situated and it does not carry with it all the background 'noise' and information that takes place within a face-to-face setting. Noting that "[t]he whole world is offered to us, but by way of a gaze...," Maurice Blanchot (1993) asks the question,

> Why take part in a street demonstration if at the same moment, secure and at rest, we are at the *demonstration* [*manifestation*] itself thanks to a television set? (240)

While this may be (virtually) true at one level, the experiential quality of actually attending a demonstration and being surrounded by activity, noise, and smells is a more complex and involving experience than the distancing achieved via the medium of a television screen. Similarly, I have argued that the enactment of relationships entirely online is a different and more one-dimensional experience than a relationship enacted entirely in the face-to-face.

Changes in the ways in which embodiment is experienced, through the application and utilization of knowledge schemas and the stretching or extension of relationships across time and space, has implications for the ways in which we understand our bodies and the relations we have with others. Some generalizations here can serve as examples. Earlier, mention was made of the detachment or reflexivity that became possible with the introduction of writing as a mediated communicative process. Mind and body became figuratively separable. This separation, it is being argued, has extended with the development of cyberspace. The interaction that takes place through a computer screen is disembodied to such an extent that it has been claimed that regular users view the body with disdain, as meat, which could be left behind or discarded if it were possible (Dery, 1996). Such views are reflected, as is often noted, in William Gibson's (1984) science fiction novel *Neuromancer*.[12]

It does not appear plausible that we have (or will ever have) reached the stage where disembodied interaction means that the body is completely left behind, as something that has to be tended to on a minimal basis to ensure its continued survival.[13] Instead, Stone (2000) argues that what is involved is a reformulating of embodiment. She writes that,

> In all, the unitary, bounded, safely warranted body constituted within the frame of bourgeois modernity is undergoing a gradual process of translation to the refigured and reinscribed embodiments of the cyberspace community. (523)

While I do not want to assert a completely new configuration of embodiment since earlier modes of being also continue to operate, there is a place for arguing that new ways of being lead to a reworking of notions and experiences of embodiment. As the individual's interactions and integrative practices become more abstracted (in some ways) from her/his body, a more detached understanding of the body is possible. The contempt, or perhaps more accurately, disengagement, that is depicted as part of the cyberspace users' attitude to the body is seen to a lesser degree in the everyday attitudes that Western contemporary individuals and societies demonstrate toward the body.[14] This does not mean that bodies become irrelevant to people. Rather, they are viewed instrumentally; as another aspect of the individual's life to be modified, managed, and transformed. Plastic surgery, weight training, and dieting are all attempts to manage, sculpt, and present the body as if it could be transcended. Physical adornment of the body—whether through the donning of physical attire or through decoration or marking upon the body—has always been a characteristic of human behavior. In more traditional settings, particularistic physical marking of the body was culturally specific and represented tribal or hierarchical significance. By contrast, in contemporary Western society, physical marking such as tattooing is approached more as a decorative device that primarily holds individual relevance. Of course, cultural markers are still used, yet there is the perception that these markers are chosen by individuals much as they would choose their wardrobe or other external representations.

This preoccupation with the body as transcendable or malleable, however, also points to the underlying essentiality of bodies—however differently conceived and experienced they might be across different ontological formations. This essentiality undermines cyber-enthusiasts' predictions of the eventual elimination of the body. And it accentuates the need to re-theorize understandings of embodiment under conditions of extended or detached integrative processes.

In Western techno-society, people interact with simulations, representations, and the extended communications of others. Whereas in tribal societies cultural and social information may have been passed on through the elders of that society, in contemporary society such information is passed on through a complex relationship with a variety of mediums: the family, the state, and the media. Contemporary subjectivity is shaped by the predominance of abstract, individualized, but also universalized integrative forms overlaying and impacting on more concrete embodied processes. What the implications of such subjective and intersubjectively constituted forms are for both individual and community relationships requires further deliberation. To begin this process, a language for discussing different intersubjective forms is required. This is the subject of the next section.

Intersubjectivity

In preceding chapters, it was pointed out that the subject is socially embedded and socially constituted. Indeed, it was noted that it is not possible to examine the individual person without recognition of her/ his social environment. There are individual influences—experiences or particularities specific to that individual—that affect that person's subjectivity, yet these are relevant primarily because of the social relevance attributed to them. Subjectivity is therefore not something that is arrived at independently—influence must also be attributed to those with whom that individual interacts. Since society does not consist of bounded isolated individuals, there are the considerations and constraints of others to be taken into account.

People live with/in relationships of dependence with emotional and physical connections to others.[15] For example, a mother's relationship to her child alters the way in which she experiences herself and her relationship to the world. The social construction of a community whereby the elders of that community are relied on for direction and advice affects the subjectivity of both the elders who experience themselves in this role and those who rely on them to fulfill those particular life roles.

A number of theorists explain these processes within their work. Jürgen Habermas's work, for example, emphasizes a dialogical subjectivity: one that is not arrived at solely through the machinations of an individual's monologic rationality, but instead arises out of communication and interaction with others. For Habermas, self and group identity—part of the subjective process—are constituted through interaction with others, since

> [n]o one can construct an identity independently of the identifications others make of him....Thus the basis for the assertion of one's own identity is not really self-identification, but intersubjectively recognized self-identification. (Habermas, 1979: 107)

Intersubjective identification is realized in part through communication processes and is an important element in this book.

Crossley (1996) notes: "By entering into dialogue, subjects transcend their individuation and become components in a larger whole" (8). This is certainly the case, *to some extent*. Subjects do indeed transcend their individuation through entering into a communication process, but successful communication requires the creation, use, and understanding of certain commonly held assumptions and understandings. These understandings are created or acquired by participants through their engagement with their social environment. Yet they are not transmitted entirely through dialogue. If this were the case, then one would have to assert that an infant is not a social subject until s/he acquires competent language skills. A statement such as Crossley's also fails to recognize that in fact the subject is socially constituted and therefore does not *become* part of the social whole, s/he is *already* part of the social whole; that this perception of self or individuation has been, to a large degree, socially constituted. To engage in dialogue therefore simply reasserts or strengthens the participant's recognition of the socially embedded nature of all persons. The term intersubjectivity very generally refers to the ways in which relations between persons are experienced and enacted.

Crossley, in *Intersubjectivity: The Fabric of Social Becoming*, divides intersubjectivity rather usefully into two types or orientations: *egoistic* and *radical*. However, he also briefly introduces a third notion—*I-It* relations—that I would like to include in the following discussion. These concepts very generally point to the differentiations that I would like to make between forms of intersubjectivity. To make this intent clearer, further examination of Crossley's approach is necessary.

The first term, *egoistic intersubjectivity*, Crossley derives from a detailed examination of Husserl's theory of intersubjectivity. The term refers to an understanding of intersubjective relations that focuses on the way in which the person experiences and interacts with others, in a manner determined by her/his own self-perceptions and worldview. That is, s/he understands and models her/his behavior and comprehension of how to relate to the Other *from* her/his particular standpoint. It is therefore a subject-focused understanding, whereby this understanding is colored by a person's perceptions and projected *outwards toward* the Other; it is largely monologic. Crossley (1996) notes that such an understanding "involves an empathic intentionality which experiences otherness by way of an imaginative transposition of self into the position of the other" (23). This transposition means that the Other is in effect shaped by the perceiving subject: "It focuses exclusively upon an individual flow of experience" since "[h]is 'other' is always necessarily created by him" (Crossley, 1996: 7). How one understands the subjectivity of actors is important in determining how useful the concept becomes. Husserl understands the subject in phenomenological terms and thus sees the subject as influenced by the experiences s/he encounters. Therefore, while these intersubjective relations are largely monologic, they are not unaffected by the experiences and interactions that the subject encounters.

The second understanding, *radical intersubjectivity*, moves the emphasis away from the subject and her/his interactions toward the Other. Radical intersubjectivity is concerned with the space *between* subjects created through their interaction. Such a space or an interval cannot be produced singularly by an individual subject; it is rather a mutual relationship (Crossley, 1996: 11). Crossley here turns to examine Martin Buber's discussion of intersubjectivity, and in particular his understanding of the "I-Thou" relation (which Crossley incorporates within his delineation of radical intersubjectivity). The interval or space between participants is presented by Buber, Crossley (1996) argues, as "an irreducible and primordial structure" (12). The intersubjective space is mutually created and mutually effective in terms of the implications for its participants and their responsibility for this space. It is constituted through the relational nature of the subjective process: "Moreover, each participant is decentred in relation to the joint situation. Their thoughts and experiences are dialogically interwoven with those of their other" (Crossley, 1996: 12). Joint actions produce unpredictable outcomes and influences that impact back on each participant, shaping their futures and ongoing interactions and perceptions. Such interaction requires both the recognition of the Other as deserving of mutual respect and the relinquishing of a focus on the self. Thus "[i]t involves a lack of self-awareness and a communicative openness toward the other, which is unconditional. Self engages with other in this modality but has no experience of them as such" (Crossley, 1996: 23). I find this an interesting idea, and one worthy of further reflection. How can/do these relations come about? What sort of conditions favor this kind of mutualistic relationship? For this mutuality has a radically democratic impetus, and it also demonstrates the essential sociality of human existence.

This (*I-Thou*, or *radical*) understanding is distinct from Buber's explanation of the *I-It* relation, whereby the space in between interactive participants is not mutually constitutive or constituted. Instead the focus is centered on the subject's perception of the Other, similarly to that within egoistic relations, inasmuch as it is subject-directed. However, in I-It relations, the Other is objectified as something through which a rational and control-oriented objective can be met. Crossley (1996) writes that Buber is "concerned that I-It relations are beginning to predominate in modern rationalised, industrialised societies and he sees this as a deterioration in the quality of human relations" (11). The Other is reduced to an object rather than another subject who has moral rights and who is an actor with whom one engages in an equal, open, and mutually effective manner. "It constitutes the other as an object (an 'It') to be *experienced* and *used*" (11).

Therefore, egological and I-It understandings of intersubjectivity are both represented as largely unidirectional in nature. Both objectify the Other through their conceptualization or projection from the self onto the Other. Crossley differentiates the two, it seems, on the basis of intent and considerations of respect. Egological intersubjectivity entails empathic intentionality—the assumption of the Other as the same as the self, or at least to treat the Other as the self would treat him/herself—and the consequent recognition of the Other as worthy of respect. I-It relations entail no such likening of self with Other, nor of granting the Other as worthy of respect. Instead the Other is viewed as an object that can further the aims of the self.

Radical intersubjectivity, on the other hand, is multidirectional, inasmuch as those interacting together are mutually constitutive of the relationship between them. Therefore, this form of intersubjectivity does not enact the same objectifying processes associated with the other two forms discussed above.

These concepts—radical, egological, and I-It relations—are useful for examining and understanding the notions of intersubjectivity presupposed in the theoretical constructions of community discussed in following chapters.[16] However, I would prefer to group these three concepts into two particular categories; to differentiate those relations that are mutually constituted from those that are projected outward from the self to the Other.[17] As such, for the rest of the book I shall refer to either radical (mutualistic) or instrumental (with the understanding that the instrumental category carries the possibility of either I-It or egological relations or both) intersubjective relations.

These concepts take us only part of the way into our examination of community and community forms. Crossley does not actively differentiate among these different types of intersubjective relations by reference to the varied framing of interactive processes.[18] Yet the structural framing of the interaction has implications for the type of intersubjective relations that are enacted. As noted above, Buber (among others) is concerned that I-It relations are beginning to predominate. What might be the impetus for such a predominance, if indeed this is the case? Is it possible that as relations become increasingly extended and mediated across time and space, and embodiment is experienced in more abstract ways, more instrumental intersubjective relations are being enacted?

What is needed is some way of considering the implications of changes in ontological categories for intersubjective relations. In the following section, I discuss the ways in which the structuring of social relations across/within ontological categories might influence the form of intersubjective relations that are enacted—for intersubjectivity is a differentiated phenomenon influenced by the structure or framing of the interaction (Schutz in Crossley, 1996: 82).

The Framing of Interactive and Integrative Processes

As explained earlier, the ontological framing of interactive and integrative processes has implications for the types of relationships that are evident, the resultant experiences of subjectivity, and the forms of community created. By framing, I am referring to the form of integration—whether it is face-to-face or mediated through some other medium (this book is concerned particularly with technological mediation)—and the way in which patterns of interaction are positioned in time and space, and through the knowledge frameworks that are employed.

Alfred Schutz distinguished at least four types of social relations that have different intersubjective implications. These four social relations are differentiated according to the way in which their relation to the Other is positioned within space and in time.

The first relation is referred to as *consociates,* and describes those relations that are enacted in the face-to-face. The category does not differentiate between levels or degrees of intimacy—although that these exist is acknowledged. It is framed simply in terms of presence: "we designate by it merely a purely formal aspect of social relationship equally applicable to an intimate talk between friends and the co-presence of strangers in a railroad car" (Schutz, 1973: 16). This is a very literal understanding, where the face-to-face denotes those situations where people are in the immediate presence of one another and thus able to discern each other's reactions, expressions, and so forth. As Schutz (1971) writes, "[i]n face-to-face situations there is an immediate reciprocity of my experiences of the Other and the Other's experiences of me" (54). This means (a little unsatisfactorily in methodological terms) that as soon as participants move out of the face-to-face situation, according to Schutz's schema, they move out of the consociates category. I would prefer to extend Schutz's notion in ways that are able to recognize the continuity of face-to-face relationships temporally as well as spatially. Degrees of intimacy or the regularity of contact might be taken into account as a measure of such continuity, thus recognizing the relation between patterns of *interaction* and forms of *integration.*

The second category is referred to as *contemporaries,* whereby people with whom you have relations exist at the same historical time as yourself but are spatially/geographically distant.[19] These relations involve some people you would know but also some whom you wouldn't (Schutz, 1971: 37–38). Since the possibilities for immediate reciprocity of observation and other-understanding are not as possible, a more objectifying or classificatory interaction is involved. The use of typifying schemes is used to understand and orient behavior with little-known others so as to fulfill anticipated and understood norms and expectations. This allows for successful communication and interaction to take place. An example would be the relationship one might have with a train conductor (if not personally known in more than his/her occupational role). You expect the conductor to collect tickets and possibly to dispense advice about train-stops and connections. If you are caught without a ticket, then you expect to be penalized. Likewise, the conductor expects that you as a passenger will hand over the ticket that you have purchased and that you will behave in a certain manner. Such typifications and their attached behavioral expectations help guide social interaction and organization.[20]

> Hence, *in a social relation between* contemporaries, I am in a They-relation. I ascribe, therefore, to my partner a scheme of typifications and expectations relative to *me* as a personal ideal type. *A social relation between contemporaries consists in the subjective chance that the reciprocally ascribed typifying schemes (and corresponding expectations) will be used congruently by the partners.* (Schutz, 1971: 54, italics in original)

The third type of social relation is referred to as *predecessors*. These are relations with people who lived before your time yet with whom you are aware of having a connection—people who are separated from you by times past. And the fourth are *successors*, or those people who will live after you (Schutz, 1972). Of course, overlap between these types may occur, and as such the categories are viewed as relatively fluid. A face-to-face situation can easily become a relationship of contemporaries, and if the death of a participant occurs, then the relationship moves into one between predecessors, and so forth.

Despite its problems, this approach begins to open up important considerations for examining the different forms of community and their dominant forms of intersubjective relations. The various dominant modes of integration practiced within different forms of community—traditional, modern, and postmodern—result in differences in the way in which these communities' intersubjective relations are practiced. The fluidity and coexistence of different forms of intersubjective relations within each form of community are also important and are explainable within Schutz's schema. For example, within the modern community of the nation, intersubjective relations are conducted between consociates—those who interact in the immediate presence with others in embodied relations—and also with contemporaries—those who exist at the same time but who are not in one another's direct presence.

What is not explicable through Schutz's schema are the ways in which these various social relations and their extension through time and space affect community forms. For Schutz, the focus is on the relational nature of individual interactions. Schutz does consider social phenomena but focuses on the individual's perspective within the social. He is not able to accommodate the ways in which communities are held together across time and space, other than through the common possession of individual "stocks of knowledge" or learned interpretive schemes. In other words, Schutz is not able to explain a socially oriented understanding of the dominant intersubjective relations that constitute communities. Although he discusses the types of relations that structure each individual interactive moment, he is not able to grapple with the larger picture and consider either the ramifications of a preponderance of a particular type of social relation, nor how this dominance may affect the individual's or the community's subjectivity and self-understanding.

Schutz differentiates between what he refers to as a We-relation and a They-relation. A We-relation equates somewhat with the radical intersubjective notion described above, since it is based in reciprocal and mutually constituted actions, and a They-relation describes either an I-It or egological (instrumental) intersubjective form, since it is objectifying and projected outward toward the Other. A We-relation, for Schutz, exists only within (some) face-to-face relations of consociates.[21] Other social relations that are stretched across time and space are all designated as They-relations.[22]

This raises again the question as to whether radical intersubjective relations can only be experienced within embodied, face-to-face social forms. According to Schutz's analysis, this would appear to be the case. Indeed, it would seem that for Schutz, these types of intersubjective experiences or a We-relation can exist only while participants are physically engaged in face-to-face interaction and communication.[23] Once the participants are out of the physical presence of one another, the possibilities of such relations are minimized or negated. If this is the case, then the spatial extension of relationships has important ramifications for the conceptualization of community. However, before accepting that all relations are objectifying to some extent outside of the face-to-face (as with egological and I-It relations), further exploration is necessary.

Schutz bases much of his analysis on participants' mutual ability to predict, anticipate, and respond to each other. In face-to-face embodied relations there are numerous signals that participants can interpret and use to guide their responses to one another. Where there are no embodied interactions, participants need to rely on typifying constructs to anticipate behavior. However, the manner in which Schutz's scheme is constructed renders it unable to analytically accommodate social cohesion, imaginings of community, or extended communicative forms in any depth. How, for example, would he explain relations that are extended technologically across time and space with those whom one has known in a face-to-face context? The telephone, which extends other behavioral indicators such as intonation and expression, is a technology that could be considered in this context. Likewise, the ways in which the Internet is being deployed by both individuals and local communities as a way of supplementing preexisting face-to-face connections require accommodation. Works by Calhoun, Wellman, Hampton, and others point to the increasing importance of intermingling forms of sociality.

Crossley (1996: 90) notes that Schutz does consider that media technologies and symbols allow for a society of contemporaries to exist. It therefore can be assumed that he does recognize that some form of connection and continuity must be operating for people who may not know one another to be part of the same community. However, Crossley goes on to note that for Schutz, mediated communication "was straightforward and theoretically uninteresting in itself" (90). I obviously disagree with this assessment. I argue that abstract or extended forms of interaction have particular subjective and intersubjective effects, but they overlay rather than completely transform or replace more embodied relations of integration.

The degree of interactivity enabled through mediated social relations may hold some intersubjective possibilities worthy of deliberation. For example, technologies that allow mutual interaction or multidirectional interaction are more likely to evoke radical intersubjective relationships than is the case when interactions are conducted through unidirectional media. These possibilities are touched on by Craig Calhoun. Calhoun's work will be discussed shortly; however, some final comments need to be made about Schutz's theoretical composition.

While Schutz is able to accommodate the fluidity and coexistence of different individual forms of interaction, he is not able to consider the implications of various socially relational forms coexisting, with variations in the dominance of particular forms being practiced at different times throughout history. It is worth considering if and how dominant intersubjective relations differ among traditional, modern, and postmodern communities. In each of these forms of community, integrative practices are enacted through different framings of presence, time, and space. For example, the types or combinations of social relations that are dominant within the nation-state are different from those that exist within a tribal system. Likewise, the understanding held by individuals and societies in terms of the framing of relations would also differ in a number of ways throughout different social formations.

Where Schutz is useful is in his recognition of different types of relations according to participants' respective positions across time and space. Schutz is also useful if we extend his analysis to accommodate the implications of extended social relations. His position adds support to my argument that as, firstly, relations are extended across time and space, and as, secondly, this dominant level increasingly reconstitutes more embodied relations of presence, the nature of community becomes more abstract and thinner. I have been arguing that where the social relations and integrative practices of a community are overwhelmingly enacted through disembodied or abstract means, a preponderance of instrumental rather than radical relations is more likely to result. Schutz writes that

> [i]t becomes apparent that an increase in anonymity involves a decrease of fullness of content. The more anonymous the typifying construct is [e.g., postman, Australian, manufacturer], the more detached it is from the uniqueness of the individual fellow man involved and the fewer aspects of his personality and behavior pattern enter the typification as being relevant for the purpose at hand, for the sake of which the type has been constructed. (Schutz, 1973: 18)

I would like to extend this statement to consider the types of relations that are involved when enacted across time and space. I would argue that as these relationships are more detached from presence and mediated through time and space, the more specific and typifying a construct becomes. Therefore, as the community relationship becomes more one-dimensional or specialized, the amount of exposure to the self and others diminishes or is relegated to that particular sphere of reference. As "a decrease of fullness in content" is experienced, "the more detached it [becomes] from the uniqueness of the individual fellow man." This leads to intersubjective relations that are more objectifying and/or less extensive.

I would further argue that as the relationships or imaginings of community are stretched further across space and time, they become more abstracted or are viewed more abstractly. This in turn leads to more detached or thin relations. The larger the community, the less possible it is to know all intimately; close relations are possible only with an intimate few, and then decreasing degrees of intimacy are manifested as the degree of contact diminishes. Typifying constructs are employed to navigate such diminishing contact. Any adequate theoretical position needs to take into account that as communities are stretched further across space and time, exposure to the face-to-face tends to be either increasingly ephemeral or fetishistically intense. Traditional, modern, and postmodern communities all display varying combinations of these social relations as outlined by Schutz, yet they differ in the degree to which certain forms predominate.

In a sophisticated and complex series of moves, Craig Calhoun (1991) begins to explore these issues through an examination of "two general features of modernity," these being "the proliferation of indirect relationships"[24] and "the production of imagined communities."[25] Calhoun argues along the same lines as this book, inasmuch as he sees the increasing dominance of extended interactive and integrative practices as having implications for social forms and intersubjective relations. He explicitly links extension with the capacities of what he refers to as *infrastructural* technology, particularly transport and communication (Calhoun, 1991: 96). While he discusses the use of technology to extend interactive and integrative processes, it is his comments about indirect relations and imagined (read extended) communities that are of particular interest.

Calhoun writes that relationships constituted outside of direct interpersonal relations are sites utilized by individuals in their search for and construction of identity. These categorical identities or imagined communities such as the nation, he argues, are confused with communities. This confusion arises because these categorical identities promote feelings of identification and commonality; characteristics of community that were discussed in Chapter One (Calhoun, 1991: 108).

> Alongside the proliferation of indirect social relationships, we have developed a variety of cultural ways for identifying similarity and difference with other people....Thus, we develop categorical identities like those of nations or within them those we ascribe to or claim as members of different ethnic groups, religions, classes, or even genders. Some of the time, at least, we imagine these categorical identities on analogy to the local communities in which we live. Even in social theory, when we identify community not as a variable structure of social relationships but as a form of common feeling, we encourage the notion that the community among neighbors and the community among citizens of the same nation are essentially similar.
>
> I want to argue, however, that there is a great deal of difference between the social groups formed out of direct relationships among their members, although often sharing an imaginatively constructed cultural identity, and social categories defined by common cultural or other external attributes of their members and not necessarily linked by any dense, multiplex, or systematic web of interpersonal relationships. (Calhoun, 1991: 107)

He thus differentiates between groups constituted through direct interpersonal relationships, such as those enacted in local communities

(what I have been calling traditional communities), with ι.
that are composed of larger indirect relations (or moαε.
postmodern communities). The first he unproblematically cα.
community, whereas the latter are seen as sites adopted in the
individual's search for identification and recognition, and are labeled
as imaginary communities (Calhoun, 1991: 108). Such distinctions, I
suggest, are not so easily drawn.

While Calhoun's assertion about the lack of density and multiplex
social relations within larger-scale imagined communities supports the
statements made so far in this book as to the types of intersubjective
relations practiced across time and space, his assertions regarding the
identificatory differences between local and direct (or in my terms,
traditional) and indirect (modern or postmodern) communities are left
sketchy. All communities, with different degrees of reflexivity, play a
part in the constitution of identity. Certainly, in contemporary society it
is unlikely that the local community of direct interpersonal relationships
is less involved than the community of indirect, extended relationships
in the constitution of member identities. The differences between
different forms of community, as expressed in the approach presented
in this book, involve different ways of living time, space, embodiment,
and knowledge.[26] If this is the case, it is possible that the reflexivity
accompanying imagined communities can be attributed in part to the
distancing achieved through the abstraction and extension of social
forms, and in part to the accompanying modes of understanding that
were discussed earlier. As extended social forms become the dominant
constitutive form of community, they become increasingly specialized
and one-dimensional in nature.[27] This compartmentalization and
specialization enables the contemporary individual to belong to
numerous communities simultaneously, each community being
accorded a special relevance in areas of the individual's life.

Calhoun differentiates between community,[28] social groupings that
are constituted by direct interpersonal relations, and imagined
community. He writes,

> [i]magined communities are essentially categorical identities. But although
> these imagined communities do not reflect dense or multiplex networks of
> direct interpersonal relationships, they still do reflect social relations.
> Imagined communities of even large scale are not simply arbitrary creatures
> of the imagination but depend upon indirect social relationships both to link
> their members and to define the fields of power within which their identities
> are relevant. (Calhoun, 1991: 108)

Calhoun also describes an understanding of community (in a
footnote) that he would like to promote. This is "a social relational

conception of community as a complex variable composed of density, multiplexity, and systematicity of interpersonal relationships" (Calhoun, 1991: 117, fn. 17). The problem with such a distinction between face-to-face communities and imagined communities is that at times it appears to stay within the limiting terms of Tönnies's differentiation of *Gemeinschaft* and *Gesellschaft*, with imagined communities falling into the *Gesellschaft* category. I agree with the characterization of modern and postmodern community forms as being largely constituted through the dominant form of extended relations. Similarly, I would agree that such extended relations result in the dominance of more specialized, less dimensional or thinner relations. However, I would not argue that these forms of community (in the sense that I employ the term) lack the systematicity of interpersonal relationships as Calhoun has suggested with imagined communities.

However, these comments are not meant to detract from the direction of Calhoun's writings on extended social relations. This book has much in common with the general thoughts and sentiments expressed in his work. Calhoun notes the increasing compartmentalization of social relations that takes place as a consequence of using communications technologies to mediate social relations and community forms.[29] He would possibly criticize my use of the term community as being too broad and failing to recognize the thinning of social forms that takes place when these forms are constituted through practices of extension. However, I would counter that the term community can be used in a way that can usefully accommodate the recognition of different forms of being-together that exist according to the dominant means of social integration around which they are organized. Indeed, this is the only way to avoid falling into the nostalgic and problematic *Gemeinschaft* and *Gesellschaft* distinction. To understand the existence of different community forms allows the releasing of the concept of community from a particularly static historical interpretation. It also allows room for the recognition of the interpenetration of these differing forms. In a later article, Calhoun (1998) notes the ways in which face-to-face social forms are increasingly supplemented by the use of communications technologies, thus indirectly acceding the permeation of dominant modes of social forms into 'earlier' forms of social relation.

In this sense, Calhoun goes further than Schutz in that he is able to consider social forms larger than individual relationships. He extends Schutz's differentiation of forms of interaction through his discussion of four types of relationships (from primary through to quaternary). These types are identified by the degree of presence involved and also the content/intent of the relationship. While I am not convinced by his model,[30] his recognition of the value of exploring the implications of mediated relations is an important starting point. His distinctions also bear on some of my earlier discussions in Chapter Two about the degrees of connectivity (interactivity) and individuation (including the technical possibilities of surveillance) that are effected by the use of technology. Calhoun recognizes the cohesive effect of the use of these technologies and of institutions in holding larger communities together. In short, he tantalizingly introduces ideas and concepts that are worth systematizing and taking even further.

I have suggested that a layered analysis be used when considering the intersubjective implications of the technological extension of community relations. A number of considerations need to be taken into account. There needs to be consideration of the dominant ontological conditions that are in place and of what they mean for understandings of social forms. The use of technology has not only ensured that extended relations have become commonplace; it has also instituted practices that affect the form and experience of such relations.

To summarize, Schutz's analysis enables some explanation of the dynamics of intersubjective relations as they are enacted in relation to immediate and direct conditions of presence. He points to the use of typifying constructs—or instrumental practices—that are practiced as relationships are extended or removed from the face-to-face. He also highlights how face-to-face relations are more likely to be of a radical nature than those that are conducted in physical absence. However, he is theoretically unable to accommodate the ongoing social practices that arise as a consequence of changing ontological understandings of presence, time, and space. Nor is he able to accommodate the ramifications of using communications technologies for the increasing extension and mediation of community relations. I argue somewhat differently from Schutz and extend his analysis to ongoing social forms (rather than instantiated individual relations), suggesting instead that those communities that are conducted predominantly through face-to-face integrative practices are *more likely* to demonstrate/enact radical relations than communities conducted through a dominance of extended or abstract practices.

Traditional, modern, and postmodern community forms all experience different perceptions and practices of time, space, embodiment, and knowledge. Calhoun recognizes some of the relational consequences of community forms that are extended across time and space. He comments on the decreasing complexity of community relations, which he attributes to an increase in extended relational forms. The proliferation of extended forms to become a dominant mode of sociality has been made possible by the development and use of technology.

A way of discussing relations that are abstracted and extended across time and space, and that is simultaneously able to accommodate the coexistence and contradictions of thicker, less extended forms of community, is needed. This is where the *Arena* perspective can prove helpful.

As mentioned in the previous chapter, part of the *Arena* perspective explains the coexistence of different although sometimes contradictory forms of social relations and social forms through a levels approach. According to this approach, as new modes of being are developed and enacted, they coexist with earlier modes simultaneously—they do not obliterate or replace these earlier modes. However, within any society, certain modes of being dominate, and these dominant forms can be said to influence the ways in which earlier modes of being are experienced and enacted. The family is one example of a form of social relation that continues to exist as a site of social reproduction. However, how family life is enacted and understood has changed over time and has been influenced by other possibilities and other modes of relating and integrating. Within increasingly abstract community forms— communities that are extended through time, space, and abstract practices—individuals become more self-oriented and compartmentalized. As the society turns to these abstract processes as the dominant mode of practice and organization, these individualistic orientations are accentuated and permeate into more embodied traditional community forms. Therefore, while families still provide an important social relational base, in contemporary Western societies the family is increasingly depicted simply as a location or grouping that provides sustenance for the *individual*. When the family relationship is no longer seen to be providing sufficient emotional return, people are encouraged to leave and form new relationships elsewhere. The more individuated, compartmentalized, and instrumental relations of extended social forms filter into the traditional face-to-face social relations and understandings, altering their form and practices in the process.

This chapter posited the notion that there can be numerous types of intersubjective relations, though we are concerned here with what are referred to as radical (mutualistic) and instrumental (egological, and I-It) intersubjective relations. It was pointed out that changes in the framing conditions of ontological categories have specific implications for the types of intersubjectivity and the types of social relations that are enacted. Radical relations are *more likely* to be practiced within social relations that are constituted through the face-to-face, although such relations are affected by the dominant mode of sociality that exists within a particular society. Instrumental relations are *more likely* to be enacted within relations that are constituted through extended means, as these relations are thinned and becoming increasingly specialized and focused.

With this in mind, let us turn to the community theorists to be considered in this book—Taylor, Nancy, and Poster—to explore if and how they tackle such considerations, and what this means for their understanding of subjectivity and community.

Notes

[1] To avoid any confusion, some distinction between technologies as physical devices that transform or extend and technologies as practices that are organized to achieve particular ends needs to be reinforced from earlier discussions. This book is particularly concerned with the role of communication technologies (physical devices) in changing forms of community. However, it is also recognized that technologies (as practices) share many characteristics with the use of physical devices. For example, as Ellul and others pointed out (discussed in the previous chapter), both demonstrate a particular mind-set or approach that is oriented toward achieving desired outcomes. Technologies as devices also are used in ways that enact or involve technologies as practices. Therefore, a strict delineation between the two is not seen as necessary—it is enough to assert that the primary focus is on technologies as devices. As such, references to technologies carry this intent (while recognizing that their use institutes certain practices).

[2] For example, Jacques Ellul (1964) points to the ways in which technological solutions are sought for any problem that may arise, even for problems caused by technology. This demonstrates, for him, a particular reliance upon or privileging of a particular knowledge framework.

[3] For example, the many debates around the notion that there has been an erosion or demise of traditions. Some argue that traditions still exist, others that routines provide the structure and certainty for the individual and society. See *Detraditionalization: Critical Reflections on Authority and Identity* (Heelas, Lash, & Morris, 1996), for an overview of some of these debates.

[4] These technologies were initially introduced as business tools with the intention of increasing efficiency and productivity. As with many technological innovations, there are frequently social adaptations or extensions to their original application/usage. See Feenberg (1995) for further discussion.

[5] Giddens (1984) argues that changes in the ways that time and space are organized enable different community forms/social orders to come into existence, and therefore also to incorporate different ways of understanding oneself.

[6] See Foucault (1977).

[7] See Poster (1990) and Lyon (1994).

[8] See also Rheingold (1993) or Poster (1995) for just two more examples of such claims. These claims are rife through the writings on technological or virtual communities.

[9] Virilio argues that we are moving toward an immobile citizenry or terminal citizen (Virilio, 1993: 11).

[10] See Mauss (1990).

[11] See Goody (1986) and McLuhan and Powers (1989).

[12] William Gibson is credited with coining the now common term cyberspace in this novel.

[13] As Stone (2000) notes, "it is important to remember that virtual community originates in, and must return to, the physical. No refigured virtual body, no matter how beautiful, will slow the death of a cyberpunk with AIDS" (525).

[14] "As the body increasingly is constructed as a commodity to be managed, designed, and parceled out to deserving recipients, pressure builds to displace identity into entities that are more flexible, easier to design, less troublesome to maintain" (Hayles, 1993: 182).

[15] Such recognition of interdependence is important. It is frequently argued by feminist writers that the notion of an autonomous, unconnected rationality is more representative of masculine experiences and fails to incorporate those elements and considerations that have been designated to the realm of the feminine. These desires, emotions toward, and concerns for the Other are important considerations and need to be recognized in any discussion of subjectivity.

[16] This discussion simplifies these concepts and lifts them out of the complex theoretical approaches within which they are situated. In some ways it is not relevant, for example, to the progression of this book, whether Crossley's representation of Husserl or Buber is accurate or not. What is helpful here is to have gathered some way of discussing and understanding the different ways in which intersubjective relations can be conceptualized and experienced.

[17] It is also important to recognize that there are important differences between I-It and egological (although both are projected outward) relations, and also that mutual radical relations may not be clearly identifiable from these, since most relations probably involve a combination of these forms.

[18] Recognition that these are important are apparent—hence Crossley's introduction of Schutz's work—but Crossley fails to develop any significant framework to work with.

[19] Note the unsatisfactory movement from spatiality to temporality as the ontological basis of connection/disconnection.

[20] For example, Giddens talks of the importance of processes of routinization for the maintenance of social systems.

[21] "The face-to-face relationship in which the partners [of a social relation and existing in the same time and place] are aware of each other and sympathetically participate in each other's lives for however short a time we shall call the 'pure We-relationship'....The directly experienced social relationship of real life is the pure We-relationship concretized and actualized to a greater or lesser degree and filled with content" (Schutz, 1972: 164). See in particular pages 163–172 for further discussion of this concept.

[22] See Schutz (1972: 181–186) for further discussion of this concept.

[23] This is not to assert, however, that only We-relations are enacted within a face-to-face context—more typifying relations are also practiced.

[24] Indirect relationships are defined as "those mediated by information technology, bureaucratic organizations, and more or less self-regulating systems such as markets" (Calhoun, 1991: 95).

[25] He writes, "people have come increasingly to conceive of themselves as members of very large collectivities linked primarily by common identities but minimally by networks of directly interpersonal relationships—nations, races, classes, genders, Republicans, Muslims, and 'civilized people'" (Calhoun, 1991: 95–96).

[26] See Heelas, Lash, & Morris (1996) for various approaches to this issue.

[27] Calhoun would also seem to concur with much of this statement. He sees extended social groupings as being less multiplex than those based around direct personal relations.

[28] Unimagined, seemingly, since they are differentiated from imagined communities. This provokes the criticism from Edward Shils (see Shils in Calhoun [1991: 129]) that Calhoun fails to incorporate recognition of the existence and practice of collective consciousness. It also fails to allow for Calhoun's own use of Anderson's imagined community definition.

[29] "This does not mean that direct relationships have been reduced in number or that they are less meaningful or attractive to individuals. Rather, it means that direct relationships tend to be compartmentalized" (Calhoun, 1991: 102–103).

[30] However, since they do not bear directly on the book discussion, I will not elaborate these differences in detail. It is sufficient to say that I perceive the framing of and differentiation between these as somewhat problematic. Using temporal and spatial situating as a basis for differentiation in some cases and then using the content/intent of relations to differentiate relations in other cases seems awkward.

Part Two

~~~

Approaches to Community

This part of the book takes the issues discussed in the previous three chapters—community, technology, and inter/subjectivity—and examines their positioning within the theories of three contemporary writers on community. The intention is to ascertain the adequacy of these three different approaches in formulating an understanding of community within contemporary techno-society. This includes consideration as to whether these theorists are able to explain the tensions between the interconnectedness between persons and within a community across space and time that is enabled by technology and the compartmentalization and individuation that I have been discussing. I will examine if they consider the consequences of using technology to mediate social relations and integrative practices within their theories or, alternately, if such consequences can be accommodated.

While this is not meant to be an all-inclusive or comprehensive survey of the many approaches to community, as noted in the Introduction, there are three current strands of theoretical approaches to community which merit further examination. I have loosely categorized these three strands as: the social communitarians, the Heideggerians, and the virtual communitarians.

Each of the next three chapters follows a similar format. First a brief overview of each strand outlining their central concerns is undertaken. Seeking greater clarity in the discussion of community and technology, each chapter then focuses upon the works of a particular theorist. I have chosen to concentrate upon the works of Charles Taylor, Jean-Luc Nancy, and Mark Poster. Each particular understanding of community is analyzed, and any concepts essential to such an understanding are also explained. The next part of the chapter examines how and if the theorist deals with the structural concerns of community discussed in previous chapters. Then an examination is undertaken of the subjective considerations of community: bonding, commonality, reciprocity and recognition, and identity. And finally, an attempt is made at determining and understanding each theorist's stance on technology. Some of the nuances and contradictions of these stances are also brought to the fore. The purpose of these explorations is to ascertain the usefulness of these theories for understanding community within technological society, and to highlight any difficulties or anomalies with their positions. Since Poster (and the virtual communitarians) is particularly interested in the implications and practices of technology, there is an added emphasis undertaken upon this area in Chapter Six. It is hoped that through this last discussion, the previous analyses of community and its relations can be enriched and broadened.

Chapter Four

~~~

Charles Taylor and the Social Communitarians

> So the culture which lives in our society shapes our private experience and constitutes our public experience, which in turn interacts profoundly with the private. So that it is no extravagant proposition to say that we are what we are in virtue of participating in the larger life of our society—or at least, being immersed in it, if our relationship to it is unconscious and passive, as is often the case. (Taylor, 1984: 183)

This chapter examines the first strand of community theory—that of the social communitarians—and asks if and how this strand considers questions of community and technology.[1] The communitarians are commonly labeled as such because of their shared underlying premise that the individual is socially constituted and socially embedded.[2] Communitarianism is therefore usually counterposed against liberalism, which instead understands the individual as self-constituted or given, and autonomous.[3]

Michael Walzer, Alisdair MacIntyre, Michael Sandel, and Charles Taylor are the theorists who have been most frequently characterized as communitarians, although this list is far from exhaustive.[4] Despite many theoretical differences in their approaches, they all share the ontological understanding of the individual outlined above. Their works on community are general and at times, philosophically abstract. There appears to be little discussion or shared understanding of what community is; if or how it differs either conceptually or practically from society; or indeed whether the discussion is focused on political or nonpolitical (or indeed any other particular type of) community.

However, for our purposes here, it is sufficient that a basic understanding of the social communitarian position be gleaned. Despite their differences, the communitarians generally share several understandings and concerns: a view of the socially constituted nature of the individual (and therefore recognition of the importance of the social); an understanding of the importance of publicly shared notions of the good life; consideration of the important role of institutions in communal life; and the importance of member participation in communities. These understandings are elaborated briefly below.

1. The Importance of the Social (for Subjectivity and Identity)

Social communitarians focus on the role of intersubjective interaction and social roles in the formation of self and group identity. They understand each person as being situated or embedded within a specific cultural, historical, and social matrix. This embeddedness in turn works to define the self-identity of each person—as they see themselves in relation to others—and also to define what the community identity consists of, what norms are collectively held, and so forth.

2. Shared Notions of the Good Life—Its Norms, Ethics, and Worldviews

Social communitarians believe that publicly shared conceptions of "the good life"—desirable material and immaterial goods—are important. Conceptions of the good life are formed through the intersection of specific historical and social forces. These forces not only shape individual subjectivity (as argued above), but they also fashion how the world is understood and where the individual and the community are positioned according to such an understanding. This approach therefore incorporates recognition of the importance of shared ethics for guiding behavior, the social formation of norms, and the possession of shared worldviews.

As Michael Sandel writes,

> [a]nd in so far as our constitutive self-understandings comprehend a wider subject than the individual alone, whether a family or tribe or city or class or nation or people, to this extent they define a community in the constitutive sense. And what marks such a community is not merely a spirit of benevolence, or the prevalence of communitarian values, or even certain 'shared final ends' alone, but a common vocabulary of discourse and a background of implicit practices and understandings within which the opacity of the participants is reduced if never finally dissolved. (Sandel, 1984: 166)

According to the communitarian position, the practices and policies of the modern world have resulted in the destruction of a publicly shared notion of the good life and of its common moral horizons—these previously depicted a specific position and behavior for each and every person in the social world.[5] Communitarians also see modern life as having created confusion about the nature of individual and group identity. With the undermining of a shared understanding of the good life and shared ethics referred to above, comes an accompanying thinning of social recognition and an emptying-out of a sense of social (as opposed to individual) identity. Such developments seriously devalue the importance of the social and of recognizing and fostering social connectedness. Instead the emphasis comes to be placed on individual and particularistic needs, desires, and rights—self-fulfillment becomes the main orientation of individual activity. Proceduralism and individual freedom of choice become the primary values that can consciously be shared.[6] As a consequence, Charles Taylor (1989b) argues,

> [a]s our public traditions of family, ecology, even polis are undermined or swept away, we need new languages of personal resonance to make crucial human goods alive for us again. (513)

Community theory can be seen as an attempt to move closer to implementing its own specific moral horizon; a horizon that incorporates recognition of such connectedness.[7]

3. Institutional Arrangements

Social communitarians see the practices and norms of a community as being incorporated within and enacted through its institutions. It is unclear whether these institutions need to be formal organizational structures or if the description also incorporates informal structures. An institutional requirement points to both a degree of complexity and temporality necessarily existing within a community: Communities are ongoing inasmuch as institutionally they are not brief moments or experiences (as alluded to by some theorists, such as Maurice Blanchot, Georges Bataille, or Martin Buber).

According to the social communitarian position, if we are to achieve more fulfilling, authentic communities, institutions need to embody such aspirations, norms, and understandings. Thus these institutions need to recognize the intertwined nature of human society, and also emphasize policies that cultivate mutualistic relations.

4. Member Participation

Social communitarians assert that community membership carries benefits, and also responsibilities and duties. They believe that since the community plays a part in the formation of both group and individual identity—it fashions the worldview and the ontology of living within that community—then each individual member has a responsibility as a group actor to that community. For example, Charles Taylor (1991) points to institutional arrangements such as juries, arguing that they form part of a socially reciprocal relationship. A person is tried by a jury of her/his peers, but this practice is only possible when her/his peers are willing to serve on such a jury.

Political participation is another area of mutual responsibility. Community members have a responsibility to participate in how they are governed. This is one of the key tenets of the Communitarian Network—headed by Amitai Etzioni—in the United States. This group argues that the American system has placed too much emphasis on the realization and enactment of individual rights while not asserting the necessity of individual responsibility. They believe that this has led to the undermining of community and of social cohesion within American society.

Having given an extremely brief overview of the social communitarian orientation, it is useful to explore some of these notions and to see how they relate to the discussion developed in the previous chapters. As stated, the social communitarians differ in their emphases and so, to enable an adequate analysis to take place, I have chosen to examine the work of Charles Taylor. Taylor is the most comprehensive theorist for the purposes of this book, and he is also one of the most commonly quoted social communitarians. He also has a limited association with the Communitarian Network in the United States, referred to above. On being questioned as to his self-categorizing as a communitarian and how this is to be understood—Taylor refers to this group:

> This group has a political agenda. One might say that they are concerned social democrats who are worried about the way that various forms of individualism are undermining the welfare state (or preventing its development in the U.S. case). They see the need for solidarity, and hence for 'community' on a number of levels, from the family to the state. I have a lot of sympathy for this group and have signed on to various of their statements. (Abbey & Taylor, 1996: 3)

Taylor on Community

To understand Taylor's notion of community, one must first understand his philosophical approach to subject formation. For Taylor, the subject is understood as an embodied agent who acts in and on the world (1995: 22). However, in keeping with the social communitarian position, this subject is not a pre-given atomistic individual, but instead is formed by and through the relations s/he holds with others, the society and culture within which s/he is born, and also the experiences s/he encounters throughout life (Taylor, 1991: 52–53). Subjective formation is therefore understood as a continual and ongoing process. Taylor describes a situated subject who participates in mutualistic and constitutive acts. These acts are referred to as dialogical acts, thereby emphasizing the participatory, interactive elements of self-constitution. They are dialogical acts not simply through the act of direct conversation and the use of spoken and written language, but also through the communication of gesture, facial expression, emotion, art, even dress (Taylor, 1991: 33). All of these languages are culturally constituted and represent a background within which an agent orients her/himself to enable participation, mutual understanding, and recognition.

Taylor argues that it is through these dialogical acts that common spaces are formed, and that a *we* is created. And it is through and within these common spaces that we are constituted as socially engaged subjects. The subject therefore cannot develop fully without the input and recognition of significant others, and without the social framework that the society, its institutions, and its members provide. Taylor (1989b) asserts that "[o]ne is a self only among other selves" (35), highlighting the sociality that is an ontologically necessary and phenomenally inescapable part of human life. Atomistic understandings of the subject are therefore not only misguided, but they encourage a social outlook that views relationships in a utilitarian manner—as oriented toward satisfying and serving the individual only. If we extend this line of thought further, we could say that such an outlook (or mode of understanding) corrupts the mutualistic process of self-constitution inasmuch as full reciprocity is hindered. Such an outlook leads to the instigation and operation of what was referred to in the previous chapter as instrumentally intersubjective relations.

Taylor (1991) writes of three "malaises of modernity" that need to be tackled if we are to adequately experience fulfilling community. These three malaises are the growth of individualism; the primacy of instrumental reason and its associated "disenchantment of the world"; and the diminishing of community political participation. Taylor understands these malaises as being brought about by mutating influences on modernity. These influences are twofold and intertwined.

One influence is the social and institutional espousal of an atomistic mode of understanding that denies recognition to the necessary and important role that others play in our identity formation (Taylor, 1995: 169). He writes that the modern sense of self that is encouraged is one that is disembedded and disengaged from embodied agency. This creates the social perception and experience (as explored in Chapter Three) of one's identity being self-authored, rather than recognizing the influence of social connections. Such perceptions undermine the sense of social embeddedness and therefore also the sense of obligation to others.

> In a flattened world, where the horizons of meaning become fainter, the ideal of self-determining freedom comes to exercise a more powerful attraction. It seems that significance can be conferred by *choice*, by making my life an exercise in freedom, even when all other sources fail. (Taylor, 1991: 69)

If self-fulfillment is the ethic underlying and directing modernity, it presupposes a certain form of individual and group subjectivity. Taylor argues that this presupposition is manifested within what he terms as the drive toward authenticity. This notion of authenticity he views as being potentially of tremendous moral value and highly worth retrieving from (what he sees as) its currently mutated forms. It is through this understanding of authenticity that Taylor is able to negotiate the integrative-differentiating dilemma that confronts all current community theoretical formulations. In *Ethics of Authenticity*, Taylor posits this notion of authenticity as a moral ideal that is located—but in a mutated form—within contemporary society. Authenticity is presented as the aim or goal of working toward achieving your uniquely individual human potentialities. However, this is not to be, and indeed cannot be, achieved in isolation—it is reached from within a socially constituted setting through communication processes. Through such a maneuver, Taylor believes he is able to dismiss the malaises of atomistic individualism and of soft relativism, and to maintain instead that the public good, or a horizon of significance, can be argued for rationally and can be commonly held. While the individual seeks unique self-realization (difference), this is (ideally) done within a cohesive social framework (integrative). Such self-realization then is only partially unconstrained; it still is bounded or guided by the social normative framework within which it is situated.

The other mutating influence Taylor refers to as the social dominance of instrumentally rational practices and policies. The development and use of technology within society falls largely within this category. Taylor incorporates Heidegger's understanding that the instrumentally rational use of technology presupposes the worldview that all things are seen as resources to be used or improved. However, Taylor believes that this understanding can be overturned or "enframed" differently to achieve more "humane" outcomes. The adequacy of this approach will be explored in a later section of the chapter.

For now, let us examine Taylor's writings in relation to some of the structural considerations raised in Chapter One.

Structural Considerations

The labeling of Taylor as a communitarian has more to do with his understanding of subject formation, social interaction, and the social practices that he advocates than with his prescription or description of a particular form of community. This lack of prescription may be due in part to his recognition of the ways in which social formation, social practices, and understandings are mobile and ever-changing. Thus Taylor describes the nation as an imagined community of a particularly modern form (Taylor, 1995: x), implicitly differentiating it from early forms of community. He talks also of political community and the need for shared goals and a shared sense of purpose to exist for such a community to attract and to hold members.

Yet while he considers the changing nature of social forms and thus of changing forms of community, he does not appear to directly accord any importance to the structural considerations discussed in Chapter One (for example, the varying communicative forms through which community relations are mediated). Instead these changing social forms are simply described in terms of historical developments, as a result of a combination of factors: the existence or development of various institutions, ideologies or horizons of significance, and objective factors such as population size. Thus he may describe the nation as above, yet he does not directly consider these differing forms of community as being attributable to changes in structural framings. Nor are the ramifications of either multiple memberships of communities or the mediation of community forms across time and space examined in any detail, apart from noting the fragmenting of a unitary social cohesiveness. He writes:

> Fragmentation arises when people come to see themselves more and more atomistically, as less and less bound to their fellow citizens in common projects and allegiances. They may indeed feel linked in some projects with others, but these come to be partial groupings rather than the whole society: a local community, an ethnic minority, the adherents of some religion or ideology, the promoters of some special interest. (1995: 282)

While atomization and fragmentation are noted, the impetus behind these outcomes is not directly explored in any comprehensive detail. This is not to assert that Taylor does not recognize that social phenomena such as increased labor mobility or the instrumental employment of technologies hold implications for social constitution. Indeed, this recognition is central to his work *Ethics of Authenticity*. Yet it takes the form of a passing (although sophisticated and intriguing) philosophical observation. Nor does it seem that Taylor's awareness of these changes or associations is connected in any way to an awareness of alterations in the framing of ontological categories. While, as I have already argued, atomization and fragmentation are brought about by changes in knowledge frameworks and through the alteration of experiences of time, space, or embodiment (or a combination), these changes are not discussed by Taylor, or at least, not in his earlier work.[8] This may well have been because of the importance he placed on ideas and philosophies as being constitutive and therefore prior to any new social form or ways of relating. Taylor (1983) writes that theories and philosophies "undercut, bolster or transform the constitutive features of practices" (2).[9] As such, his suggestions for overcoming the three malaises of modernity, or the fragmentation of modern or postmodern community and the alienation of its members, are to be achieved through the societal adoption of certain "benevolent" moral emphases and humane understandings as a framework for society to operate within. This is important but partial. The privileging of ideas over practices was problematized in the last chapter, where I argued that ideas do not arise out of a vacuum and that ideas and practices were mutually implicated and intertwined. However, in his most recent work, *Modern Social Imaginaries*, Taylor also stresses the intertwined nature of ideas and practices. He writes, somewhat emphatically, that

> [c]ertain moral self-understandings are embedded in certain practices, which can mean both that they shape the practices and help them get established. It is equally absurd to believe that the practices always come first, or to adopt the opposite view, that ideas somehow drive history. (2004: 63)

Indeed, Taylor goes further and labels any strict delineation as to the import of one or the other of these as

> a false dichotomy, that between ideas and material factors as rival causal agencies. In fact, what we see in human history is ranges of human practices that are both at one, that is, material practices carried out by human beings in space and time, and very often coercively maintained, and at the same time, self-conceptions, modes of understanding. (2004: 31)

Thus, *Modern Social Imaginaries* (published during the final stages of this book) is an important addition to Taylor's work. It addresses and clarifies some of the areas that were absent and/or of concern to my discussion here.

I want to reorient and extend Taylor's phenomenal and philosophical observations and moral debate, to consider more closely the technological influences on community and intersubjective relations. This also means that I will attempt to make explicit many of the implicit characteristics and observations about community and human relations that Taylor makes, but does not explicitly develop.

For instance, he notes the importance of institutions embodying social goals for the maintenance of community cohesion. These institutions reproduce community norms and values, and thus ensure the continual integration and reproduction of community forms. Yet he does not explore in any detail the ways in which institutions allow the extension of community relations and integrative practices across time and space. Nor does he link the changing ways in which time and space are lived explicitly to the form or types of intersubjective relations that are practiced. He does make the observation that people living in cities are unable to know one another as intimately as they would in smaller communities, and notes that increasing individuation, atomization, and fragmentation are the outcome of capitalistic practices and particular historical and philosophical developments. Implicit within these observations is an awareness that experiences and practices of time and space and the modes of presence have changed. With acknowledgment to Benedict Anderson's work *Imagined Communities*, Taylor (2004) notes the existence of different forms of time—profane, secular, higher—linked to changed understandings of the moral order from earlier times to modernity (or in my terms, changed modes of understanding intersecting with changed modes of organization). But nowhere is there discussion or recognition of how different forms of community and social organization coexist (even if in tension) simultaneously, even as they are affected by the dominant modes of constitutive practice.

This renders his structural analysis of community inadequate for my discussion of the coexistence of traditional, modern, and postmodern communities and the various constitutive modes that these forms utilize. It is also inadequate for exploring the tensions that exist among such community forms. I would suggest an alternative approach—one that is able to recognize the existence and coexistence of different forms of community within any historical time period. Such recognition would enable a closer analysis of the varying influences on and consequences for community relations and practices. By failing to make this distinction, Taylor's generalization results in the representation of a particular community form and is thus able to note only where there is partial adherence to or complete failure to adhere to this form. For example, see his earlier comment as to the existence of partial groupings:

> They may indeed feel linked in some projects with others, but these come to be partial groupings rather than the whole society: a local community, an

ethnic minority, the adherents of some religion or ideology, the promoters of some special interest. (Taylor, 1995: 282)

Rather than partial groupings, perhaps it would be more useful to understand these as particular modern or postmodern forms of community with specific characteristics as a consequence. As noted, Taylor does indirectly point to the existence of different forms of community. Thus it would be interesting to learn more about why the term "partial groupings" has been employed, for example, or why 'community that does not equal society' is seen as a partial grouping. Further clarification would be useful, and so it is to the subjective considerations of community that I now turn.

Subjective Considerations

In the first chapter, I introduced several subjective elements of community to enable a close analysis of the concept and practice of community to be undertaken. These elements were bonding, commonality, reciprocity and recognition, and identity. This section takes these elements as analytical devices to explore Taylor's understanding of community in more detail.

Bonding

Taylor understands community as something beyond a connection existing between people because of a particular utilitarian orientation that all may possess. He would instead describe community as consisting of a group of people who share some "irreducibly social goods." These social goods are more than the provision of public utilities or other utilitarian measures that would benefit a large number of people. It is rather the possession of a common culture, commonly esteemed emotions and value systems that are referred to (Taylor, 1995: 137–138). Thus we could suppose that members are bonded together through the process of recognizing and sharing these social goods.

Language is one way through which we connect with one another: "language creates a kind of bond, a common understanding between those who share it" (Taylor, 1995: 86).[10] Taylor's understanding of the subject as embedded and socially constituted, and of the importance placed on dialogical acts in such a constitutive process, has already been noted. The creation of a mutual space, or of radical and egological forms of intersubjectivity, is created/enhanced through dialogical acts of conversation. Whether such acts are conducted predominantly or entirely within the sphere of the face-to-face is inferred to some degree (although not explicitly discussed), although Taylor's discussion of communication technologies would seem to indicate that mutualistic dialogical acts are not necessarily so spatially restricted. Such vagaries require greater clarification.[11] The possibility that different modes of communication enacted through varying degrees of mediation have implications for the ways in which such acts are experienced—a proposition advanced within this book—also requires greater exploration.

Taylor emphasizes that it is only through the common possession of shared visions, goals, or horizons of significance (including having a faith in the institutions that reproduce and enact these), that people will align themselves with or belong to a political community. Values that are mediated through institutions via a common language therefore provide the cohesion or bonding of community. Horizons of significance are fairly central to Taylor's understanding of the degree of cohesion experienced among people within a society or community. Horizons of significance refers to the central value system and cultural understandings held by a group of people or a society. In more traditional times, Taylor explains, a horizon of significance provided the framework within which people were situated in terms of expected behavior, social standing, and occupation. Taylor, along with others like MacIntyre, argue that contemporary society has eroded its horizons of significance and that this is much of the reason for the commonly proclaimed absence of meaning in society today.

> To take a salient example, just because we no longer believe in the doctrines of the Great Chain of Being, we don't need to see ourselves as set in a universe that we consider simply as a source of raw materials for our projects. We may still need to see ourselves as part of a larger order that can make claims on us. (Taylor, 1991: 89)[12]

Mention of society *or* community is also relevant here, for Taylor does not overtly, in the readings I have undertaken, differentiate between his understanding of the concepts of society and community. It is possible to infer that they can be one and the same, possessing the same cultural and ethical values in common, or they can be quite different, falling more generally into Tönnies's differentiation between *Gemeinschaft* and *Gesellschaft*. Taylor would see current Western society as being closer to a *Gesellschaft*, more commonly composed of people grouped together for more utilitarian reasons. Having made such an assertion, it must be qualified by his acknowledgment of the necessity for some level of bonding existing between members of a nation-state. For example, Taylor (1995: 276) writes that within liberal-democratic societies there must be some shared horizons, a sense of bonding and of membership, for the participants in that society to follow its rules and norms. He also notes that participation in democratic societies indicates an acceptance of "a kind of belonging much stronger than that of any chance group that might come together" (Taylor, 2004: 189–190).

How these horizons are mediated across community or society—apart from institutionally—would benefit from further examination. Again, his recent work begins this task through an examination of the importance of "social imaginaries" and the mapping of the development and transmission of certain social imaginaries within Western society. Social imaginaries will be explained in more detail below. However, for now it must be noted that, for Taylor, these can be usefully analyzed to help explain tensions between contemporary individualization and the accompanying, but often unacknowledged, idea of equality and social benevolence.

> Our embedding in modern categories makes it very easy for us to entertain a quite distorted view of the process and this in two respects. First, we tend to read the march of this new [modern] principle of order, and its displacing of traditional modes of complementarity, as the rise of "individualism" at the expense of "community." Yet, the new understanding of the individual has as its inevitable flip-side a new understanding of sociality, the society of mutual benefit, whose functional differentiations are ultimately contingent and whose members are fundamentally equal. This generally gets lost from view. (Taylor, 2004: 17–18)

Indeed, Taylor argues that the (modern) social imaginaries within Western society assume social beings; that the individual is positioned within an understanding that takes as its very foundation a particular notion of sociality. This notion of sociality is one that sees all persons as worthy of equal and mutual respect and as of necessity enmeshed in reciprocal relations.

> [T]he basic point of the new [modern, social] normative order is the mutual respect and mutual service of the individuals who make up the society. (Taylor, 2004: 12)

However, within the Western contemporary setting, Taylor depicts three malaises of modernity as corroding relations between people and damaging the possibilities for healthier, more fulfilling communities. These malaises have occurred in part through a societal emphasis on the individual, and his/her right to pursue his/her own goals and values while failing to recognize the situating of such values within a wider social context. The effects of mobile labor and consequent mobile social relations, as well as the consequences of living en masse in cities, accentuate this development. Taylor argues that such situations create the conditions for accepting more utilitarian understandings of our relations with others, and the necessity of more revocable associations:[13]

> the individual has been taken out of a rich community life and now enters instead into a series of mobile, changing, revocable associations, often designed merely for highly specific ends. We end up relating to each other through a series of partial roles. (Taylor, 1989b: 502)

I have already argued that changes in the ways in which ontological categories are experienced and understood have implications for intersubjective relations and social organization. This is related to the way that the technologically accentuated processes of abstraction, mediation, and extension encourage an individualistic and more instrumental approach toward the self and others. This argument is in accord with Taylor's assertions that such an individually oriented focus encourages atomistic developments and instrumentally rational relationships. Unfortunately for the purposes of this book, however, Taylor's analysis of this phenomenon does not take us any further. He makes a case that the central moral values necessary for valuable horizons of significance do exist in contemporary society within such individualistic and rationalistic emphases, though in a somewhat elusive and distorted fashion, and that what is necessary is an exercise in retrieval and restoration. Indeed, while he may consider modern Western society as containing these modern malaises, he also sees incredible potential for the full self-realization of individuals—a development that, for Taylor, is to be encouraged.

> Modern individualism, as a moral ideal, doesn't mean ceasing to belong at all—that's the individualism of anomie and breakdown—but imagining oneself as belonging to ever wider and more impersonal entities: the state, the movement, the community of humankind. (Taylor, 2004: 160)

Taylor's work allows more nuanced and often positive understandings of key theoretical suppositions and social understandings to be undertaken. For example, within both *Ethics of Authenticity* and *Modern Social Imaginaries*, he points to valuable elements and ideas that are either subsumed or unacknowledged within the dominant discourses. His work can thus be seen as a political exercise aiming to reinvigorate or excavate these—more socially aware—ideas and practices. Yet the question of how this is to be achieved within techno-society without addressing some of the issues raised in this book remains problematic.

Commonality

Taylor accentuates that it is important not only to recognize the differences and unique qualities that various and different people and cultures may hold, but also to recognize and foster the commonalities. He argues that there is a need for commonality: that this is necessary for us to be able to relate and have meaning in our lives. If there are no commonly shared values or principles, then, according to Taylor, there is little or no value available for us individually. Things do not acquire value just because we singularly decide that they do. They are instead situated within a social and cultural system that gives meaning to things according to commonly shared values, ideals, or processes. These are the horizons of significance referred to earlier. Elsewhere Taylor refers to these horizons as providing a framework for both social and individual behavior. As he states,

> I want to defend the strong thesis that doing without frameworks is utterly impossible for us; otherwise put, that the horizons within which we live our lives and which make sense of them have to include these strong qualitative discriminations....that living within such strongly qualified horizons is constitutive of human agency, that stepping outside these limits would be tantamount to stepping outside of what we would recognize as integral, that is, undamaged human personhood. (Taylor, 1989b: 27)

We acquire these values through involvement within our environment and through our interaction and engagement with our significant others, who likewise are embedded within particular cultural and social systems. Taylor draws our attention to the socially constituted understanding of value that subjects hold and reminds us that these are not atomistically or individually constructed. These values necessarily have to be shared for them to be of significance for participants: They would not be significant if only a sole individual held them. Shared values enable members to feel satisfaction, pride, honor, or shame. This contextualizing of value is an important move. Taylor makes the key point that things, values, and practices have meaning for us because of their shared social significance. Therefore it is shortsighted and nonsensical to theorize the individual outside of these social settings. Indeed, Taylor's notion of the social imaginary stresses the ways in which moral and social understandings are 'adopted' within a society and held in common (by social individuals).

The notion of social imaginaries in Taylor's most recent book is sufficiently important to warrant a brief digressive explanation. He writes,

> By social imaginary, I mean something much broader and deeper than the intellectual schemes people may entertain when they think about social reality in a disengaged mode. I am thinking, rather, of the ways people imagine their social existence, how they fit together with others, how things go on between them and their fellows, the expectations that are normally met, and the deeper normative notions and images that underlie these expectations. (2004: 23)

Social imaginaries are necessarily shared even where/when that imaginary asserts the primacy of the individual or where it fails to explicitly acknowledge the importance of the social. Though individuals may understand and experience themselves as discrete units, their practices and conceptions of themselves are in common with others. Taylor's description of the social imaginary articulates clearly what I have been (less clearly) describing with my knowledge schemas or modes of understanding. These understandings are like shared maps that aid navigation and agency in everyday life. These maps are necessarily held in common.

According to Taylor, it is only through the recognition of commonalities that the possibilities of open dialogue and constructive community building are made possible. He writes, "[s]omething is common when it exists not just for me and for you, but for *us*, acknowledged as such" (Taylor, 1995: 139). Therefore, it is not enough that something is mutually beneficial in the sense that you and I both gain something for ourselves that we individually desire. Rather, Taylor is referring to a process whereby *we* share something that enriches *us*. And it is through the processes of dialogue, according to Taylor, that a common space for sharing is created.

> We can speak of a common space when people come together in a common act of focus for whatever purpose....Their focus is common, as against merely convergent, because it is part of what is commonly understood that they are attending to, the common object or purpose, together, as against each person just happening, on his own or her own, to be concerned with the same thing. (Taylor, 2004: 85)

This idea is explored a little further in Taylor's discussion of the public sphere.

> The public sphere is a common space in which the members of society are deemed to meet through a variety of media: print, electronic, and also face-to-face encounters; to discuss matters of common interest; and thus to be able to form a common mind about these. I say "*a* common space" because although the media are multiple, as are the exchanges that take place in them,

they are deemed to be in principle intercommunicating. The discussion we're having on television now takes account of what was said in the newspaper this morning, which in turn reports on the radio debate yesterday, and so on. That's why we usually speak of the public sphere in the singular. (Taylor, 2004: 83)

Common space allows for the possibility of radical relations to be enacted—where the conversation can be mutually constituted. However, it can be completely radical only when both participants in the conversation are unconstrained by considerations of equity, where each is able to express her/himself freely and equally.[14] It would not be radical if one participant felt at a disadvantage to or under the power of the other. Such inequities and power differentials also need to be considered in association with the idea of a mutualistic we. Recognition of a mutual dialogic space with the presupposition of equal participation is politically important. However, as noted in many critiques of the public sphere discourse, relations enacted within and across this sphere are not unaffected by various power relations, despite being understood in this way.

Taylor (2004: 89) notes that the public sphere "is a space of discussion that is self-consciously seen as being outside of power. It is supposed to be listened to by power, but it is not itself an exercise in power." While operating with a very particular representation of power, this view of the public sphere articulates an underlying ideal, rather than being representative of the reality of media(ted) public dialogue. However, Taylor's acknowledgment of the creation of a space that allows difference and diversity to appear within its boundaries is an important and conceptually interesting move. This move allows the recognition of, and possibilities for, divergent individual actions and understandings (difference) taking place within a socially bounded and socially imagined arena (integrative): in other words, possibilities for difference framed by common understandings and practices. Within this understanding, the two aspects of sociality—the integrative and the different—are understood as mutually constitutive themselves; that is, each impacts on the other. This understanding is articulated in various ways throughout his work.

A question comes to mind: Is it only through communication conducted in the face-to-face that a *we* is constructed and experienced as such, or can it be extended across time and space? According to Taylor's account of the public sphere, it can be extended. *We* construct, participate, and share in the metatopical space of the public sphere. Indeed, "Such spaces are partly constituted by common understandings;

that is, they are not reducible to but cannot exist without such understandings" (Taylor, 2004: 86).

Yet according to Schutz's understanding of contemporaries, as discussed in the previous chapter, relations conducted within the face-to-face are the only location of We-relations. While I do not wish to be so absolute—it seems possible that mutualistic relations can certainly be conducted and experienced outside of the realm of the face-to-face— Schutz's arguments about typification are also valid. Practices and communication enacted within the realm of the face-to-face are embedded in a more multiplex environment than those that are segregated or lifted-out of such embedded settings to be enacted within/ across a mediated field. This leads one to consider the possibility that those relations that are entirely or even predominantly mediated are more likely to display instrumental intersubjective tendencies. Taylor is unable to help this book explore such possibilities.

Reciprocity and Recognition

> The importance of recognition is now universally acknowledged in one form or another; on an intimate plane, we are all aware of how identity can be formed or malformed in our contact with significant others. On the social plane, we have a continuing politics of equal recognition. Both have been shaped by the growing ideal of authenticity, and recognition plays an essential role in the culture that has arisen around it. (Taylor, 1991: 49)

Reciprocity and recognition are necessarily invoked through the processes of dialogical action. Of particular importance is dialogue with those who are one's significant others. Taylor maintains these are essential for identity construction and social function. Yet dialogue is possible only where there exists some level of mutual understanding or commonality, since it needs to be situated within mutually recognized and understood contexts.

Full and equal reciprocity is also necessary if participants are to be accorded equal status within any dialogue. Dialogue involves not only speaking but also being heard; someone who is not accorded equal status to speak or be heard cannot participate fully. The degree of reciprocity enacted therefore depends on the type of relationship that is being engaged. Taylor infers that some of the reasons behind the current fragmentation and alienation felt by members of society can be attributed to them not being accorded an acceptable level of reciprocity by/within the system. This is different in a community that experiences a certain degree of bonding, recognition, and appreciation. "People [in a community] can have a sense that they are heard because they know themselves to be valued in a certain way, even when some particular demands are not met" (Taylor, 1995: 277). Taylor would appear to be referring to radical intersubjective relations necessarily taking place within an effective community. As such the dialogical space is mutually constituted and maintained, rather than manipulated by some at the expense of others, as is the case in I-It (and to some degree, in egological) relations.

Taylor sees the possibilities for democratic society as being entwined with the possibilities for all receiving equal recognition; it is only achievable where all citizens are necessarily accorded equal status and dignity. He argues that with the contemporary focus on personally derived individual identity, the notion of identity has been problematized, and identity recognition has become an issue. This is a different situation from that in previous societies, where recognition was integral to the social hierarchy. "Social recognition was built in to the socially derived identity from the very fact that it was based on social categories everyone took for granted" (Taylor, 1991: 48). With the contemporary focus on individuality and uniqueness, Taylor suggests that social recognition has become more problematic—lacking overt socially shared value systems and knowledge frameworks through which to negotiate recognition. I am less convinced by this claim, since as Taylor himself has acknowledged, social horizons of significance (shared knowledge frameworks) are essential for any society. Such difficulties with equal recognition could be explained through reference to the accentuated individual (and the diminished focus on the importance of the social), heightened through the use of technology to extend and mediate social relations across increasing expanses of time and space.

As a possible solution to finding or creating the types of radical community to which Taylor refers, uncritical advocates of communications technologies argue that while they perceive equal recognition and reciprocity as being limited or unavailable within modern forms of community, this can be overcome by the possibilities enabled through technology. For example, the Internet is promoted as enabling the possibilities for enhanced democratic participation and the removal of barriers—such as external hierarchical structures—to full and equal participation in the political system. However, as I have already discussed, while such technologies increase possibilities for interconnectivity and participation to some degree, simultaneously their use leads to subjective and intersubjective pressures that discourage involvement.

Identity

> Modern societies have moved toward much greater homogeneity and greater
> interdependence, so that partial communities lose their autonomy and to some
> extent their identity. (Taylor, 1984: 193–194)

I have outlined above much of Taylor's understanding of identity
formation. It is an understanding that recognizes an embodied, socially
and culturally embedded, dialogical subject. Her/his identity is
formed—and constantly being formed, undergoing alterations and
changes—through an ongoing dialogue with others, particularly with
those who are significant others. It is thus a subject who cannot be
analyzed individually without some regard to the social environment
within which s/he is immersed.

Our identities are shaped through social interaction, our particular
environs, and the communities within which we are situated. These
identities require some degree of self-understanding: an understanding
of ourselves, of our position within the society in which we interact,
and of the societies themselves. Taylor (1995) believes that this self-
understanding is necessary because "there can't be a community in any
meaningful sense that doesn't come to understand itself to be such"
(276).

This self-understanding is also relevant in a politically
transformative sense. Practices, he explains, take place within a
framework of certain self-understandings and self-descriptions on the
part of the participants: "These self-descriptions can be called
constitutive"(Taylor, 1983: 3). As already mentioned, Taylor argues the
significance of political and social theories for the transformation of
social practices. Theories alter self-understandings and self-descriptions.
Therefore Taylor's writings can be seen as a political exercise with the
intention of bringing about a more holistic approach to social
understanding and practices within societies. A holistic approach would
be one that recognizes the embedded, embodied, interrelational nature
of people and their communities.

Taylor's emphasis on the necessity of recognizing our embodied
nature and its relevance for our perception of our world is quite explicit.
For Taylor, there are complex structures within which an agent operates,
and where s/he is aware of the limitations and possibilities of being
within the world with a particular body.

> Here is a 'world shaped' by embodiment in the sense that the way of
> experiencing or living the world is essentially that of an agent with this
> particular kind of body. It is an agent who acts to maintain equilibrium upright,
> who can deal with things close up immediately, and has to move to get to

things farther away, who can grasp certain kinds of things easily and others not, can move to make a scene more perspicuous; and so on. (Taylor, 1995: 62)

Thus he says that we are not essentially disengaged reason, as Descartes theorized. Our minds cannot be separated from our bodies (Taylor, 1991: 101–102). This point is particularly relevant when we come to consider the segregation or further separation of mind/body from embodied social contexts that is enacted via technologically extended mediation and interaction.

Taylor and Technology

Taylor's understanding of the importance of embodiment for identity formation and interaction is adequate until the element of technologically mediated communication is introduced. Here things become more confused and contradictory, and certainly require further development. Taylor uses the term technological society quite freely, acknowledging the centrality of technological development and its utilization within Western society, and also the instrumentally rational practices that are accentuated through the use of technology. But he fails to work through the implications of this for social formation, social practices, and social relations. For example, his writings on the public sphere infer that interaction through the electronic and print media is the same as face-to-face interaction, in that both enact the dialogical functions that are so important to his understanding of human ontology; in many cases technologically enabled media constitute the public sphere. It is through this public sphere function and its development of and sharing of common ideas that bonding and membership are enacted. Taylor's definition of the public sphere is worth re-quoting:

> What is a public sphere? I want to describe it as a common space in which members of society meet, through a variety of media (print, electronic) and also in face-to-face encounters, to discuss matters of common interest; and thus to be able to form a common mind about those matters. I say 'a common space' because, although the media are multiple, as well as the exchanges taking place in them, they are deemed to be in principle intercommunicating. (Taylor, 1995: 259)[15]

Here, Taylor represents the media as simply a continuation of the face-to-face by other means, or as a tool by which to transcend space. There is the sense here too that this use of technology is seen in wholly positive terms, as a sign of the enhancement of both individual freedom and of the public sphere. This is similar to the argument put forward by Jürgen Habermas and expanded by Mark Poster, that technology is providing a space or means for the widening of public debate.[16] However, there is no consideration by Taylor of the ways in which such an extension could impact on subjectivity, social relations, and community forms. Nor is there any consideration of the ways in which surveillance and the promotion of individualism are entwined with the use of these technologies.

An interesting idea that Taylor mentions in *Modern Social Imaginaries* is of a "horizontal, simultaneous, mutual presence, which is not that of a common action, but rather of mutual display"(Taylor, 2004: 168). I would like to explore this brief mention a little further. Taylor points to the ways in which we use fashion as a way of presenting or re-presenting ourselves to others—to display ourselves (but also to influence) in the presence of others. He continues, "It matters to each of us as we act that the others are there, as witnesses of what we are doing and thus co-determiners of the meaning of our action" (2004: 168), thus pointing to the socially ascribed/constituted nature of meaning. However, his discussion of these city dwellers, "urban monads," or "lonely crowd" who share "[t]his strange zone between loneliness and communication" (Taylor, 2004: 168–169), is suggestive in terms of the ideas that I have been exploring about mediated interaction and integrative processes and the tensions that are invoked through these processes. For Taylor, communication technology has

> produced metatopical variants [of the nineteenth-century topical spaces of the flâneur or dandy], when for instance, we can lob a stone at the soldiers before the cameras of CNN, knowing that this act will resonate around the world. The meaning of our participation in the event is shaped by the whole vast dispersed audience we share with it. (Taylor, 2004: 169)

Again, here, the technology appears to be accorded a connecting potential that enables or opens up spaces for mutual action or moments of togetherness. It also provides spaces for more destructive activities, or expressions of strong shared emotion, leading Taylor to state that, "one has as much cause for fear as hope in these wild, kairotic moments"(Taylor, 2004: 170). However, Taylor hints at, but does not develop or examine, the ways in which such possibilities may impact/ shape subjectivity or impact on the types of social relations and social practices.

This approach is also in tension with the way in which, elsewhere, Taylor contends that the instrumentally rational ways in which much technology is employed promote social fragmentation and atomism.

He suggests that an instrumentally rational outlook fails to take into account the embedded, embodied social person. Using the example of the medical profession, Taylor argues that the profession has emphasized a problem-solving approach that ignores the client as a whole person, treating her/him instead in a very localized or compartmentalized manner (with parts to be fixed). Here Taylor seems to be incorporating a Heideggerian emphasis that sees instrumental reason leading to a view of others as raw materials or standing reserves; as simply a means to achieve one's individual goals.[17] When coupled with the drive for individualism, this understanding results in relationships of all types being seen also as raw materials available for the individual's enjoyment.[18] Yet this instrumentalism is criticized by Taylor as being antithetical to the ideal of authenticity, which necessarily requires the recognition and valuing of a rich social setting.

> In the light of the ideal of authenticity, it would seem that having merely instrumental relationships is to act in a self-stultifying way. The notion that one can pursue one's fulfilment in this way seems illusory, in somewhat the same way as the idea that one can choose oneself without recognizing a horizon of significance beyond choice. (Taylor, 1991: 53)

Taylor's proposed solution to this dilemma is to encourage a different enframing of the uses of technology; to situate it within a more benevolent caring framework that recognizes the complexity of the person (or even the humanness of the person). He explains that there is also a benevolent moral ideal behind the use of instrumental reason—the ideal of improving people's lives—and that this is often overshadowed by the dominance of the idea and use of technology to control nature and circumstances. Taylor argues that as long as we remember this benevolent ideal and take into account the "embodied, dialogical, temporal nature" of human beings, this will constrain technological uses and therefore achieve alternate outcomes. As he writes (and it is worth quoting at length):

> What we are looking for here is an alternative enframing of technology. Instead of seeing it purely in the context of an enterprise of ever-increasing control, of an ever-receding frontier of resistant nature, perhaps animated by a sense of power and freedom, we have come to understand it as well in the moral frame of the ethic of practical benevolence, which is also one of the sources in our culture from which instrumental reason has acquired its salient importance for us. But we have to place this benevolence in turn in the framework of a proper understanding of human agency, not in relation to the disembodied ghost of disengaged reason, inhabiting an objectified machine. We have to relate technology as well to this very ideal of disengaged reason, but now as an ideal, rather than as a distorted picture of the human essence.

> Technology in the service of an ethic of benevolence towards real flesh and blood people; technological, calculative thinking as a rare and admirable achievement of a being who lives in the medium of a quite different kind of thinking: to live instrumental reason from out of these frameworks would be to live our technology very differently. (Taylor, 1991: 106–107)

Taylor asserts that these more benevolent intentions will always be in tension with the dominating or controlling aspects of instrumental rationality. However, he believes that simply looking at technological application differently will permeate through to more humane practices and social relations. Following this logic, it is possible to argue that Taylor might see virtual communities, the rationale and use of communications technologies, and the practices of a mediated public sphere as operating within frameworks that are not instrumental or domineering. As we have already seen, proponents of virtual communities maintain that the technology allows them to associate with others in a manner that is egalitarian and liberating and that increases relationship possibilities. As such, they could argue that they are framing the uses of the technology differently and thereby subverting the instrumentally rationalized processes that Taylor problematizes. However, the nature of many relationships within virtual communities—which are specific, revocable, and transitory—raises questions as to the degree of instrumentality invoked within and toward online relations. As discussed in Chapter Three, the extension of relationships also encourages the enactment of instrumental relations. And the removal of the body from interactions also does not necessarily equate with removal of hierarchical or domineering practices. Likewise, the ways in which communication technologies have been individualized and applied encourage instrumental approaches to the technology and the relations it engenders. And I have already addressed some of the critiques of the discourse surrounding the public sphere and the ways in which the actuality of a mass media(ted) public sphere are influenced by varying power relations with their own specific instrumental aims and purposes.

In Chapter Two, in the section on social forms, the ways in which the telephone has been utilized were examined. It became obvious that while the telephone was invented and perceived by its developers as a technology that would be utilized as a business tool, it was also appropriated as a valuable tool for maintaining social connections. Similarly, while the Internet was initially funded by the U.S. Defense Department in an attempt to overcome security concerns, it is increasingly becoming an important resource for social extension. These changed or widened uses of technology are not unusual occurrences.[19]

The social appropriations of these technologies could be argued to be enframing the technology more benevolently. They also would fit within Taylor's thesis about the social connectiveness and dialogical nature of desirable human activity. However, this understanding fails to recognize the paradoxes of such extended social forms. While Taylor addresses issues of technology and instrumental rationality, the other processes discussed in Chapter Two, such as abstraction and extension, are left unexamined.

As mentioned above, Taylor places immense faith in the belief that thoughts and philosophies are ultimately behind social transformation. While there is obviously some force to his stress on the importance of social philosophies and worldviews, some further explanation that is able to recognize and incorporate an understanding of the implications of changing ontological categories is also needed. There is also more than an ideal at work here—the structural practicalities and cognitive changes that are a result of the use of technological communications have implications for the enactment of increased individuation and compartmentalization, while simultaneously enhancing interactive possibilities: Increased communication and integration possibilities intersect with disembedded, disembodied communication conditions. Simply understanding or enframing the use of technology differently will be insufficient to resolve such tensions.

The atomism of which Taylor is critical is accentuated by the disconnection or detachment that results from the utilization of disembodied processes and changing ontological categories of time and space. As argued in the previous chapter, the use of communications technology extends relationships and integrative possibilities across space and time, thus enabling the operation and reproduction of postmodern community forms. However, it was also posited that such extended interconnection has an effect on the experience and depth of such relationships. It was argued that such community forms are thinner and more specialized than within traditional community forms constituted through the face-to-face, a phenomenon that Taylor infers but does not develop (nor associate specifically with processes of extension or abstraction).[20] Yet he argues that

> those who condemn the fruits of disengaged reason in technological society or political atomism make the world simpler than it is when they see their opponents as motivated by a drive to "dominate nature" or to deny all dependence on others, and in fact conveniently occlude the complex connections in the modern understanding of the self between disengagement and self-responsible freedom and individual rights, or those between instrumental reason and the affirmation of ordinary life. (Taylor, 1989b: 504)

I have frequently asserted both the increased interconnective possibilities enabled by the use of these technologies as well as the individuating tendencies that are accentuated. I have also stressed the changing nature of ontological categories, in part through the possibilities enabled by the use of technologies. As explained in Chapter Three, changes in modes of understanding both reflect these ontological changes and are a factor in their development. Hence, Taylor's self-responsible freedom and individual rights can easily be encompassed within such an approach. However, this fails to address the intersubjective consequences that are implicated by these developments. Nor does it assist in recognizing the important role that technology— through its impact on the way the various ontological categories are experienced—plays in changing community forms and changing social relations. These require further attention. While the importance of interconnectedness is marketed as achievable through technological means—indicating the perception of a general desire or need for such interconnectivity among many contemporary individuals—this book also argues that technology's use has wider ramifications that are not as apparent and that coexist in uneasy relation with interconnectivity.

So where do we go from here? How do we understand and negotiate through more enriching and valuable ways of being-together? Taylor advocates an exercise in retrieval, yet in many ways this proposal fails to recognize and address many of the structural concerns and issues raised in this book. What *is* valuable is his stress on the importance of recognizing the value of commonality as the underlying basis on which we structure our lives. His emphases on the essential sociality of the individual and the key role of language are also important. The recognition of the role technology plays in the growth of instrumentally rational practices also supports some of the central contentions contained in this book. However, Taylor's analysis of the use of technology is problematic in a number of ways. While he recognizes both the increased technological possibilities for interconnectivity (his discussion of the public sphere) and for instrumentally rational approaches (his example of the medical profession), certain anomalies and contradictions are apparent. Although he may believe that his approach to the communicative possibilities of technology addresses the movement of ideas and language, while his assertions as to technologically invoked instrumental rationalization refer to the application of physical practices, such distinctions between language and practices are—as he himself recognizes—not so easily made. Communication, ideas, and language are also practices. Further discussion and analysis of these seemingly inherent contradictions are required.

This takes us to the next strand of community theory—that of the Heideggerians—to see if they are able to provide a better understanding of the consequences of the intersection of community and technology.

Notes

[1] Social communitarian is not the common label for this group. However, I have decided to append the term 'social' to the term 'communitarian' in this book simply to enable a clearer delineation to be seen between these communitarians and those I refer to as virtual communitarians. It is also a useful way to demarcate these theorists from so-called 'political communitarians,' e.g., Etzioni, Glendon, or Galston (Bell, 2001).

[2] This is despite many other differences within individual theories.

[3] Taylor explains that such a distinction is not straightforward or unproblematic. He makes a further distinction between ontological and advocacy approaches. See Taylor (1989a).

[4] Sociologist Amitai Etzioni and others who subscribe to the Communitarian Network in the United States are also frequently added to this list.

[5] See MacIntyre (1981) in particular for this approach.

[6] See MacIntyre (1981) on proceduralism and Taylor (1991) on procedural justice, choice, and instrumental rationality.

[7] Although, as I clarify later in this chapter, for Taylor, all horizons are necessarily understood as being socially constituted and socially contextualized.

[8] Apart from some discussion of changing knowledge frameworks in *Sources of the Self*.

[9] While Taylor does assert exactly as quoted, elsewhere he also notes (though doesn't examine) the importance of other factors such as the constant interaction of and relation between ideas and practices. See Taylor (1989) and (1983).

[10] Although in this reference the bonding referred to is not restricted to the human species, nor even like species. Taylor mentions the rapport that is developed through some level of communication between a dog and its human trainer. Yet he goes on to talk about the necessity of understanding the language within its specific contextual framing, i.e., as understanding its meanings and cultural/social significance…a trait he is surely not extending to dogs.

[11] The anomalies between Taylor's representation of the use of technology to mediate discourse and create a public sphere and his assessment of the instrumental impact of the use of technologies on human social relations is examined in more detail in the later section on technology.

[12] Although elsewhere, in *Sources of the Self*, Taylor claims that it is not possible for human action to take place outside of a framework of some degree (1989: 26–27).

[13] As noted in Chapter Three, Taylor writes (and it is worth repeating here) that, "[m]obility is in a sense forced on us. Old ties are broken down. At the same time, city dwelling is transformed by the immense concentrations of populations of the modern metropolis. By its very nature, this involves more impersonal and casual contact, in place of the more intense, face-to-face relations in earlier times. All this cannot but generate a culture in which the outlook of social atomism becomes more and more entrenched" (Taylor, 1991: 59).

[14] Such inequity possibilities are not discussed by Taylor.

[15] The same definition is used in *Modern Social Imaginaries* (2004: 83), suggesting that his understanding on these issue is unchanged.

[16] See Poster (1995).

[17] Taylor (1991) writes: "In addition, our technocratic, bureaucratic society gives more and more importance to instrumental reason. This cannot but fortify atomism, because it induces us to see our communities, like so much else, in an instrumental perspective. But it also breeds anthropocentrism, in making us take an instrumental stance to all facets of our life and surroundings: to the past, to nature, as well as to our social arrangements" (59).

[18] "If my self-exploration takes the form of such serial and in principle temporary relationships, then it is not my identity that I am exploring, but some modality of enjoyment" (Taylor, 1991: 53).

[19] See Feenberg and Hannay (1995), particularly Chapter One, for a discussion of the social appropriation of technology.

[20] He appears to associate such developments more with the privileging of instrumental reason than with related processes of extension or abstraction.

Chapter Five

~~~

Jean-Luc Nancy's Notion of Community

Different theoretical approaches to community have been undertaken by a number of European theorists—I will call them, for lack of a better name, the Heideggerians.[1] Several theorists fall into this category, but those with the highest profile include the following: Jean-Luc Nancy, Maurice Blanchot, Emmanuel Levinas, and Jacques Derrida. Nancy and Blanchot, in particular, have engaged in a public (textual) dialogue about the philosophical understanding of community. Each of the above theorists has his own particular approach to the conceptualization and practice of community; however, some generalizations can be drawn about the overall emphases they share.

Most of these theorists became prominent within academia after the revelations of the Holocaust, and the disaster/demise of the practice of communism in Eastern Europe. The dangers of an understanding of community based around a singular notion of identity, of totalitarianism, and of undertaking projects of community that became apparent as a result of these events are very evident in the direction of their work. As a consequence, all seek to understand a way of being-together that is able to accommodate the Other in a manner that is not repressive.[2] Therefore these theorists similarly face the integrative/differentiating dilemma of all contemporary community theorists. In particular, they place an emphasis on recognizing multiplicity and singularity, and on the importance of non-totalizing approaches; there is some stress on the momentary or fleeting nature of community; and also recognition of the importance of finitude/death. Some of these themes emerge (or are influenced) either directly or indirectly by the work of Martin Heidegger (hence the appellation "Heideggerians").

In the following sections of this chapter, I turn to discuss Jean-Luc Nancy in more detail. Nancy is the most prominent writer on community and has dedicated a number of his writings to exploring the experience and understanding of community and/or of ways of being-together. But first a qualification must be made. Nancy's work is deliberately attempting to stretch and rework concepts such as community to find new ways to discuss and understand them. For example, he states:

> the sole task for an ontology of community is, through thinking about being and its difference, to radicalize or to aggravate Hegelian thinking about the Self until it caves in. (Nancy, 1991a: 3)

This pushing of concepts to their limits makes any textual analysis difficult, since the work is full of contradictions, clarifications, and overlap. However, there are sufficient consistencies and inferences to enable a sense of what Nancy is attempting to emerge. Nancy's work is particularly interesting within the context of this book's focus on the relational. Whether discussions of sociality (or intersubjectivity) are able to accommodate or assist with understandings of the intersection of technology and sociality will become increasingly apparent as the chapter unfolds. However, before such an analysis can be undertaken, some explanation of Nancy's understanding of community is warranted.

Nancy on Community

> Community is given to us—or we are given and abandoned to the community: a gift to be renewed and communicated, it is not a work to be done or produced. But it is a task, which is different—an infinite task at the heart of finitude. (Nancy, 1991b: 35)

Nancy claims that theoretical discussions centered on the recapturing of, or nostalgia for, lost community have been recurrent throughout Western history, and are to be viewed with suspicion (1991b: 10).[3] According to Nancy, the Western understanding of community is that,

> community is not only intimate communication between its members, but also its organic communion with its own essence. It is constituted not only by a fair distribution of tasks and goods, or by a happy equilibrium of forces and authorities: it is made up principally of the sharing, diffusion, or impregnation of an identity by a plurality wherein each member identifies himself only through the supplementary mediation of his identification with the living body of the community. (1991b: 9)

This notion of community, Nancy (1991b:10) argues, can be attributed to the Christian understanding of community-as-communion, more recently translatable within modernity as the desire for immanence and a defying of the finitude that is the reality of each human being. For Nancy, community is not communion.[4] This form of community (as communion) constrains a group of people into a monolithic form or identity, suppressing difference and promoting exclusionary practices.

The double structure of community, as Nancy refers to it, is that to be able to exclude the Other, the community must first fix or name the Other. Therefore,

> [t]he crucial double question of the in-common would thus be: how to exclude without fixing (*figurer*)? and how to fix without excluding? Exclusion without fixing is to legitimate (*faire droit*) the absence of grounding, or of presupposition, to legitimate being together. Fixing without excluding is to uphold the lines of exteriority, the two sides of the same edge. (Nancy, 1992: 393)

Nancy's work can be seen as the beginnings of an attempt to find an answer to, or way of thinking about, such dilemmas. He argues for an understanding of community as the *incomplete* sharing of the relation between beings, where there exists sharing and separation or resistance of beings simultaneously.[5] For Nancy, being is not common, since it differs with each experience of existence, but being is *in* common: It is in the *in* where community 'resides.' Community exists in/as a relation between being, existence (which Nancy seems to almost equate with being), and finitude. Yet at the same time it differs in each presentation or appearance, because of the differences existing within these experiences (since each being is different). The danger is in prescribing or categorizing an essence or form to both community and the beings it includes.

Nancy's discussion emphasizes the fluidity and singularity of being, and the importance of the relation between beings. The emphasis on singularity and the absence of ties between these beings allows a nonprescriptive form of relation to exist. Christopher Fynsk explains Nancy's community thus:

> [C]ommunity names a relation that cannot be thought as a subsistent ground or common measure for a "being-in-common." While a singular being may come to its existence as a subject only in this relation (and it is crucial, in a political perspective, to note that Nancy thus starts from the *relation* and not from the solitary subject or individual), this communitary "ground" or condition of existence is an unsublatable differential relation that "is" only in and by its multiple singular articulations (though it is always irreducible to these) and thus differs constantly from itself. (Fynsk,1991: x)

For Nancy, community is not a *thing* that can be consciously created or artificially imposed. Nor is it a property or essence that can be measured or described in terms of certain common attributes. As such, the foregoing discussion, in which I attempted to outline the general understanding of the concept of community in terms of the subjective elements of bonding, commonality, and so forth, would be viewed problematically by Nancy: Community cannot be encapsulated by such elements. Indeed, for him, if community is encapsulated, then it is lost in that process, for it cannot be reproduced or fixed as it differs with each occurrence or presentation (Nancy uses the word *compearance*).[6] Also, to fix community is to lay the groundwork for the attempt to retain or make community in a particular form (which is work), yet Nancy believes community does not/cannot be derived through work. To work to create community is to actively constrain the relation between beings by ascribing particular qualities or restrictions, thus undermining community.[7] It is within or through such work that many of the atrocities of the past, such as the Holocaust, have been committed. I will return to this point later. For the moment it is sufficient to counter that, for the purposes of this book, the identification and use of community elements serve a useful analytical purpose.

The terms *compearance* and *compear* are used throughout Nancy's work and are therefore worth a brief digressive comment at this stage. Tracy Strong, a translator of one of Nancy's articles (1992), writes that compearance "refers to the act of appearing before a court having been summoned" (Nancy, 1992: 371, translator's note). Nancy uses the term quite specifically in this sense—invoking notions of judgment, presentation, and reception simultaneously. He employs the term rhetorically to ask: "Have we done right (*droit*) by that which still has no right? right [sic] by existence itself—or since this word is subject to misuse in the singular, by our existences, by their community" (Nancy, 1992: 372). Compearance is a complex notion that points to (perhaps) an ontological justice (though I am uncomfortable with this term)—of which there is no prescription, just a continual questioning. This questioning not only calls upon existence or existences but also upon relations between these. To compear is thus to present oneself (and to be called upon or invoked) as both a singularity and as *in*-common.

> We compear: we come together (in)to the world. It is not that there is a simultaneous arrival of distinct units (as when we go to see a film "together") but that there is not a coming (in)to the world that is not radically *common*: it is even the "common" itself. (Nancy, 1992: 373–374)[8]

Nancy thus attempts to overcome the integrative/differentiating dilemma faced by community theory through asserting the impossibility of either individuals without relations, or of collectives without singularities, through the notion of singular beings. For Nancy, community exists in/on the limit where singular beings meet. To understand this statement, it is necessary to investigate the meaning of these terms—*limit* and *singular beings*—further.[9]

Singular beings is a term used to describe presences or entities, yet even these terms appear too fixed; multiple, singular presentations of being would perhaps be more appropriate. Nancy does not restrict the use of this term to the human species alone, nor is it seemingly restricted to living objects.[10] Indeed, a community restricted to humans is problematic, as human communities work to reproduce their own essence. (Nancy 1991b: 3)

Singular beings are not fixed totalities: They exist in and through their relations with other singular beings. Indeed, the use of the term emphasizes these beings' difference, their multiplicity, and their relations. A singular being ends at the point where it meets other singular being/s. This is the *limit* where the possibility of one or another singular being exists simultaneously. The limit refers to a mutual exposure whereby both presence and absence exist simultaneously; at the point where a singular being is stretched toward its crisis or dissolution point whereby it has cause to both question and acknowledge its own and the Other's existence. The limit is where there exists a consciousness of both separation and togetherness at the same time—it is where beings compear together and to each other. Nancy's use of these concepts in his discussions of community, and his denunciation of the possibility of the existence of the individual as an absolute totality without relations, highlights the relations *between* beings. Likewise, he asserts that singularity can exist only within a relationship among a multiplicity of singular beings and that it is through/within this relationship that singularity *compears*.

> The 'someone' does not enter into a relation with other 'someones,' nor is there a 'community' that precedes interrelated individuals: the singular is not the particular, not a *part* of a group (species, gender, class, order). The relation is contemporaneous with the singularities. 'One' means: some ones *and* some other ones, or some ones *with* other one. (Nancy, 1997: 71)

For Nancy, the focus of community is therefore on the relational, the ontological (in the traditional philosophical sense of the term) necessity of the relational, and at the same time, the difference in each presentation or experience of the relational. His understanding of incomplete sharing stresses both the relational and also the resistant nature of being in the world. Such an assertion about the necessity of the relational acknowledges the uniqueness of other beings and imposes an implicit ethical responsibility to allow and respect differences. To ignore these differences, or attempt to consume them within a totalized whole, is to undermine the experience of community.

Structural Considerations

There are difficulties in applying a naive version of my earlier theoretical approach to community, to understanding or explaining Nancy's approach to community. My discussion of a differential structure of community or recognition of different forms of community as constituted through different modes of interaction and integration across time and space is not easily transposed onto Nancy's work.

Nancy does differentiate, as made apparent above, between community-as-communion and the inoperative community. The first, following Nancy's definition, could be applied in some degree to a modern community such as the nation-state, where all members identify themselves partly through their belonging to a particular nation-state. For example, while I may see myself in a number of different ways, I also understand myself as being Australian. This forms an integral part of my self-identity much as "each member identifies himself only through the supplementary mediation of his identification with the living body of the community" (Nancy, 1991b: 9). Australian is also part of the identity that others attribute to me. However, Nancy could easily point to the fissures that exist within such a community form; where there exist different and contesting understandings and experiences of such Australian-ness. Hitler's Germany and its Holocaust were the result of attempts to realize community-as-communion, with disastrous consequences for those who did not fit within a desired image or identity. Yet Hitler was unable to realize such a dream; his ideal of an Aryan Germany was unable to withstand its own internal scrutiny and resistances. As nationalists in areas such as Rwanda or Bosnia found, the conjunction of the ideal and of the actual realization of a particular nation are not straightforward projects. Identities do not fall neatly into clear-cut categories. Communion is not possible without suppression (using that term impossibly broadly), and suppression necessarily invokes resistance. The community-as-communion ideal is as unachievable as it is undesirable.

The second of Nancy's definitions of community, the inoperative community, comes closer to some theorists' description of a postmodern community. Mark Poster, for example, refers to Nancy's inoperative community to support his argument for virtual communities as possible postmodern communities.[11] Georges Van Den Abbeele points to Nancy's positing of community within the spaces between singularities, and writes:

> What Nancy thus deftly disconnects, although he never says so explicitly, is the assumed immanence of communal identities to demarcated geographical spaces in the form of towns, lands or nations. (Van Den Abbeele, 1997: 15)

This detachment from geographical space would also fall comfortably in line with the approach taken by those who argue for a postnational imaginary; as postmodern community. There is a resonance here too with Nancy's emphasis on the multiplicity and singularity of experiences of community. However, as will become apparent through the discussion in this chapter, Nancy's analysis is posited at a different—even prior—level than such postnational or postmodern deliberations. For Nancy, community is experienced or exists *before* the imposition of political organization, or indeed before the constitution or formation of subjects and their subjectivity. The difficulties of this approach will be deliberated in more detail, but first I wish to continue discussing Nancy's approach to community and structural analysis.

Nancy does talk briefly about a social form existing prior to modern society that was unlike the nostalgic construction of community or community-as-communion that Western tradition promotes.

> It would undoubtedly be more accurate to say…that *Gesellschaft*—"society," the disassociating association of forces, needs, and signs—has taken the place of something for which we have no name or concept, something that issued at once from a much more extensive communication than that of a mere social bond (a communication with the gods, the cosmos, animals, the dead, the unknown) *and* from much more piercing and dispersed segmentation of this same bond, often involving much harsher effects (solitude, rejection, admonition, helplessness) than what we expect from a communitarian minimum in the social bond. (Nancy, 1991b: 11)

This argument posits the possibility of different social forms existing historically. Nancy also writes of community (in the inoperative sense) as following after modern society, or as yet to come. Therefore, it seems that he wants to include consideration of historical influences and developments in his analysis. However, this emphasis on historicity is in tension with his positioning of community as existing or residing at the limit between singular beings and prior to social or political organization. Such positioning infers that community, in Nancy's sense, is always existent and underlying all social forms. The difference becomes then one of degree—more or less community—as a consequence of practices and projects.

> Community is given to us with being and as being, well in advance of all our projects, desires, and undertakings. At bottom, it is impossible for us to lose community. ... Only the fascist masses tend to annihilate community in the delirium of an incarnated communion. Symmetrically, the concentration camp—and the extermination camp, the camp of exterminating concentration—is in essence the will to destroy community. But even in the camp itself, undoubtedly, community never entirely ceases to resist this will. (Nancy, 1991b: 35)

Yet this understanding is difficult because of where Nancy's community is positioned. Despite a certain ambiguity around his conception of singular beings, Nancy posits his analysis at the level of the ontological. Indeed, his singular beings could be described as ahistorical, because historical and cultural forces are not attributed a direct and formative influence on them; these forces are enacted on or experienced through already existent singular beings (and in turn, creating subjects?). Such an understanding, while devoid of generalizations and oppressive classifications, makes any critique of singularity and community extremely difficult. It also renders any historically situated analysis of community problematic, since community is assumed to be always existent or prior to and underlying all such influences.

Nevertheless, for Nancy, the task is to understand the experience of community rather than describing or creating community through a particular politics or organizational schema. As noted above, for Nancy, community cannot be made: It cannot be a project. It exists at an ontological level within the relation between beings. Social forms or organization are imposed on singular beings and on the experience of community. Yet these forms also affect community through their enabling or constraining of the relation between beings of community; they intersect with the ontological.

Nancy's understanding of ontology in *Being Singular Plural* highlights the interconnection of the ontological and the phenomenal (or the impact of social forms and social practices) when he writes,

> "Ontology" does not occur at a level reserved for principles, a level that is withdrawn, speculative, and altogether abstract. Its name means the thinking of existence. And today, the situation of ontology signifies the following: to think existence at the height of this challenge to thinking that is globalness [*mondialité*] as such (which is designated as "capital," "(de-) Westernization," "technology," "rupture of history," and so forth). (Nancy, 2000: 46–47)

The ontological situating of multiple singular being/s, and community, as prior to, yet impacted on/influenced by phenomenal happenings, requires further clarification. The imperative would seem to be to encourage social forms that allow greater expressions of community. What these forms might be is unclear…and indeed this is the intention of starting to think in these terms for Nancy: It is a task. What these forms are *not* is made very clear—they should not be a production, the making of a project, or the realization or production of a human essence. Such an approach evokes a withdrawal from the political arena and thus disregards the possibilities for realizing actual practical benefits or change. Yet practical action is precisely what Nancy sees as dangerous. To attempt to make something happen, to make something work, is to override or suppress the differences that exist into a totality. Such an orientation is open to the criticism of being politically disengaged and apathetic; of being so careful in description that the theory disempowers political direction or incentive.[12] If community is always there, it risks negating the political and ethical value of community—reducing it to an inescapable part of life.

What is valuable in Nancy's discussion (1991b: 23) is his emphasis that a focus on the subject or on the individual circumvents a thinking of community, and that instead one must focus more on the relationship *between* beings. Indeed, he goes further and suggests, much like Taylor, that contemporary ways of understanding and theorizing the individual and also the community are themselves fundamentally flawed, leading to particular political outcomes.

> Co-appearing does not simply signify that subjects appear together. In that case (which is the "social contract"), it would still need to be asked from where it is they "appear," from which remote depth do they come into being-social as such, from what origin. [Such questions point to] the dead ends of a metaphysics—and its politics—in which (1) social co-appearance is only ever thought of as a transitory epiphenomenon, and (2) society itself is thought of as a step in a process that always leads either to a hypostasis of togetherness or the common (community, communion), or to the hypostasis of the individual. (Nancy, 2000: 59)

Instead, Nancy wants to shift the focus of understanding to recognize the actuality of being with, and the impossibility of being alone. At the same time he wishes to emphasize the uniqueness of that relationship within each occurrence or experience between different beings. Thus, community cannot be encapsulated within a single identity or collectivity.

Nancy does not appear to consider the implications that have been discussed so far regarding the extension, abstraction, or mediation of community relations and practices across time and space, nor does he consider the ways in which embodiment or presence are experienced. His attention instead is turned toward the importance of spontaneous/

playful/unworked communication and literature for the exposure and communication of community.

All communication is an abstraction/extension beyond the self to some degree. It is extended both in practice and intent beyond the articulator to an other/s. Communication exists or takes place in the space between participants—between speaker and receiver—and its message or communication is mutually derived. By this I mean that the speaker can only communicate as effectively as he or she can to the receiver, but s/he cannot absolutely determine the manner in which the receiver understands or experiences the communication. Therefore, the communication can be said to be incompletely shared as it is extended across the space between participants.

Nancy would appear to agree with such an interpretation, arguing that "[c]ommunication is the constitutive fact of an exposition to the outside that defines singularity" (Nancy, 1991b: 29).[13] However, he does not appear to differentiate between communication that takes place across space between those in embodied presence and that which takes place across extended space through mediums such as the text (and by extension, through communications technologies). For him, all communication that exposes our singularity in relation, and our finitude, exposes and expresses community. And as such, it is to be encouraged. He writes:

> Instead of getting upset over the gigantic (or so they say) growth in our means of communication, and fearing through this the weakening of the message, we should rather rejoice over it, serenely: communication "itself" is infinite between finite beings. Provided these beings do not try to communicate to one another myths about their own infinity, for in such a case they instantly disconnect the communication. But communication takes place on the limit, or on the common limits where we are exposed and where it exposes us. (Nancy, 1991b: 67)

Technology has enhanced our ability to communicate across time and space and has thus enhanced our communicative abilities. Yet I have argued that to remove presence from the communication—as a dominant mode of practice—is to change the nature and the receipt of such communication. An effective example is to point to the way in which we find it more difficult to turn away someone in distress or refuse help when faced with their embodied presence, than to ignore the same requests in written or extended/disembodied form. Using communications technologies can, as has been covered in Chapter Two, increase the perception of individual freedom through the removal of the face-to-face. However, such freedom can also involve a feeling of decreased responsibility, obligation, or commitment to the Other or to the society/community.

Alphonso Lingis points to the ways in which technology, despite compressing time and space, has not resulted in the production of a world citizenry (Lingis, 1997: 210). Instead, he argues that the rapid introduction of technology has led to a decline in the quality of communication, and by inference, in the quality of relationships accommodated within and across such techniques.

> Technologies multiply and render one another obsolete at an even faster pace before adjustment to them can integrate one's force, one's skill, one's thought and imagination into the enjoyment of a singular presence. The technologically equipped performance required for an individual to be active expropriates him or her of his or her force, his or her labour, his or her body, his or her sensibility — the space-time of his or her singularity. (Lingis, 1997: 210)

It may be possible to argue, as Nancy does, that the work (or unworking, as the case may more accurately be expressed) of literature touches us through its revealing of our community and our finitude. Such revelations arguably become more accessible or prolific because of the possibilities of technology. But I would argue that such a reaching out, or touching, is effective only because of our immersion in and familiarity with a concrete embodied social environment. And as Lingis and others have pointed out, the quality of much of the communication that takes place through technology is questionable. Nancy is not able to accommodate the intricacies of different relationships, since he is interested only in asserting the singularity and multiplicity of each exposure and the ways in which different social organizations/forms or processes undermine, negate, or encourage opportunities for community. But if we unpack some of these concepts and Nancy's language a bit further, some interesting anomalies arise. These are explored in the later discussion of Nancy and technology.

As has been noted, for Nancy community exists or *is* at a fundamental ontological level — it exists *prior* to any political or social agenda/practices. Therefore, those theorists who attempt to create or find community through the implementation or realization of certain forms of spirituality, politics, or morality (such as the communitarians) are deluded, if not dangerous. Yet Nancy himself appears to use the term community at this other (more superficial and compromised) level when he implies that community is an identity — a being itself. For example, both he and Blanchot talk of the community of lovers defined by the sharing of the experience or sense of love. This use of community is problematic because of the way in which Nancy presents the notion of community as indefinable, ungraspable, and yet fundamental to the relation between/of Being/s.[14] The concept cannot be used to signify a singularly total condition or identity—a situation that Nancy constantly asserts is not community. It could be argued that Nancy uses the two notions of community interchangeably—community-as-communion and community-as-inoperative—and in an undifferentiated manner. Again, this is problematic insofar as it is seemingly left to the reader to discern which form of community is being referred to. And Nancy seems to use this first notion of community-as-communion quite comfortably, despite his protestations in *The Inoperative Community* about its totalizing and problematic form.

There are also inconsistencies between Nancy's assertions that community is not limited to—indeed is constrained by the thought of a limiting to—human beings, and his use of the term. Often, he talks of community in a way that implies human communities (for he does not consider non-humans in much of his discussions). He continuously uses situations between humans as examples, and writes from his perspective—as a human. If Nancy is correct that a thinking of community that is restricted to humans is detrimental to an understanding of community, then my focus on human communities, including technologically extended human communities, is inherently flawed from the outset. For not only is the thought restricted to humans flawed, this problem is compounded further by the incorporation of technology; since the technology itself is seen (sometimes) as a presentation or reproduction of this human essence.

If, however, we ignore this assertion about the detrimental impact of thoughts of community limited to humans, in line with Nancy's own inconsistencies, and attempt to draw out other implications around technological interaction, then difficulties arise as to the nature or understanding of singular beings. Is this understanding of singular beings and their exposure to include only humans interacting via technology whose limits are exposed through their use of the technology, or is one to include the actual technology itself? It is unclear whether humans interacting through technological mediums are to be considered in relation; or if each human and the technology itself must be seen in relation; or indeed whether the technology that communicates to other technological entities need also be considered in relation. Perhaps the communication acts themselves are included within the concept of singular beings.

> What is *a* body, *a* face, *a* voice, *a* death, *a* writing—not indivisible, but singular? What is their singular necessity in the sharing that divides and that puts in

communication bodies, voices, and writings in general and in totality? (Nancy, 1991b: 6)

The inclusion of communicative acts and of technology within an understanding of singular beings would further widen the relational possibilities and thus the potential or compearance of community. This will be discussed in more detail.

Despite Nancy's protestations against defining community, it is interesting to take those elements from our previous discussion and see what can be drawn from his writings. Such an exercise, I believe, is plausible in light of Nancy's inconsistencies and his unacknowledged ascription of commonalities.

Subjective Considerations

Before commencing discussion of the subjective considerations of community, Nancy's understanding of the subject and of subjectivity must be explored. Nancy wishes to deny a subject except as a construction. Therefore, subjectivity and identity are seen as fixing/ imposing an essence on being. For Nancy, to concentrate on the subject is to center this subject as separate to and different from the rest of the world. And it is to render the Other as object. When the theoretical focus is centered on the subject, the subject is the primary object of attention and the origin of consciousness. In rejecting this sense of the subject, Nancy is denying the basis on which liberal theory is premised, whereby the subject is understood as being atomistic and ontologically given, and he also denies the communitarian understanding of the subject as historically, culturally, and communally determined. Instead, his understanding of the *singular being* is determined in relation with/ to the Other. How this relation with the Other is to be understood is discussed in the following subsection on bonding.

Bonding
Nancy writes about a fundamental sociality that underlies all social organization or social forms. As such, he does not write of a need to cohere or to frame beings/people together—in some fundamental ways, they are already and continually together. This togetherness is expressed through literature. Literature, for Nancy, seems to be understood as an expression of or communication about being, existence and finitude.

The type of bonding required by a community-as-communion social form is explicitly rejected. Instead, Nancy outlines an understanding of togetherness that is fleeting, singular, but multiple—unique in each of its experiences or presentations. Through his understanding of exposure to and communication with the Other there is the implicit recognition of respect for the Other. The space between self and Other is incompletely shared—it is not to be fused together, or absorbed completely, into a totality of any form. Bonding in terms of an intersubjective recognition or an emotional investment in the connection—even if only in an abstract sense—between those members of community/ies is also explicitly rejected:

> The metaphor of the "social bond" unhappily superimposes upon "subjects" (that is to say, objects) a hypothetical reality (that of the "bond") upon which some have attempted to confer a dubious "intersubjective" nature that would have the virtue of attaching these objects to one another. This would be the economic link or the bond of recognition. But compearance is of a more originary order than that of a bond. (Nancy, 1991b: 29)

As noted, compearance is used by Nancy to describe an appearance, presentation, or exposure between/to singular beings. As such it implies a certain type of recognition or acknowledgment but, according to Nancy, not a recognition that creates ties or attachments that are binding. 'Non-tying' bonding exists in and through the relation between different singular beings; through the actuality of being-in-common. He speaks

> of a bond that unbinds by binding, that reunites through the infinite exposition of an irreducible finitude. How can we be receptive to the *meaning* of our multiple, dispersed, mortally fragmented existences, which nonetheless only make sense by existing in common? (Nancy, 1991b: xl)

… and only make sense through sharing. Nancy posits bonding at a level that is *prior* to the formation of the self or the subject, as an earlier quote indicated. Indeed it could be argued to take place at that point—at the limit—where connection and disconnection exist simultaneously between singular beings. This would seem to indicate momentary or fleeting connection or recognition, and exposure to and before the Other. A bond implies a connection between, but also, therefore, an exclusion or absence of those outside of the connection. This notion of connection/ exclusion fits within Nancy's approach, since for him, all connections are fleeting or momentary—although absence describes such situations just as accurately.

Literature and communication therefore express and expose community. Literature (in Nancy's sense) and communication bond or connect—we recognize, understand, and are touched by expressions of existence, finitude, and singularity. Literature *is* because of our fundamental sociality—we are singular beings among, and only among, other singular beings. (Nancy, 1991b: 66–67) This understanding resonates with Taylor's emphasis on our ontological sociality, when he writes that we are only selves among other selves. Taylor's writing suggests an important, indeed ontologically necessary, dialogical process of communication. Communication is therefore important to both Nancy and Taylor. Other similarities are also apparent. Both Taylor and Nancy are concerned with the effects of instrumental rationality (or in Nancy's sense, work). This similarity will be discussed further in the following section on technology. However, for the moment, let us recall that for Nancy, the communication of community is not achieved through work. As such, it is not the writing, conversation, or painting in and of itself that expresses community — it is the intent or content of the *unwork* that is important.

Because of the level at which Nancy positions his analysis, there is little if any discussion of integrative practices, social forms, or practical day-to-day living. However, this does not preclude consideration of the relations between singular beings. These relations could be described according to our earlier designation of radical intersubjectivity (with the exception that Nancy posits his singular beings as existing and relating prior to the formation of the subject and thus intersubjective relations).[15] The limit between singular beings is understood as mutually constituted and incompletely shared. Implicit within Nancy's understanding of exposure/encounter with others is consideration and respect for the existence of the Other. Indeed, this is the primary emphasis of his attempt to understand community: For him a community does not constrain or suppress the Other and allows the Other *to be*. What is of value in Nancy's formulation is thus the emphasis on a radical relationship between beings and the implicit requirement of respect for and recognition of the Other. This relationship can be either undermined or accentuated by the social forms that are in place.

So can my argument about extended relations be accommodated here? Where does this fit into Nancy's understanding? The notion that I put forward — that as relations are extended further in space and time and abstracted from the body, such relations are prone to becoming more instrumental in nature, are thinner in experience and practice, and encourage individuation — is in keeping to some degree with Nancy's formulations. But it is only to some degree. First, Nancy does not understand the relation between singular beings (or community), as more than an exposure to others[16] — it is not an ongoing relationship that carries over time. Therefore, community is not seen as thinner or thicker — it is there to a greater or lesser degree.[17] However, such degrees are effected through the imposition of certain social forms and certain social processes. This means that it may be possible to assert that technological processes of abstraction, extension, and rationalization do diminish the *amount* of community experienced. Second, my notion differs from Nancy's in that his position on technology is ambiguous, as will be explored in a later section. Nancy infers that using technology can lead to more instrumental relations through the production of projects of community, but it can also lead to the accentuation of radical relations through the facilitating of literature and communication. The use of technology for administrative and surveillance functions could therefore be seen as diminishing community through expanding the sphere of instrumental relations, whereas communication through virtual communities could be seen as increasing the radical potentials of community.[18] His stance accords to some degree with this book, but I also assert that there is an increased tendency or possibility for the dominance of instrumental relations even within virtual communities. Nancy is not able to discuss such possibilities in any detail because, as asserted, he talks of community only as ontological and as diminished by certain actions, processes, or forms.

Nancy's writing is also able to accommodate the compartmentalization argument that I have been advocating, although he takes a slightly different approach. He argues that the individuation or compartmentalization of individuals is accentuated or created through practices and processes such as capitalism. Capitalism overrides singularity—imposing universality, generality, and creating the individual in the process. It thus undermines/negates community. (Nancy, 1991b: 75) This is similar to Foucault's understanding of individuation and the universalization/standardization that takes place as a result of surveillance and other production processes.

Commonality
There are difficulties with Nancy's exposition of community. He wishes to avoid definitions that designate or prescribe any givens or commonalities for community, yet implicitly he does exactly that. He continuously asserts the singularity (uniqueness) of each/all experience; for example, being is *in* common (not the being itself that is common, but both the relationship and the singularity of being that is *in* common), yet this experience or relationship is never experienced in the same way because being itself is not common. So while he undertakes this rigorous, even convoluted construction, he manages to avoid confronting explicitly the implications that such a construction inherently carries. For it could be argued that, if being is *in* common, then surely there

must be some thing, some essence, quality, procedure, or element that is shared—even if only incompletely—that enables Nancy to say that "being is *in* common." For without commonality, how can beings be identified or labeled as such, and how can they be ontologically in common if there is not some element of commonality or sameness? What would differentiate being from community, or any other concept, if there is not some sense (which is ascribable commonly) of the potentialities of being? In his cautious attempt not to reify or inscribe certain tendencies or attributes to community, Nancy is unable to prevent himself from doing exactly that (although these common attributes are not described; rather, they are ignored, as if the fact of saying that these experiences are different is able to obscure any commonality).

For example, he hints at commonality when discussing the sharing that takes place within community. That being is in common and that this is incompletely shared can be drawn within the description of commonality. The fact that beings are finite, that they are born and also die, is in common even if such realities are experienced differently each time.[19] Nancy would want to deny that this commonality, this incomplete sharing, would create pressures or obligations that suppress or are totalizing. Instead, this commonality is seen as an essential part of the ontological actuality of being, and is thus viewed by Nancy as positive.

This interplay between integrative and differentiating forms or practices is characteristic of Nancy's work. Things, beings, exposures, existences, and community are frequently asserted as *in* common, but are also represented as singularly different. Literature, which communicates community, would signify a degree of commonality, since it commonly communicates (i.e., it is read and understood). As Nancy writes: "There must be some 'common' stuff (*il y ait du commun*), whatever it be for there to be communication"(1992: 384). Yet this literature is also stressed by Nancy as singular in its expression and in its reception.

Similarly, while community may be in common, community itself is not common. This means that it cannot be attributed common virtues, qualities, or essence. As Nancy writes,

> thinking of community as essence—is in effect the closure of the political. Such a thinking constitutes closure because it assigns to a community a *common being*, whereas community is a matter of something quite different, namely, of existence inasmuch as it is *in* common, but without letting itself be absorbed into a common substance. (Nancy, 1991b: xxxviii)

This is an attempt to prevent the naming or ascribing of an identity to community—to fix it into *some-thing* that could be readily identified, made, and so forth. Naming would recreate the totalizing and suppressive conditions that Nancy is attempting to avoid. Rather, "[c]ommunity is made of what retreats from it: the hypostasis of the 'common,' and its work" (Nancy, 1991b: xxxix).

In the previous chapter, Taylor's argument that socially derived understandings of commonality are required for the assignation and perception of values was discussed: He asks how anything can have value without context. Context, for Taylor, is socially derived and commonly recognized as such. We can ask here how it is that Nancy understands and ascribes values, for there are implicit values being asserted throughout his work. For example, the experience of community and also respect for the Other are set up as implicitly good, and fusion with or absorption of the Other is bad (although Nancy also seems to argue that this is not possible, that there are always resistances). Taylor asserts that individual autonomy or difference is worthwhile and valuable, yet it is constrained by operating within a social framework that ascertains what is valuable and what is not (including his own assertions as to its value?). Likewise, Nancy asserts the uniqueness or difference of everything, arguing that it is not possible to generalize or ascribe common qualities; yet there are inescapable or implicit commonalities within his formulation.

Therefore, while Nancy is focused on continually asserting the differences between beings and their existences, I would argue that an emphasis on commonality can also be valuable. This is where the assertion of the *in* common becomes relevant. However, Nancy is being so careful not to obscure or impede difference that he is not able to fully draw out the importance of such commonality.

Reciprocity and Recognition
Nancy barely touches on the issues or practices of recognition or reciprocity in his work on community. However, a form of recognition is implicit within his understanding of singular beings. Singular beings end where they encounter other singular being/s; therefore, some form of recognition is enacted through their exposure. Nancy writes that

> [n]evertheless, before recognition [the Hegelian desire for recognition], there is knowing: knowing without knowledge, and without 'consciousness', that *I* am first of all exposed to the other, and exposed to the exposure of the other. (Nancy, 1991b: 31)

Recognition, as Nancy employs the term, could generally be said to describe the enactment of radical relations.[20] The sense that is derived from Nancy's writing is that the danger of a loss of respect or denial of the possibilities of being comes when such singularity is forced, pressured, or totalized into an identity or subject. Nancy calls our attention to a prior recognition of and respect for the Other that underlies or precedes the formation of the subject (and the Other's creation). This interpretation has led to claims that Nancy in fact does not allow respect for the Other because—through his understanding of recognition and singularity as prior—he renders the Other as essentially the Same.[21] Yet I believe that such criticisms fail to recognize Nancy's emphases on both singularity and multiplicity. This understanding ties in with our discussion of commonality above and the tensions that arise through an explicit assertion of difference yet an implicit recognition of commonality. In a way, Nancy's work can be characterized as a struggle to uncover and work through to an understanding of such (irreconcilable?) factors/pressures.[22]

Tensions of a different sort arise when we introduce technologically mediated practices and relations into the equation. While it is extremely unlikely that there will be a time when we will not be exposed to other people at the most immediate and intimate levels, questions arise about the capacity for such recognition to take place when encounters are mediated across time and space. Does the recognition that we experience in intimate and personal encounters assume the same characteristics when projected onto similar relationships enacted through a computer screen, or via a mobile phone? Nancy's understanding of recognition becomes difficult to comprehend when extended outside the realm of philosophy and abstract conceptualizations, to be situated within a complex and structured system of varying social relations and practices across time and space. Taking, for example, Mark Poster's representation of postmodern community (explored in more detail in the next chapter), it could be argued that the asserted fluidity and multiplicity of identity exhibited through online interactions allow this recognition to be realized in a less constrained manner. Such an argument suggests that the recognition that takes place—for example, through words and images on a screen—demonstrates this recognition of singular beings (all communication is, after all, mediated to some extent). While I do not believe that the direct transposition of a complex philosophical formulation onto a particular online scenario is as simple as outlining descriptive resonances between Nancy's formulation and analyses of online interaction (through assertions about multiplicity and singularity), consideration needs to be given to the consequences of technological mediation for human social forms. Consideration also needs to be given to the implications of the ways in which what I have referred to as different forms of community coexist and interact.

Reciprocity plays an important role in the continuation of relationships. While relationships carry many potential dangers for the integrity and singularity of the self, they also offer many rewarding and important elements to that self. Nancy's understanding of reciprocity is complicated. While his notion of recognition necessarily implies a reciprocal process — the recognition of the Other and allowing the Other to 'be' — reciprocity is not a concept that is explicitly explored. It is, however, implicit within Nancy's notion of communication and indeed within his understanding of community. However, this understanding is not as straightforward as seeing reciprocity as a simple and uncomplicated process of exchange. As with much of Nancy's work, there is evidence of the same tensions between commonality and difference for understandings of reciprocity. For example, while Nancy proposes that literature is the way in which community is experienced and communicated among beings, it is also understood as experienced differently by each receiver. Yet again, while there is this difference, literature similarly touches us through some commonality.[23] It is enough perhaps to state that the importance of literature is that it touches us because it speaks of the unrecognized recognition that takes place at such a deep level.

The difficulty with Nancy's struggle with multiplicity, singularity, and togetherness (evident in the above discussion) is his lack of consideration of emotional connections. Where and how, for example, would Nancy accommodate such valuable relationships as those that take place between parent and child? Or is it upon that first precognitive recognition that a child experiences toward its mother that Nancy is abstracting as his understanding of singularity? Either way, the concept of recognition needs to be taken beyond the theorization of a momentary preconscious experience. This brings the discussion around to the issue of identity and how Nancy understands the relationship between identity and community.

Identity

[H]ow could one understand the agent transforming "himself," or being transformed, without introducing an otherness older and more "constitutive" than his identity (and *of* his identity)? The reality of this otherness, that which makes it "other" and not just a simple provisional distance in the heart of the Same, is the *in*-common of a plurality of agents and of their compearance. (Nancy, 1992: 382)

Nancy is interested in the relations between singular beings. Indeed, as the quote above indicates, such relations not only underlie or precede the formation of identities; they play a part in their formations. That community exists prior to the formation of identities is also important.

Identity involves the accentuation of particular characteristics and the suppression of other characteristics. For Nancy, therefore, the danger of identity is that it is totalizing, or prescriptive, to the self and similarly to relations between the self and the community. This argument is similar to that in Georgio Agamben's book *The Coming Community*. In this work, Agamben attempts to reformulate or come to an understanding of community that is without an identity that does not belong to any particularity or classification. He turns instead to what he refers to as "whatever singularity," which is singularity *as it is* (i.e., with all of its characteristics and qualities, rather than an emphasis on one particular quality). "Whatever singularity" does not belong to a particular group or even a particular linguistic designation (Agamben, 1993).

Nancy's work carries a similar intent; to avoid the prescription of an essence to his singular beings or their communities. Community identity usually applies to community-as-communion — where the community is seen as one or a totality. But this notion of identity is not applicable where community is used in Nancy's sense, that is, as differently relational.

Can postmodern (virtual) communities, in the way that people like Sherry Turkle, Mark Poster, or Howard Rheingold understand them (discussed in the following chapter), be accommodated within Nancy's understanding of the inoperative community? Poster writes that "[c]ommunity for him [Nancy] then is paradoxically the absence of community. It is rather the matrix of fragmented identities, each pointing toward the other, which he chooses to term 'writing'" (Poster, 1995: 34).[24] Poster and Rheingold, as mentioned previously, argue that the possibilities of multiple appearances or representations through virtual communities allows for the proliferation of multiple identities and multiple communities, thereby avoiding the dangers of both a monolithic community identity or a modern, fixed, and centered individual identity. Similarly, Sherry Turkle draws on Frederic Jameson to argue that participation in virtual communities is like the practical realization of postmodern theory — where multiple fluid identities navigate surfaces (Turkle, 1995). Yet as I have mentioned, Nancy's writing is not so easily appropriated by or transposed onto such practices. Postmodern or virtual communities do indeed enable possibilities at one level for multiple and singular articulations. But the operation of self-consciously constructed subject identities in virtual communities is problematic for Nancy's formulation.[25] So too is the fact of online communication that is directed toward a specific audience; an audience that allows for the avoidance of the Other in favor of the Same. Further exploration of Nancy's view of technology is required.

Nancy and Technology

> Ecotechnics privileges…a primacy of the combinatory over the discriminating, the contractual over the hierarchical, the network over the organism, more generally the spatial over the historical, and within the spatial a multiple and delocalized spatiality over a unitary and concentrated spatiality. These motifs compose an epochal necessity. (Nancy, 1993: 53)

Despite his assertions of an "epochal necessity," Nancy does not analyze the impacts or consequences of the uses of technology in an extensive manner. Instead, it is left to the reader to draw conclusions from the occasional remarks about technology made throughout his writings. My impression is that Nancy has an ambiguous view of technology: It can be either positive or negative, or both, in its impact on community, depending on how it is used. This ambiguity was touched on in the earlier section on bonding. There, it was noted that the use of technology to do "work," such as projects of community, undermines community, while increased communication possibilities enabled by the technology are, in Nancy's view, seen as positive for community. Let us explore these points in a little more detail.

On the one hand, Nancy makes it very clear that technological usage and orientation holds negative implications for community. Within his understanding, technological development and use are an extension of a human essence and a consequence of work—both are orientations or outcomes that erode or undermine the possibilities for a questioning of community.

Whether this negativity is premised on a Heideggerian understanding of technology as the transformation of nature (including humanity) into resources or standing reserve or, alternately, on a perception of the rationalization and demystification of the social order and social relations that is problematic, is not clear. Perhaps it is both. Both understandings could be drawn from Nancy's work. On this front, Nancy shares many of the same emphases as Charles Taylor. Both focus on the value of communication (Taylor stresses the importance of language or dialogue; Nancy, that of writing and literature). Taylor sees technology as enhancing possibilities of dialogue, while Nancy sees enhanced opportunities for communication. Both too stress the dangers of instrumental rationality, or "work" in Nancy's sense, for the experience of community. Taylor criticizes instrumental rationality when applied in a controlling and dehumanizing manner for the ways in which it undermines community, but he also sees the possibilities of a more benevolent application of instrumental rationality being attainable through the implementation of a different understanding or enframing of technology. Nancy sees technology as an extension of humanness, and, one suspects, in line with Heidegger, the turning of all into standing reserve. Rationalization and bureaucratic practices are also problematic for Nancy, because they delineate and fix understandings or modes of practice in ways that are totalizing in outcome (and involve the suppression or exclusion of differences). As David Ingram (1998) notes,

> [n]otwithstanding its apparent opposition to totalitarianism, Nancy insists that Western democracy is structured by a similar logic. In this instance, however, the reorganization of society is not accomplished by restoring traditional forms of authority and identity. Rather, lack of identity, loss of certitude, and fragmentation are exploited to good advantage by filling the void vacated by a once vibrant political culture with bureaucratic administration. Nancy here draws on Lyotard's analysis of the collusion between the ideology of "performativity" (technological efficiency) and cybernetics in characterizing capitalist society as a closed, self-regulating exchange system oriented toward stability and homogeneity. (96)

On the other hand, Nancy simultaneously celebrates the opening up of the possibilities for infinite communication enabled by technological forms. As asserted earlier, there is no consideration or concern about the disembodied nature of communicative forms in his work. Nor is there evidence of concern about the fact that social mediation is increasingly taking place through such mediums. Recall these words, cited earlier:

> Instead of getting upset over the gigantic (or so they say) growth in our means of communication, and fearing through this the weakening of the message, we should rather rejoice over it, serenely: communication "itself" is infinite between finite beings. (Nancy, 1991b: 67)

The technology is therefore not the issue per se, it is the uses or ways in which the technology is employed that are of concern. Maybe it is a paradoxical situation where both tendencies exist simultaneously. This ambiguity resonates with my approach in Chapter Two where I argued that the uses to which technology is employed both extend the relational possibilities of community and enhance the individuation tendencies that are apparent. However, neither Taylor nor Nancy consider the implications of extending communicative forms across time and space, nor the implications of an increasing dominance of the extended mode of interaction and integration. Nancy's focus appears to be on the content of communication itself and is unconcerned with its form or manner of conveyance. For example, he sees community and an awareness of finitude being communicated within literature. This is to perceive communication as having a similar outcome regardless of the medium through which it takes place. While in some senses this is indeed true, there are other implications—with which this book is concerned—that are not accommodated so easily within such a framework. Communication taking place via the medium of computer-mediated communication is similar to communication via textual means inasmuch as it is not tied to presence—the communicator does not have to be physically present for the communication to take place. Yet the way in which it contracts time and space on such a large scale, lifting the main form of communication out of its embedded social and cultural context, necessarily has an effect on the ways in which participants see themselves and their relations with Others.

However, while at times Nancy does embrace these forms of communication, this assertion must be qualified to some degree. Nancy would have some problems with the formation and understanding of virtual communities and the writings of the virtual communitarians. This can be argued from a number of perspectives—primarily that which is related to his assertion that community cannot be fixed, made, or named as such. Also, the often functional or instrumental nature of much electronic communication, and the self-interested behavior of (virtual) communicants, would presumably be viewed as undermining the realization or experience of community. Therefore, it may be that Nancy would differentiate between those who play within such medium, and those who communicate for functional reasons. The fact of, and need for, spontaneity and irrepressibility of communication in all its forms certainly requires some consideration. It highlights the communal and social necessity of communicative acts for people; the need for a connection or contact, no matter how fleeting, as being fundamentally important for persons. This is one of the difficulties in discussing the relations constituted within virtual communities. Both forms or communicative intents (work and unwork) take place.

As pointed out earlier, Mark Poster asserts that because of the multiple and fragmented identities that interact within such communities, fixity, and its totalizing tendencies are avoided. Multiple and fluid identities can join, form, or leave communities at will, consequently changing the nature of the community through each interaction. However, the way in which he posits this claim does not hold when subjected to closer analysis. Poster (1995) writes:

Nancy denies the relation I am drawing between a postmodern constitution of the subject and bidirectional communications media. The important point, however, is that in order to do so he first posits the subject as "multiple, dispersed, mortally fragmented" in an ontological statement. (34)

Setting aside his lack of references as to where such a denial has been noted, Poster actually misreads/misquotes Nancy. Nancy does not posit the subject as dispersed or multiple, he writes instead of existences that are before the formation of the subject. For Nancy, there is a distinct difference between the subject, whose implications I have discussed, and singular beings. Poster appears to tackle the one as if it is the other and thus ignores the entire point and intention of Nancy's work. Even by referring to a decentered subject, Poster still focuses on the subject and thus centers the discussion around it. He thus fails to acknowledge the importance—indeed necessity—of the relations between beings.

Poster (1995) goes on to say:

To this extent he removes the question of community from the arena of history and politics, the exact purpose of his critique of the essentialist community in the first place. While presenting an effective critique of the essentialist community, Nancy reinstates the problem at the level of the subject by ontologizing its *in*essentialism. My preference is rather to specify the historical emergence of the decentered subject and explore its links with new communications situations. (35)

Nancy's comment that to focus on the subject is to thwart thoughts of community is particularly apt here, for where does the interest in community lie in Poster's statement?

I would agree with Poster's assertion—and indeed have myself argued—that Nancy removes community from politics and history by abstractly ontologizing it. I also noted that Nancy is not consistent with his usage of the concept and does not consistently keep his discussion at the level of ontology. For example, as was noted, his discussion of capitalism's negation of community intersects the phenomenal with the ontological. Such conceptual maneuvers create difficulties in understanding the ways in which these levels interact and are to be interpreted. These would benefit from greater clarification.

However, to return to Nancy's understanding of technology, it also seems that at times, for Nancy, to examine technology is to displace attention from the more basic human or ontological concerns that are always evident regardless of technologies or techniques. Technology is simply a secondary instrument that is used to enact basic human functions. He writes:

And communication is neither better nor worse when it is carried by optic fibers than when it is carried by messengers on foot. Of importance is that we find out what something like "communication" means. If "technological" civilization displaces the concepts of war and communication (and health, and life, and so on) such as they are, then it ought to be a question of these concepts themselves, of their "becoming-technological" within a general space of the becoming-technological of the world. But it is not a matter of evaluating new instruments for the unchanged purposes of a world that is forever old. (Nancy, 1993: 39)

Here is a serious contention that this book necessarily must recognize and address. If communication is always mediated—whether through language, culture, or subjectivity—and it is simply the medium through which communication takes place that has changed, then is there a point to examinations of technology and community? This book argues that in fact the use of technology for enacting communication and integrative practices holds implications for the ways in which we experience certain ontological categories, and thus also for the ways in which we understand and experience our relationships with others. As such, it is not the technology per se—it is not the instrument—that is being examined; it is the possibilities, potentialities, and outcomes of the use of technology that are deemed to be worthy of further investigation. This is not to see technology as a neutral tool, but to recognize that different technologies carry different *possible* consequences with their use. Such potentialities and possibilities alter our perception and conceptualization of the world; for example, the ways in which our understanding of presence and of time is altered as a consequence of changes in the ways in which we can technically navigate such phenomena. Nancy uses the example of photography:

Photography passionately exposes the real, its fragility, its grace, its transience. Somewhere, for a moment, something or someone has appeared. Photography shows us that it took place and that it resists our doubts, our forgetfulness, our interpretations. It offers us this evidence. (Quoted in Francis Fischer, 1997: 36)[26]

As Nancy (1993) wrote,

[o]ne has not correctly raised the "question of technology" as long as one still considers technologies as means in the service of ends.... If, then, there is a "question of technology," it begins only at the moment when technology is accounted for as finishing of being, and not as a means to some other end (e.g., science, mastery, happiness), and consequently as an end in itself, *sui generis*. (40–41)

What can we learn from Nancy's approach to community and technology? Nancy's work is useful for a number of reasons. His arguments about the inherent sociality of beings accord closely (though conducted at a more abstract level) with Taylor's. His stress on the singularity of each and every presentation of being—yet also on the ways in which singularities are situated among others—draws the discussion away from a focus on the individual alone, to recognize the importance of the social. However, for this book, perhaps the most important aspect of Nancy's work is his struggle with the tensions of singularity and commonality, of integration and difference. What Nancy's struggle illustrates is that there is no absolutely satisfactory resolution that can be achieved. The struggle is interminable and unresolvable. Yet it is not a struggle that we should abandon because of this fact. Nancy's work is in some ways most valuable because of its underlying philosophical approach: that we should continue to struggle with such tensions despite the impossibility of resolution. This does not also mean that we should find the most satisfactory solution and leave it at that. Rather, it means that whatever solutions we arrive at need to be continually questioned, inspected, and altered to allow the struggle to continue.

This struggle is represented throughout his work, not only in its methodology but also in the politics that it advocates. Despite the value of Nancy's approach, however, there are also inherent dangers in undertaking such abstract philosophical processes with the intention of improving our understanding of community. For example, recognition of an inherent respect for the Other in the abstract runs the risk of obfuscating the need for any direct political or social action (community is always there no matter what). As I argued at the beginning of this book with reference to the work of Stephen White, there is an ethical responsibility to the Other, but there is also an ethical responsibility to act. While Nancy might assert the political nature of his writing (as differentiated from his project?), I have already questioned the degree to which processes of abstraction undermine or negate the possibilities for direct political action.

Nancy is valuable for his recognition of the existence and importance of the space (relations) between beings as mutually constituted and mutually recognized. It is in this spacing or at this limit where the philosophical and ontological potential of radical relations exists. However, more needs to be done for radical relations to be conceptualized as a more practicable reality.

Further work is also needed on the implications of technology for social relations, the different forms of community that result, and what it means to have various forms of community intersecting. In this respect, Nancy's discussion of technology does not take us any further than does Taylor's analysis. Therefore, it seems appropriate to turn now to theorists who deal more explicitly with the issue of technology: the virtual communitarians.

Notes

[1] This label is used advisedly, given the revelations about Heidegger's own political past and these theorists' struggles to overcome the possibilities of such practices.

[2] See May's (1993: 283) discussion of Lyotard, Nancy, and Lacoue-Labarthe.

[3] Yet it is interesting that Nancy himself appears to be caught up with the search for a (better) understanding of community and could possibly be said to possess a fascination with the notion similar to the fascination of those he questions.

[4] Although, at times, Nancy does appear to use the term community in this way — community-as-communion. This is similar to Maurice Blanchot's use of community to indicate both the community of communion and also the community of "those who have no community" — in the sense of those who are not "communed." See *The Unavowable Community* (Blanchot, 1988), Blanchot's response to Nancy's book *The Inoperative Community*.

[5] It is incomplete, since to be complete would be to absorb and thus annihilate the Other.

[6] Nancy wishes to avoid the dangers inherent in prescriptions and reification. Such dangers were manifested in the movement of communism from a theory to a practice, and in the outcome of Nazi political practice during Hitler's rule.

[7] "This is why community cannot arise from the domain of work. One does not produce it, one experiences or one is constituted by it as the experience of finitude. Community understood as a work or through its works would presuppose that the common being, as such, be objectifiable and producible (in sites, persons, buildings, discourses, institutions, symbols: in short, in subjects)" (Nancy, 1991b: 31).

[8] He also writes that compearance "does not set itself up, it does not establish itself, it does not emerge *among* already given subjects (objects). It consists in the appearance of the *between* as such: you *and* I (between us) — a formula in which the *and* does not imply juxtaposition, but exposition" (Nancy, 1992: 29).

[9] It is difficult to explain these terms or concepts clearly or decisively, since there is slippage in the ways Nancy uses and describes them.

[10] "The 'singular being' is not a kind of being among beings. In a sense, every being is absolutely singular: a stone never occupies the space of another stone" (Nancy, 1991b: 77).

[11] See Poster (1995) and Chapter Six of this book.

[12] It should be noted, however, that Nancy's writing is described as bringing the political back into philosophy (Fynsk, 1991: x-xi, xxvi-xxvii).

[13] Although he does make mention that the communication he is interested in describing takes place prior to the subject.

[14] Fynsk writes that Nancy unceasingly pushes concepts to the limit and as such, "he does not shy from risks of redundancy or even outright contradiction — he is aiming for the *chance* exposure of a limit." Further, "There is no language for what Nancy is trying to think that does not at some point inhibit this thought, reinscribe in it the

classical conceptual systems Nancy is trying to work past. The tension keeps us from seizing too easily upon the formulas with which Nancy seeks to define his notion of difference" (both from Fynsk, 1991: ix).

[15] For Nancy, the formation of the subject also results in the creation of the Other as an object: "This other is no longer an other, but an object of a subject's representation (or, in a more complicated way, the representative object of another subject for the subject's representation)" (Nancy, 1991b: 24). As such, Nancy prefers to use the notion of the 'being-communicating.'

[16] Although there are ethical implications built into such a notion of exposure to and between.

[17] This is difficult to explain. While community can exist in greater or lesser degrees, this does not mean that it is thinned in the usual understanding of thick or thin community (changes form in any way). Community as relation does not change; for Nancy, there are simply greater or lesser relational possibilities enabled or constrained by the social forms in place.

[18] However, Nancy is difficult to pin down here. It seems that communication that is functionally communicative is not what he means by literature or the communication of community.

[19] "What could be more common than to be, than being? We are. Being, or existence, is what we share....But being is not a thing that we could possess in common. Being is in no way different from existence, which is singular each time. We shall say then that being is not common in the sense of a common property, but that it is in common" (Nancy, 1991a: 1).

[20] Instrumental relations are instituted once the formation of the subject and the creation/constitution of an identity take place.

[21] Bernasconi (1993) claims that Nancy is unable to accommodate the Other because of his refusal to recognize "radical alterity" (4, 12).

[22] Or it could be seen as an unwillingness to force singularity into any category or constraint. Fischer writes that "[t]his is not a passion for seeing, but a letting-be of this existing in the multiple brilliance of its singular exposure. Every body, however ordinary, is also absolutely singular. And the image is neither empty nor simulation, hence his [Nancy's] refusal of all those denunciations of our world as spectacle or simulation" (Fischer, 1997: 36).

[23] Much as the commonality of our existence, even though it is always experienced differently, touches us.

[24] I believe that Poster misreads and misinterprets Nancy's work. For example, it is neither accurate nor appropriate to use the term "identity" in the way that Poster does. This misuse is discussed in more detail in the following section.

[25] See Whitely (1997) for a critique of these identity processes.

[26] Photography—and its ability to capture a piece of the real and to immobilize—changes the ways that we understand such possibilities.

Chapter Six

~~~

Mark Poster and Virtual Community/ies

The appeal for community...must take into account the forms of identity and communication in the mode of information, and resist nostalgia for the face-to-face intimacy of the ancient Greek agora. In the era of cyborgs, cyberspace and virtual realities, the face of community is not discerned easily through the mists of history, however materialist and dialectical it may be. (Poster, 1995: 93–94)

But the dramatic spread of electronic communication systems which will undoubtedly rise even more precipitously once the computer, the telephone and the television are systematically integrated toll the end of community in any shape it has hitherto been imagined. (Poster, 1995: 52)

Mark Poster, Sherry Turkle, and Howard Rheingold are just a few of the theorists who embrace an understanding of virtual communities as possible postmodern communities. These writers see virtual communities as a way to overcome the integrative/differentiating dilemma. Therefore I have chosen to categorize them under the umbrella of a virtual communitarian position.

The virtual communitarians' main emphases are on the following: the proliferation of multiple identities that can be enacted through the use of the Internet; the removal of the constraints on embodied identity and the ability to play with alternate forms of identity; and the removal of the constraints of time and space from social relations and practices. All these have been covered in some detail in earlier chapters (particularly Chapters Two and Three) and thus do not warrant detailed attention here. Suffice it to say that these writers see the technology enabling the possibility for more liberating and more postmodern communities (in the sense of multiple, decentered identities and unconstrained relations).

As in the preceding two chapters, I have chosen to focus on the work of one theorist in particular. Therefore, I now turn to the discussion of community undertaken by Mark Poster. Poster's stance on community is not well defined; community is not the focus of, or indeed central to, his work. However, the few statements that he has made, when coupled with an understanding of his social theory, enable some assumptions to be drawn out. In discussions, some people have expressed surprise at my decision to focus on Poster's work in relation to virtual communities. I have chosen to examine Poster's work for a number of reasons. Even though Howard Rheingold, for example, deals more explicitly and extensively with the topic of virtual communities, he does this more in the style of observation and description. And while Poster has not written much about community—indeed, his writings are quite minimal in this area when contrasted with writers such as Rheingold, Nancy Baym, Barry Wellman, and colleagues—he is the only theorist who concentrates in sufficient detail on issues such as the interplay of technology and subjectivity or who moves beyond empirically descriptive social analysis. Poster is not only more theoretically sophisticated in his analysis, he is also more useful in terms of the argument within this book. His underlying methodology and theoretical approach are also more clearly explicated. While I have some differences with his approach, there are sufficient commonalities and overlaps in interest to warrant subjecting his theory to a closer analysis.

Poster on Community

Poster works with a general understanding of what he calls an improved critical social theory—critical theory that is broadened to take into account the implications of changing language structures and the impact of communication technologies. This improved critical social theory combines some of the elements of critical theory and its recognition of the social and cultural implications for the subject, with the poststructuralist (primarily Foucauldian) notions of the impact of discursive practices on the subject.[1] The manner in which Poster attempts this combination is open to question and deserves further analysis.[22] The manner in which he outlines this improved critical theory is rather confusing. In some of his writing he argues that the problem of critical theory is that it is premised on a rational, centered subject who is positioned within the binary of autonomous/heteronomous. He argues that the poststructural emphasis on decentered and multiple representations of the subject is more appropriate and can more easily be used to gain some understanding of the ramifications of the uses of different communications technologies (and also avoids totalizing theoretical approaches).

However, he argues that the increase in social interconnectivity and the changes in language structures resulting from the use of new communication technologies make analysis of the implications of these media important. He believes that critical theory in its unimproved state is unable to accommodate this type of analysis, and therefore such a theoretical combination is necessary.

In some ways, Poster's understanding of both the subject and community falls within the social communitarian understanding—with a difference. For Poster, the subject, and thus the subject of a community, is influenced by the use and form of language, institutions, cultural practices, and historical developments. The difference derives from the importance he places on the formative role that language and its "wrappings" play in the constitution of the individual and her/his cultural understandings and practices. Communication technologies are credited with impacting on these language-wrapping configurations.

> Electronic communication machines reconfigure space and time coordinates, restructure the relation of the body and mind to the practice (of writing), redesign relations of inside and outside through what I call the wrappings of language. In these ways the conditions of culture are shifted. (Poster, *Seulemonde*)

Poster seems more optimistic about the possibilities for community in contemporary society than many of the social communitarian theorists. Poster sees contemporary technological society enabling the freeing up of social roles and the multiplication of worldviews. These developments are understood as reconstituting the individual and the community in new and liberating forms, rather than as undermining the possibilities for community and emptying out the meaning of life for its subjects (as depicted by the social communitarians).

Poster (1995: 34) adopts Nancy's conception of communities "in the older sense" as constituted through the production of a fixed essence with which each member identifies, and subsequently structures their own identity around. However, he believes the potentialities of current technologies of communication alter this relation among community, identity, and membership. According to Poster, the dynamics of electronically mediated communications and their languages structure participant identities in such a way as to undermine the rational autonomous subject central to modernity and the Enlightenment project.[3] For Poster, as for Rheingold, real (traditional and modern) communities entail fixed stable identities, while virtual (postmodern) communities consist of fluid or transient identities. His justifications for such an assertion are, I argue, lacking in depth; however, this will be discussed in more detail later on.

Poster deals with the integrative/differentiating dilemma of community theory in several ways. First, he posits the subject of postmodernity/mode of information as dispersed, decentered, and multiple. As such, he believes the postmodern subject is itself less repressed or totalized than the centered and rational subject of modernity. Second, he believes that communications technologies enable new structures of language that encourage these multiple articulations of the self. Virtual communities are thus depicted, by Poster and others, as the location or site for togetherness with difference. This togetherness with difference is seen as realizable both when interacting within individual virtual community sites and also through interacting within and between a multiplicity of these sites.

All three theorists considered within this book—Poster, Taylor, and Nancy—emphasize the importance of language and communication in one form or another, for the practice and understanding of community. Taylor stressed the importance of a dialogic relationship with others mediated through the communication of language or conversation. As noted in Chapter Four, this understanding of language incorporated consideration of nonlinguistic communication devices—body language, dress, tonal emphasis, and so forth. For Nancy, writing was represented or understood as the means by which we recognize our togetherness, our existence, and our finitude. This approach, like Taylor's, also focused on the social nature of subjects and of community. Poster also stresses the importance of language in self-constitutive processes, arguing that language and discursive practices are integrally involved in the construction of the subject and his/her identities. Yet differences become apparent when all the approaches are aligned side by side. Taylor and Poster are both interested in the constitutive processes of the subject, whereas Nancy posits his analysis at a more 'fundamental' level of singular beings (arguing that a focus on the subject undermines community). Taylor and Nancy emphasize the necessity and importance of the social and the importance of the relationships that take place *between* beings, whereas Poster is focused more on the impact on the individual and the individual subject's interaction with technological processes. Poster's is an instrumental or utilitarian approach toward the Other whereby s/he is seen as useful only for self-constitutive processes. Indeed, while Poster's focus on language and discursive practices implicitly recognizes the existence and necessity of others, relations with these others are not discussed. To be fair, as stated above, Poster does not declare community to be his central concern; he is more interested in the relationship possibilities he sees developing between subjects and machines than he is in the exploring relationships between people. Therefore, he goes to great lengths to stress the multiplicity and fluidity of identity constituted through the processes enabled by the mode of information (a concept that will be discussed shortly). This approach argues for a freedom from restrictions on the self, including restrictions created by relationships with others. One is drawn to wonder how, for example, the fleeting and unconstrained interactions that Poster depicts as taking place within virtual communities can sustain or be the basis for rewarding, ongoing relationships—relationships that can foster important human emotions such as compassion and empathy. This will be discussed further in the technology section.

Poster is attempting to do a multitude of different things within his work. As a consequence, a number of ideas are tantalizingly presented but undeveloped. These would benefit from further elaboration. For example, he argues at one stage for a differentiated cosmopolitanism that is able to accommodate and recognize gendered and ethnic subjects. It would be interesting to know more about this idea and to understand how Poster reconciles this notion with his understanding of multiple subjects. The relationship or interconnection of cosmopolitanism with another brief proposition, that of the coming of a second media age, would also be worthy of further exploration. Poster writes,

> Differentiated cosmopolitanism is furthered by the thickening and intensification of communication across boundaries of locality, a process enabled but not completely shaped by electronic forms of communication. (1995: 51)

Obviously, further work is required to make these connections and relationships clearer. However, having stated some of its limitations, this is not to negate the relevance of Poster's writings for this book. His work attempts to theorize contemporary technological society, asserting that understanding the consequences of using these technologies is important for understanding social forms.

Structural Considerations

> Electronically mediated languages constitute a new social region distinct from but overlapping with the capitalist economy, the welfare state, and the nuclear family. Structurally distinct from face-to-face interactions and from printed communications, they emerge into technically advanced societies, undermining the boundary between public and private space. (Poster, 1989: 69)[4]

> The mode of information designates social relations mediated by electronic
> communication systems, which constitute new patterns of language. It is my
> hypothesis that an important new dimension of advanced society concerns
> language and can only be investigated by means of linguistically based
> concepts. (Poster, 1989: 126)

Poster explores the ways in which different communicative forms result
in different understandings and practices of the subject. He does this
by asserting the importance of language structures and the discursive
effects of these structures on the subject, and by linking changes in
language structure to the use of different communicative technologies.
As a result, he argues for constitutive differences in the subjects of oral,
print, and electronic communications.[5] Thus he is in accord with part of
the argument of this book; that communications technologies have
implications for subjectivity and (for Poster, by inference) on
intersubjective relations. He does this through employing a conceptual
schema that he entitles *the mode of information*.

In his book, *The Mode of Information*, the concept is used to "suggest
that history may be periodized by variations in the structure in this
case of symbolic exchange, but also that the current culture gives a
certain fetishistic importance to 'information' " (Poster, 1990: 6). He
analytically differentiates between different stages in the mode of
information. These stages are tentatively divided into the "face-to-face,
orally mediated exchange; written exchanges mediated by print; and
electronically mediated exchange" (Poster, 1990: 6). This division is not
sequential but coterminous and not real but analytical.[6] Such a division—
made on the basis of differing communicative forms—appears similar
to the manner in which I have differentiated between forms of
community. I argued for the analytical distinctions of traditional,
modern, and postmodern forms of community partly by the dominant
means through which communicative and integrative practices are
enacted. However, my use of these distinctions incorporates recognition
and analysis of changes in the ontological forms that intersect with or
underlie these practices. While Poster does not explicitly draw such a
correlation between changing ontological forms and forms of
community, he does assert that each stage of the mode of information is
accompanied by the constitution and presentation of a different form
of the self.[7] This would suggest that the relations between these differing
selves are also differently experienced.

However, while there are seeming similarities in Poster's and my
own approach, each position is handled slightly differently. Poster
maintains that changes in communicative forms result in changes to
the language structures, and thus too in changes to the form of the
subject. Almost implicitly these changes are noted as also providing

different ways of negotiating time, space, and embodiment, though these are not directly theorized. I argue that changes in the ways in which communicative forms and integrative practices are structured and experienced through time, space, and presence have an effect on subjectivity and intersubjective relations. Poster interposes the additional step of changing language structure to mediate or explain these alterations; an addition I feel is unnecessarily complicating. Whereas I argue for the effect on community forms and social relations, Poster comments on the effect on the subject. It is difficult to ascertain, then, how he understands the interconnection or overlay of the various modes of communication and their associated social forms, or indeed how he sees the subject-in-relation, if these modes are understood as coexistent. He does note that

> [w]e need to study the interweaving of electronic associations with older forms of community to see if the effects are complementary, antagonistic or non-relational. (Poster, 2001a: 140)

Some way of accommodating and explaining the interrelation of these differing forms would be useful. How, for example, does Poster reconcile the concept of the subject of electronic communications who is also engaged with print and oral forms of communication? If the subject of print culture is understood as centered and rational, how is the subject of electronic communications—as multiple and dispersed—similarly constituted through her/his interaction through print and oral forms?[8] These questions highlight the importance of a theoretical emphasis on or recognition of the dominance of particular modes of communication within social forms. Such recognition enables discussion of the ways in which dominance and coexistence are structured and experienced.

In *The Second Media Age*, Poster introduces, albeit only briefly, the consideration that we may have reached or are in the process of becoming a second media age, whereby "Subject constitution in the second media age occurs through the mechanism of interactivity" (1995: 33). Here he makes the same mistake as other technological utopians in his overemphasis on the role of disembodied or extended interactivity as being solely constitutive. Interactivity always plays a part in the constitution of the subject and her/his relations. However, other practices and processes are also involved. Such an overemphasis overlooks the existence of these other important constitutive processes.[9]

Poster stresses interactivity—and the possibilities of a second media age—because of the role he sees interactive communicative forms playing in the constitutive and constituting possibilities for the self. He differentiates between the first and second media age on the basis of interactivity (the first media age being one-directional) and the differences he depicts between the various selves of such ages. Apart from the reservations expressed above, I also have difficulties with some of his other assertions. For example, I am less than convinced about the basis for which he asserts multiplicity and the difference between the modern subject of print culture and the postmodern subject of electronic communications. Poster argues the difference on the basis of interactivity and fluidity: Print culture defines the subject and subject identity as fixed, whereas electronic (interactive) communication problematizes individual identity, allowing multiple articulations. Interactive communication is depicted as throwing into question the author/reader designations. Yet I do not see the divide between these two forms being as unproblematic or decisive as Poster describes. Indeed, as he himself points out, Derrida's work argues against such readings of print culture (1995: 71–72). I would agree that there are important differences between each form of communication, but not entirely on the basis that Poster claims. The reconfiguring of different ontological forms through the dominance of differing forms of relating across time and space provides a more useful explanation than basing claims on fluidity and interactivity alone.

In *The Second Media Age*, Poster sees similarities between real communities and virtual communities. He claims that the opposing of the two forms of community on the grounds of differing realities is problematic since, following from Benedict Anderson's work, the role of the imaginary plays an important part in both forms (Poster, 1995: 34). Poster also refers to Stone's point regarding the juxtaposition that takes place within virtual communities whereby these communities are ascribed real life characteristics and attributes.[10] Having made such an assertion, and also outlining how this opposition between real and virtual hinders analysis of forms of bonding and identity (Poster, 1995: 35), he then proceeds to the use the term quite unproblematically, as if the existence of virtual communities—in the sense that they are communities that are virtual—were a *fait accompli*. More analysis of the concept of community itself—and particularly his notion of a postmodern community—would be worthwhile, as would more explicit discussion as to the relations that are experienced or practiced between members of the community. While he adopts Nancy's description for real communities, he fails to explain why or how the new forms of interaction enabled through communication technologies can accurately be encompassed within a concept of virtual (postmodern) communities. Poster (1995) is willing to accept that the destruction or loss of so-called real communities could be part of the allure of virtual forms of community, but he prefers "to explore the new territory and define its possibilities" (35). What these possibilities might be with regard to community, we are given little indication. However, he does write that

> [w]hile this form of computer writing [computer conferencing] *may* never fully replace traditional community, it offers an alternative to synchronous meeting that meliorates the *increasing isolation* of the information age. (Poster, 1995: 71, my emphasis)

And therefore, he is seemingly unwilling to rule out the possibility that this new form of community may in fact fully replace those of earlier community forms. Here too Poster points to "the increasing isolation" that is experienced within the contemporary information society, and yet this isolation is not theorized. How does he explain such increasing isolation if the new communicative technologies increase social interconnectivity and interactivity? This is one of the anomalies of contemporary life worthy of further exploration. I have suggested in this book that both compartmentalization and interconnectivity result from the use of technologies to extend and abstract relationships and integrative practices, altering the experiences of embodiment and time and space in the process.

Of the implications of electronically mediated communications, Poster says that while it may not appear to effect change at an ontological level, there is change at the phenomenal level at which the subject experiences itself and the world. "Like other domains of the mode of information, the computer draws attention to the subject as a constituted phenomenon, undermining the illusory assurance of the fixed, defined individual" (Poster, 1989: 139). This is to focus on the content/process of the communication acts themselves and the possibilities enabled by the technology. While I would question the degree of reflexivity that the subject enacts in his/her self-constitution I would also argue that change or effect on the subject and her/his intersubjective relations takes place at both a phenomenal and an ontological level. Considerations of the processes of abstraction and extension—which Poster also comments on—need to be taken more fully into account, as do the implications of changes in the ways in which the ontological categories of time and space and embodiment are experienced. For Poster, "[l]anguage and action are interrelated aspects of experience" (1989: 127).[11] Therefore, the implications of technologically mediated language must be included within any account of subjectivity. The removal of presence, the constraints and discourse of the technology itself, the potential for interactivity and the altering of time and space are all mentioned in Poster's account of individual subjectivity (as evidenced in the quotation above). However, these changes in the understanding and experience of ontological forms are not granted more than a brief comment about their phenomenal impact. For example, although Poster notes the technological compression and mediation of time and space that is enacted, he does not give this fact anything more than passing attention.[12] Yet these categories—whether they are understood as ontological or phenomenal—are completely implicated in Poster's use of the concept of language and its wrappings.

To try to gain a fuller understanding of Poster's own conception of postmodern/virtual communities (accepting that his understanding of the traditional or real community would tend to fall within that of everyday usage), I once again turn to the subjective elements from earlier discussions of bonding, commonality, reciprocity and recognition, and identity.

Subjective Considerations

Bonding

Poster's entire position rests on the supposition that changes in language structure and changes in the *way* that communicative acts take place affect subject constitution. Speech transmitted in face-to-face situations acts as a tie or bond, since it is able to be attached to concretely identifiable persons/identities. Print isolates the individual from the immersive qualities of face-to-face situations; enabling them to still be treated as integrated and unitary subjects, yet also allowing some detachment from the communicative process. And communication through electronic media disperses or fragments the communicative subject, offering no concrete identity or particularity to which to tie or bond with others—fluidity and impermanence characterize such relations (Poster, 1990: 46). One assumes that all linguistic experience and communicative acts, regardless of medium, are carried out either directly or indirectly with others: communication and language are interactive, dialogic processes. Thus—of necessity—Poster implicitly recognizes the importance of others in the process of self-constitution. However, the necessity of involvement with others is either taken for granted by Poster and is not mentioned, or else the analysis is so subject-oriented that the types of intersubjective relations are viewed either procedurally or in a utilitarian manner, whereby the interchange is carried on solely for the subject's benefit.

The multiplicity and fragmentation of the postmodern subject, which Poster posits as an increasing phenomenon, would lead one to assume that, as for Nancy, any bonding would be tenuous and singular. It would be limited to exposure of one fragmented part of a subject to another's or group of another's fragmented part/s. However, what is unclear is how—or what—constitutes community among such dispersed and multiple selves/subjects. If there is no defined referentiality, if subject identity is fluid—and thus one would assume the connections with others must necessarily be similarly fluid—then what holds these actors together? Is it possible to extend this understanding to encapsulate some form of community in any meaningful sense?

Poster explains that the role of the imaginary plays an important part in the constitution and cohesion of many forms of community. Therefore, noting the group identification achieved through the operation of a national imagination enabled by print technology, likewise it would seem that Poster is implicitly acknowledging a certain level of group identification enacted within technologically mediated communities. But what is unclear is how such group identification is constituted. Is it through entering into the space of communication as a participant? Maybe it is formed around common intent, being within a common space, or sharing an ideology or purpose. This would seem to posit group identities as coherently held by participants in a relatively stable though changeable form. Yet members' relationships (and member identities) are not depicted by Poster as stable or unitary, but instead as fleeting, tenuous, and multiple. Isn't Poster undermining his argument with this implicit assumption of commonly held identification—a commonly held essence—of the community, a quality that he explicitly uses to distinguish between traditional and postmodern communities? Perhaps this is too simplistic a reading. He might say that because people may hold multiple memberships, these memberships are not as totalizing as belonging simply to one community in which all facets of life are enveloped and defined.

Poster (1995) writes that "what makes a community vital to its members is their treatment of the communications as meaningful and important" (36). Yet he fails to elaborate how this meaningfulness is achieved. Is it to be understood as solely subject-oriented, whereby the subject derives satisfaction through an outward participation in dialogue? Does acknowledgment or response from others to individual communicative initiatives denote the importance of that communication? It is simplistic to assert that to be heard and acknowledged is sufficient for the experience of meaningful communication to take place. Such experience is meaningful only if those who respond are perceived as important, or when being heard in a particular place is seen as valuable.

In short, meaningful communication is situated within a framework of already shared and valued goals or ethics. To be heard and recognized by those who were viewed as unimportant, or indeed less than that, would not be valued. It would be held to be irrelevant or even detrimental. Poster appears to argue that if the communication is valued in itself, then it is simply the act of communication being valued that makes such acts meaningful. This would indicate that the content of the communication is not relevant, and that participant values or orientations are not important. A focus on the act of communication being seen as sufficiently valuable in itself conjures up images of poorly socialized, isolated subjects whose sole worth comes from being heard, regardless of by whom, and regardless of their communicative content or the setting in which their communicative acts take place. Although there are writers, such as Sherry Turkle, who suggest that some participants in virtual communities demonstrate a lack of social skills, this is not a sufficient explanation for these communities' growing appeal within techno-society or for their description as a community. A wider analysis of why such communication is important and meaningful is required. Perhaps it might be suggested that through the communicative process, relationships are formed — and bonding takes place — rendering the reception of such communicative acts as meaningful. This raises questions as to assertions about the fleeting and transient nature of subject identity and subject relations.

Poster is difficult to pin down in these areas, since he hints at possibilities, makes tentative suggestions, and then fails to develop any of them further. This is explained away by Poster's immersion in modernity and its conceptual baggage, which does not allow him to fully appreciate or analyze new developments without constraining them, and by the tentativeness of these developments and the hint of early possibilities (Poster, 1995: 35). While I recognize that his primary interest is in human-machinic relations, discussion and analysis of the relation of being-together is necessary for him to fulfill some of his other intentions. If he focuses just on self-constitution, then his attempts to distance himself from the liberal atomistic understanding of the self are undermined, and he negates the role of the social and of language, both elements that he asserts as being so important for his analysis.

Commonality

Like the poststructuralists, Poster does not accentuate the importance of commonality. This raises the criticism again, as Taylor has pointed out, that socially constructed and shared values and norms are the means by which individuals formulate their own understanding of what is important and meaningful. Therefore, commonality is an essential part of human life. What such commonalities also do is enable the *means* for the development and maintenance of relationships between individuals. For Poster, the recognition or characterizing of a commonality could be understood as actively imposing an essence. The perception of commonality—or the theoretical acknowledgment of commonality—could be deemed an arbitrary construction undertaken for the purposes of totalization, domination, and the categorizing of identities. Yet in a postmodern world of fragmented identities, where individual choice is open to many possibilities, commonality would also provide the means for (possibly) fleeting bonds. Fleeting ties raise the question of participants' commitment to these relationships and also of their ability to acknowledge responsibility to the Other. Poster's failure to explore the connections and commonalities between subjects leaves such questions unanswered.

Poster does not examine the way in which technology enables the occlusion of the Other through the seeking out and maintaining of relations with those who are the Same. The potential to isolate and protect the individual from disruptive or alternate subjects and social forms does not bode well for the celebration of difference or for the ability to interact sensitively and compassionately with those who are different. It is obviously possible to argue that segregation and exclusive behavior can be and are enacted outside of these media. It is also obvious that these forms of technology have—through enabling the compression of time and space—brought us much closer to the Other on numerous levels. However, as noted in Chapter Two, the flip side of these technologies is the ability to isolate, protect, and exclude the individual from unwanted contact.

Poster and other proponents of virtual communities argue that because bodily recognizable differences are excluded and the individual is able to present his/herself in different forms, this is generally not the case.[13] However, anecdotal and empirical evidence suggests that it is simply the criteria for recognition or differentiation that changes.[14] The forms and types of exclusions are transformed instead to Net behavior, ideas, and goals. Poster is too astute a theorist to rest his argument simply on the removal of the body from communicative processes. However, such inferences can easily be drawn from his writings. For example, he notes:

> New qualities of community relations develop in this cyberspace. Without the cues of body language, status, force of personality, gender, clothing style—all present in face-to-face situations—conversation changes in character.

Interventions are less conventional, less deferential, as social authority is cancelled through computer writing. (1995: 71)

These inferences require qualification or elaboration.

Poster focuses on difference to the detriment of commonality. However, there are still common elements implicit in his analysis. For example, the emphasis on the constitutive role of language relies on the existence of commonality for it to operate successfully. Therefore, what is required is recognition and analysis of the role that commonality plays in community forms.

Reciprocity and Recognition

An understanding and recognition of the relation between subjects (or self, or being, wherever one chooses to locate sociality) is vitally important for the project that Poster has set up. Reciprocity and recognition play an important part in this process. Since Poster does not pay much attention to subject relations, his approaches to issues of reciprocity and recognition are difficult to ascertain. Again, I reassert that I see this lack of interest in the social forms and practices of subjects as problematic.

Implicit within Poster's analysis of language are these very notions of reciprocity and recognition. These could be productively explicated to enable analysis and consideration of the types and forms of reciprocal practices that are enacted within the different community forms. Issues of recognition are also important because recognition involves processes of inclusion and exclusion—to not be recognized as a participant in a conversation, for example, is to be excluded and denied a voice. Poster's analysis would benefit from such a discussion. As presently expressed, his analysis suggests a positive but rather narrow understanding of communication whereby individuals relish their own productions and expressions, but it misses the essential core of intersubjective communication. Nancy's point about the importance of the incomplete sharing of the in-between of singular beings is worth raising again. Poster's representation of communication, in its present form, is not able to accommodate the possibility of such incomplete sharing, or the recognition of the Other that this sharing enables.

As Nancy claimed, a focus on the individual subject and subject-constitution undermines a thinking of community. With such a subject-oriented focus, Poster diminishes the importance or ability to adequately theorize relations between subjects and thus to theorize ethical relations. This may be because he places an emphasis on subject fluidity and multiplicity and he does not, like Nancy (although in a more theoretically superficial manner), wish to prescribe certain characteristics or behaviors to dispersed subjects. However, this reluctance leads to the same lack of ethical or political direction that Poster is critical of and wishing to supplement in poststructuralist positions. And while he notes the potential for transformation in social forms, this potential is posited entirely within the ambit of the changing subject. Such a focus on the subject fails to consider relations with the Other or indeed the importance of such relations for subject formation. If the focus of community analysis is on the individual and the effects on/for the individual, then the Other becomes a utilitarian instrument for the achievement of the individual's own ends. This focus leads to an instrumental understanding of relations, where the intersubjective relation is one that is subject-directed and subject-oriented—it is not a radical relationship inasmuch as these relations are not depicted as being mutually constituted. By focusing purely on the lack of restrictions placed on the self, considerations of notions of responsibility, respect, or concern for the Other are unable to be situated within any particular social form or practice. Poster's analysis fails to make a space for relationships to be formed or understood. This inadequacy accentuates the further compartmentalization and totalization of the individual (despite the potential of fluidity and multiplicity enabled by the technology).

Identity
Community identity is something that Poster sees as one of the dangers of modernity, and it is responsible for many totalitarian and repressive actions. To talk of community identity would be seen to fix an essence. Instead, Poster's interest is centered on the identity/ies of the postmodern individual and how these identities are constituted. The postmodern individual is described, as has been already mentioned, as possessing multiple, fluid, and fragmented identities that are not confined within bodily constraints.[15] Electronically mediated language structures self-constitution in two ways. First as a consumer, and second,

> the individual must also play with the very process of self-constitution; in this respect, the mode of information undermines the cultural basis of dominant structures.... Watching television (especially ads), being monitored by computerized data bases, participating in computer conferencing, or even using computers—all these experiences enact asynchronous discursive practices that heighten the self-referentiality of language and undermine the earlier stability of the subject, the sense of having a continuous identity rooted in time, in space, and in relations with others and things. (Poster, 1989: 68)

While they have their own particular identities fashioned from shared interest, virtual communities are communities in which participants create their own identity self-presentation. They can also choose their participation in any of these community activities or discussions.

> In the small communities of tribal society, individuals are "known" from birth, enmeshed in extensive kinship structures that reproduce identity in daily experience. In this context the subject is social, constructed and reproduced as a relational self. In cities, by contrast, the individual is extracted from such identity reproduction, but here conversations, before the mode of information, required face-to-face positioning and therefore bodily "signatures" which specified the individual so that, if necessary, actual identities could later be recalled. With writing and print, identity is further removed from communication, but authorship, even under assumed names, serves to fix identity. With computer message services, language use is radically separated from biographical identity. Identity is dispersed in the electronic network of communications and computer storage systems. (Poster, 1990: 117)

Poster discusses how the opportunities afforded by enacting social activity external to the body—in a disembodied form—not only enable one to play with alternate presentations of the self but also lead to a more reflexive approach to issues such as gender. Through participation in a textually interactive medium, a representation of self must be consciously chosen: a participant must decide in what form, gender, and other characteristics s/he may choose to present. Poster, Turkle, and others argue that the ability to consciously and also reflectively present as alternate genders opens up possibilities for the undermining of prejudice and for more open forms of community. Indeed, these writers go so far as to state that it is possible for a participant to actually experience what it is like to *be* another gender, thus allowing more compassionate and egalitarian forms of relating and understanding to be developed. As already discussed in Chapter Two, such representations fail to acknowledge the embodied and biological particularities that contribute to one's interpretation and experience of being in a gendered body. They also fail to recognize that the social and cultural complexities of gender go further than textual attempts in a virtual world could possibly replicate and/or experience. Edgar Whitley (1997) refers to this as the "flawed logic of moving from the removal of physical cues to the claim that new identities can be created simply by changing the words that are uttered" (152). He also notes that for the argument of those who believe in the easy creation of online identities to succeed,

> it has to be shown that choosing the words for a different identity is unproblematic. Unfortunately...the choice of words is not something that can be learned in a formal manner; rather the choice of words is the result of

a process of socialization associated with a particular identity. It is therefore very difficult to learn a new identity without being socialized into that role. It may be possible to make a passable attempt at mimicking the identity, but such mimicry is limited and is not the same as creating a viable, permanent new identity. (Whitley, 1997: 148)

Indeed, I would go even further than Whitley and argue that understandings of being in a gendered body have more to do with the existence and experience of ontological boundaries in general (and how the body is lived) and social behavior than with the existence or removal at one level of one set of ontological boundaries—the spatial.

Virtual communities have been presented by proponents as less restrictive than traditional communities, because of the possibilities of fashioning one's representation of oneself unconstrained by embodied characteristics, where such options are not as freely available. However, if the basis for such a determination is positioned solely around the freeing up of bodily constraints on identity formation, this is negated by the continuing function of other restrictive processes existing within both forms of community (although the actual presentation or manifestation may differ in form, rather than in kind). It is also a fairly superficial and simplistic understanding of the way in which exclusionary practices function. To remove certain features that have been the basis for exclusionary or discriminating factors in the past is not to remove the underlying repressive or domineering tendencies behind their utilization. These simply reform and attach themselves through other characteristics or practices. What is being suggested addresses the symptoms and not the cause. Further examination of the dynamics of power relations within and between individuals and communities is certainly required.

Poster and Technology

[A] new planetary relation of humans to machines based on the emergence of new kinds of information machines as well as a continuing, rapid dissemination of both industrial and postindustrial machines. By the late twentieth century machines populate the earth in considerable numbers and variety. Two basic questions that needed to be posed about technology at this point are, Synchronically, how do we understand the combinations of humans and machines? And diachronically, do we dare ask if humans are a stage in a development of which machines are the inheritors of the planet? (Poster, 2001b: 26)

> It is now imperative to study a new region of experience, the domain of the
> mediated, a domain that is imbricated with everyday life in a manner that is
> different from industrial society's man-machine relation. (Poster, 2001b: 12)

Technology—in particular, electronic communications technology—and
its implications for the subject are the main focus of Poster's work. Since
this is the case, some of Poster's understanding of technology has already
been explored in this chapter. This section therefore is intended to fill
in a few gaps to help us gain a more comprehensive understanding of
his position on technology and to highlight some of the insights and
omissions of this position.

Several points need to be made. First, Poster claims that we should
not be approaching our studies of technology as if technology was
homogenous in form. He asserts that the difference in the way the subject
interacts and is acted on varies according to the technologies
encountered in each particular instance. Poster adopts Foucault's
understanding of self-constitution as influenced by discursive practices.
This means that consideration of both the surveillance and
communicative implications of these technologies are noted.[16] He asserts
that different forms of technology and the languages that are utilized
within these technologies create differing outcomes in the construction
and self-constitution of the subject. They involve different technologies
of power. For example, databases construct multiple identities often
unbeknownst to the referent subject. Television advertisements both
constitute the subject and lead to her/his self-construction as a consumer.
Interactive technologies such as interaction via the Internet constitute
multiple and dispersed identities. As has already been discussed, these
identities, along with those freely chosen by the subject in a society
where social roles are less prescriptive and open to choice, are the basis
for Poster's assertion of a second media age and provide the potential
for postmodern communities.

I prefer, rather than stressing the difference of each technology, to
examine the processes that are involved/implicated in their usage, since
it is rare that simply one process applies to one technology. For example,
as was explained in Chapter Two, the Internet enacts a number of
processes and degrees of interactivity. Surveillance, communication,
information retrieval and creation, and commercial transactions all take
place. These different activities involve different consequences and
different degrees of interactivity, making it difficult to adequately assess
the technology's particular discursive impact. However, it is possible to
suggest the consequences of the generalized and dominant use of certain
processes (as opposed to particular technologies) on inter/subjectivity.

Second, Poster argues that "[t]he body is no longer an effective limit of the subject position" (1990: 15). Technologically mediated interaction means that the subject is extended beyond his/her body to participate in a social space outside of immediate face-to-face or embodied interactions. For Poster, technology in such situations must be understood as more than simply a tool that extends or expands human behavior. Instead, as outlined in Chapter Two, he claims that cyberspace, or the space that is constituted within the Net, must be viewed as a cultural space. He likens the effect of interacting within cyberspace to the experience of being in Germany, whereby being located within such a space confers exposure to and the formation of certain cultural attitudes, behaviors, and understandings on inhabitants (1997: 216). Yet to fit within Poster's other formulations, "somewhere like Germany" can not be seen as referring to an essence, or he would be reproducing the totalizing discourse that he is so critical of—again, some clearer explanation of these ideas is required. The issue of cyberspace, of a new relationship or ontological understanding of time and space, does require further consideration; however, inconsistencies undermine Poster's analysis.

Poster does not just believe that the subject is extended beyond the body (a process that could also be argued as being initiated with print media) but also that the subject is physically changed by such interactions. He draws attention to the increasingly common phenomenon of the cyborg, where technology and the human body are physically intertwined.[17] This use of technology to not only extend the body and its practices outward, but to colonize within, raises important questions about our understanding of what it means to be human, and of our attitude toward our relationship to technology. A turn to technology to solve the problem of perceived constraints of the body or to improve on its biological capacities reflects both our valorization of all things technological (as Ellul feared) and our increasing abstraction from embedded and embodied realities.

Poster argues that a new understanding of the relation between humans and machines is necessary. He believes humanist orientations to be limiting and not able to accommodate the changes taking place within techno-society. Instead, he sees the works of theorists such as Guattari or Haraway as promising (1995: 19–20) and argues that a theoretical focus on the interface—that point where human and machine meet—may provide some understanding of the connection and divide between space and cyberspace. He writes, "Interfaces are the sensitive boundary zone of negotiation between the human and the machinic as well as the pivot of a new set of human/machine relations" (Poster,

1995: 21). His later work develops this notion of machinic assemblages further.

This approach raises some interesting questions for Poster's work and also for my attempts to understand the forms and potential of community. Does Poster, for example, see machines as entities or as part of particular assemblages that need to be taken into account in community formulations? In *What's the Matter with the Internet?* he writes:

> The question concerning technology, then, is no mere exercise about the destruction of nature by the irresponsible deployment of machines or the loss of human reality into machines or even the cultural "misshaping" of the human by its descent into the instrumental, the bringing forth or challenging or enframing of the human by the technological. Instead the conservative, "sensible" question of technology is now one of the nature of the cyborg, of the new order of humachines. And the rigorous or outrageous question of technology must be the possible inheritance of the globe by a species we call "machines" but whose nature we can barely foresee. (Poster, 2001b: 27–28)

While the "rigorous or outrageous" question still belongs to the realm of science fiction, the relationship we have with our machines has become an important consideration. Certainly the ways in which we structure and manage our lives are increasingly mediated through technology and technological processes. Mobile phones, ATM machines, and the Internet, for example, all extend or mediate interactions and practices that once would have taken place in a face-to-face context. While face-to-face interactions are increasingly appropriated to become enacted as abstract or extended forms, these forms still intersect with those practices that are embedded, embodied, and concrete. This intersection of the embodied and disembodied (or concrete and abstract) also requires both recognition and theorizing.[18] And the issue of the cyborg—where increasingly these face-to-face interactions are undertaken by those who incorporate the outcomes of abstract processes within their bodies—raises further areas of deliberation. The cyborg is an example of the way that more abstract or extended forms of the social overlay less abstract forms, affecting the experience and understanding of these less abstract forms. The cyborg—broadly understood— is also an interesting way into thinking about postmodern community: If technologically mediated social practices are the dominant social form, then the subject/individual/self's incorporation of technological practices becomes an increasingly important consideration.

Another area that I would question is Poster's representation and explanation of the reflexive self-constitutive practices enabled and enacted through these new technologies. Poster writes that "[l]inguistic experience in the mode of information is *about self-constitution*, whereas in earlier epochs that process was only implicit" (Poster, 1989: 139, italics in original). He bases much of his argument on the fact that subjects who interact through these technologies are required to consciously create themselves in a chosen form(s). As such, they are called on to be linguistically reflexive about the impression they wish to project.

> In electronic cafés one cannot be authentic or be present in full presence since one's body is not there and one's identity is fabricated by design. Individuals may "feel" more real in cyberspace or more artificial, alienated, disjointed. Yet the machinic solicitation is to reveal to oneself that one is never oneself and that this is legitimate, a condition of the new human-machine interface, the being of technology that has seduced humanity into its own heterogenesis. And what is more, things have only begun to get interesting because the current state of the Internet is clearly a bare beginning of things to come. (Poster, 2001b: 37–38)

I would suggest that the processes that lie behind such self-reflexivity would be better argued as resulting from changes in the ontological categories of time and space, embodiment, and knowledge. These categories intersect with the enactment of abstraction, extension, and rationalization processes, resulting in different ways of perceiving oneself and one's relations with others. While one may be required to be linguistically reflexive when consciously representing oneself through textual means (a process of abstraction), this is simply an accentuation of the self-conscious representation that the post/modern individual is forced to make in all areas of life (both embodied and disembodied) as a consequence of such ontological changes.

Poster is also one-sided, perhaps even empirically wrong, in his assertion that processes such as instrumental rationality are not involved in the utilization of the communication/information technologies. He makes this claim on the basis of what he sees as the changing relationship between humans and technology. He differentiates between mechanical machines that are applied in an instrumentally rational manner, and information machines that enact subject-constitutive processes. He writes,

> Ellul (1964) defines technology (*la technique*) not as machinery but as instrumental-rational practice. "In our technological society," he writes, "*technique* is the *totality of methods rationally arrived at and having absolute efficiency* (for a given stage of development) in *every* field of human activity" (xxv; italics in original). His purpose in *The Technological Society* is to gauge the effects of technology thus understood upon economics, politics and society in general. In each case the effects he discerns are baleful. But can the same complaint be raised against information machines? On this question Ellul is

silent. The issue is particularly grave because information machines upset the position from which the critique of mechanical machines was raised, the view of humans as agents or subjects distinct from and in a stance of opposition to a world of objects. Information machines put into question humanity as instrumental agent and thereby disqualify the critique of technology as "dehumanizing." (Poster, 2001b: 23)

I'm not sure exactly what Poster means by the last sentence. This quotation, with its undertones of technological determinism, asserts a merger of the human with the technological—a merger that removes agency or autonomy from the subject. And that through this removal of a differentiation between human and machine, the human subject can no longer be deemed to be acting instrumentally. Instead, the human is seen as operating from within a particular configuration of technological practices.

The result [of the ways the Internet differs from broadcast and print media] is a more completely postmodern subject or, better, a self that is no longer a subject since it no longer subtends the world as if from the outside but operates within a machine apparatus as a point in a circuit. (Poster, 2001b: 16)

These assertions, when added to the constitutive role he sees as being played by the new media, cloud distinctions and boundaries. It seems that Poster moves between asserting the role that changes in language structures have upon social practices as a consequence of these new technologies, and asserting that the technology itself in some way has agency.[19] Though his position on machine-human interrelations seems to have shifted between his earlier work on language practices and his later work on machinic assemblages or machine apparatus and on technological beings, this is not sufficient to explain a differentiation of mechanical and information machines (as currently formulated). A focus on practices and processes enhanced by technologies, as has taken place in this book, removes this focus on technology itself as agent, a focus that is inherently problematic. The conception, development, and utilization of *all* technology—even communications technologies— involves instrumentally rational processes and outcomes. Indeed, according to the approach taken by this book, it potentially results in *increasingly* instrumentally rational social practices and intersubjective relations.

Processes of abstraction, extension, compression, and mediation are also enacted. These processes and their intersection with changing ontological categories have consequences for human subjectivity. This book is therefore in full accord with Poster (1990) when he asserts,

[b]ut such communications at a distance are *in practice* new structures of discourse. Older models of communicative interactions based on face-to-face or print situations are not simply expanded or multiplied by their electronic mediation. The mediation changes the structure, the conditions that underlie symbolic exchanges. It may be the case that anyone may now talk with anyone else at any time but the words will no longer mean exactly the same things. (45)

What is required is an analytical structure that is able to analyze and discuss the complex interconnection and sometimes contradictory outcomes and implications of such technologies, particularly when they are used to extend, mediate, or replace social forms. Poster's work, in its present form, is unable to fulfill such a requirement.

However, his work is helpful in a number of ways. Unlike the previous two theoretical strands, he focuses considerable attention on the consequences of the social adoption and utilization of technology. For example, he recognizes the importance of considering the subjective changes that result as a consequence of the possibilities of the use of communication technologies—a recognition clearly lacking development within both Taylor's and Nancy's work. While there are some contradictions and confusions evident in his work, his recognition of changing subjectivity as a consequence of changes in communicative processes accords with much of the approach taken within this book.

Poster's failure to consider more than the individual consequences of such processes is, however, problematic (particularly in light of his claims about changes to social forms). The individual cannot be adequately theorized as outside of the social environment within which s/he is embedded. As both Taylor and Nancy have asserted, one is indeed only one among many. Consideration of the relations *between* these many necessarily requires theoretical consideration. Poster appears to believe in the potential or possibilities of a new form of community—indeed also a new form of subject within that community—being enabled through technological communication. Such a community would not be centered around a fixed essence, supposedly,[20] and would consist of people who have more control and freedom over their participation and their self-constitution. Whether such a community is achievable or valid is debatable. Poster gives no real indication of why in fact the concept of community is employed at all. Although he asserts that the technologies under discussion may, and do, work to reproduce modern institutions and practices, he has not suggested or adequately outlined what the potential difference for the postmodern community may be. Nor has he suggested either how the subject may negotiate through these differing communities nor indeed how these differing community forms may intersect with one another. Such a lack of attention to these issues demonstrates a theoretical need for further work in this area.

This chapter, like the two chapters before it, has attempted to draw out the strengths and weaknesses of a key theorist writing in the area of theories of community and subjectivity. All three chapters—Four, Five, and Six—discussed how the various theorists approached the implications of technology for understandings of community. This exploration revealed both valuable insights and notable omissions. While each theorist—Taylor, Nancy, and Poster—has made significant contributions to the analysis of community, I argued that none were able to adequately encompass an appropriate understanding of communities within techno-society. Importantly, all three stressed the role of communication for the operation of and possibilities for community. However, community involves more than interaction or communication alone—none of the theorists adequately dealt with the importance of the structural framing of either communication or other integrative practices.

Other positive and negative attributes were noted. For example, Taylor and Nancy were valuable in their assertions as to the socially essential character of human existence. This character necessitates recognition of such sociality in any study of community. Taylor and Nancy also stressed the importance of mutually constitutive or radical interpersonal relations. The existence of such relations seems to be a necessary prerequisite for a mutually respectful and unrestrictive understanding or experience of community. However, I noted that while such formulations may work as an ideal, more work needs to be undertaken on understanding the possibilities of and for such relations. For example, while Taylor asserted the importance of dialogical relations, he did not pay attention to other influences on these relations, such as the inequities of power structures or the framing of these relations across time and space and the possible consequences of such framing. Nancy removed consideration of working on or the political realization of mutualistic community relations through positing them at the level of the ontological—as always already there. While he also recognized the importance of the intersection of the ontological with the phenomenal (although in a way that is theoretically problematic), this is coordinated in such a way that the social simply removes more or less of this essential mutuality. Nancy did add the important point that community cannot be a project that is self-consciously or collectively constructed. This extends to an understanding that technologically mediated communities, such as virtual communities, are not necessarily of themselves, nor can they be made into, communities.

However, while Poster was valuable in terms of his assertions as to the subjective implications of technologically extended social forms, his work was inadequate in terms of a recognition or analysis of this sociality. Most of his analysis was oriented around implications of the changes in communication structures for the self-constitutive capacities of the individual. Little consideration of the ramifications of these subjective changes for the types of social relations and the forms of community was undertaken. Nor were the ways in which the various levels or types of community interact or coexist explored sufficiently. Yet he went further than the other theorists considered here in terms of his analysis of the different constitutive effects of alterations in time, space, and the body (through the use of technology to mediate social practices). All of the theorists discussed, however, failed to accommodate this book's concerns—of sociality, radical relations, and technologically extended social forms—into a cohesive theoretical position.

Notes

[1] He also points to the need for an ethical emphasis he believes is largely missing from poststructuralist theories. He sees critical theory as enabling such an emphasis to be made.

Elsewhere, he writes that the problem with critical theory is that it is not able to account for the different changes in language structures that are effected through alternative communications technologies. The difficulties I have with the manner in which Poster depicts and understands these theories and with what I perceive as theoretical incompatibilities are numerous. However, despite these theoretical weaknesses, Poster brings some valuable insights to the issues of technological communication, and it is thus well worth undertaking some engagement with his central points. My reservations with Poster's approach do not extend to dismissing a possible (but differently framed) amalgamation of these theories.

[2] The manner in which he outlines this improved critical theory is rather confusing. In some of his writing he argues that the problem of critical theory is that it is premised on a rational, centered subject who is positioned within the binary of autonomous/ heteronomous. He argues that the poststructural emphasis on decentered and multiple representations of the subject is more appropriate and can more easily be used to gain some understanding of the ramifications of the uses of different communications technologies (and also avoids totalizing theoretical approaches).

[3] It must be acknowledged that Poster represents much of his work as suppositions and possibilities, since in his view the second media age is still only in its early stages of development. It is yet to be fully realized as the predominant form orienting social life and the constitution of the individual.

[4] I don't think the public/private boundary, however, has ever been really there in the way posited by some theorists, including Poster. It was certainly being undermined by the welfare state and its use of written records and overt and covert surveillance of its population prior to the introduction of computer systems. This is just one example

of what I see as Poster's tendency to exaggerate or uncritically adopt the characteristics or claims of theorists despite their contradicting his other theoretical presuppositions.

[5] In particular see Poster (1995) for elaboration of this position, although it can be found in varying forms and emphases through much of his work.

[6] There are inconsistencies evident with both Poster's description and his use of the concept. For example, in *Critical Theory and Poststructuralism* (1989), he writes: "[T]he mode of information does not designate a new period of history" (82) yet "[t]he mode of information marks a new epoch" (139). He also writes that "It [the mode of information] is designed to open as wide a field of investigation into the changes in social relations that accompany the introduction of electronically mediated communication" (130) and "all [its parts] are mediated electronically" (139); while in *The Mode of Information* he writes, "By mode of information I similarly suggest that history may be periodized by variations in the structure in this case of symbolic exchange…. Stages in the mode of information may be tentatively designated as follows: face-to-face…." (6). While some development of the theory over time is likely, there is a necessity for more careful attention to detail in order to avoid contradiction or confusion.

[7] "In the first, oral stage the self is constituted as a position of enunciation through its embeddedness in a totality of face-to-face relations. In the second, print stage the self is constructed as an agent centered in rational/imaginary autonomy. In the third, electronic stage the self is decentered, dispersed, and multiplied in continuous instability" (Poster, 1990: 6).

[8] Or is Poster making epochal claims as to different subjects existing in different historical periods, despite his assertions as to being unwilling to ontologize a particular type of subject at any time?

[9] For example, see Scanlon (2000) and Sharp (2000) for their discussions about the need to recognize other more concretely grounded social practices.

[10] "Just as virtual communities are understood as having the attributes of 'real' communities, so 'real' communities can be seen to depend on the imaginary: what makes a community vital to its members is their treatment of the communications as meaningful and important. Virtual and real communities mirror each other in chiasmic juxtaposition" (Poster, 1995: 36).

[11] See Poster (1989: 124–142) for further discussion of this approach.

[12] For example, Poster (1989: 127–129) discusses the distancing achieved through writing, and now through electronically mediated communications, but he does not develop or analyze this phenomenon in detail. He writes: "The close connection between thoughts and speech, which had perhaps always been desired or even socially prescribed, rather than naturally existing, is supplanted by the separation of thought and expression inherent in writing," and "The enormous temporal and spatial distances by which the senders and receivers of written messages may be separated introduce the possibility for structural changes in language and in the ways individuals are constituted by language" (128).

[13] Poster does note that some of the characteristics of modernity can still be found in this media. However, he argues that there is also the potential to move beyond such behavior. This book obviously questions the degree to which such liberatory outcomes can be achieved through technological means.

[14] For example, see Kollock (1999).

[15] "The body then is no longer an effective limit of the subject's position" (Poster, 1990: 15).

[16] Although, there exists something of a disjuncture between Poster's recognition of the surveillance implications of electronic technologies and his depiction of the communicative and subjective implications of interaction through such technologies. Part of this problem is due to the methodology he utilizes and his understanding of the subject.

[17] Technological devices, such as pacemakers or hearing implants, are increasingly being adopted by/within the human body.

[18] See Sharp (1993).

[19] "Information machines in particular resist instrumental enframing, especially those that are embedded within complex congeries of technologies, and they do so particularly in their interface with humans" (Poster, 2001b:37). He backs this comment up with accounts of how technology is appropriated and changed from its original intention. However, this would seem more to fit into accounts of social agency and changing social forms. Because technology is not used strictly in the ways that its developers intend does not mean that they resist instrumental enframing. Feenberg (1995) uses the example of the bicycle (7) and Minitel (9), and I have already referred to the telephone (in the social form section) to demonstrate changes in design and application according to social usage.

[20] I say supposedly, for Poster does not actually outline or even suggest if and how this would be the case. The only hint we are given is that members of this form of community are able to operate freed from the constraints of real-life biological and social identities.

Chapter Seven

~~~

A Question of Theory and Practice

And so there is little else we can do, except to carry our hopes to where the last chance of the moral community, evicted from bankrupt shelters and a fugitive from treacherous ones, has recoiled: to the moral capacity of the self, instead of to the legislating and policing capacities of supra-individual powers; to the wondrous aptitudes of sociation, rather than the coercive resourcefulness of socialization. This could be a descent into hell, we are warned. But it may also be the moral person's voyage of self-discovery. (Bauman, 1996: 58)

One thing at least is clear: if we do not face up to such questions, the political will soon desert us completely, if it has not done so already. It will abandon us to political and technological economies, if it has not already done so. And this will be the end of our communities, if this has not yet come about. (Nancy, 1991b: xli)

In the last chapter, I argued that while Poster studied many of the same phenomenal and ontological concerns that have been the focus of this book, his concentration on the subject obfuscated consideration of the relations between subjects/selves. The challenge that arises now is to move some way toward addressing the relationship of community and technology within a more useful explanatory framework. While this book is not attempting more than the beginnings of such an ambitious enterprise, this chapter hopes to make some suggestions for future efforts in that direction. As such, it recognizes the difficulties of the integrative/differentiating dilemma faced in attempts at community reformulation. My emphasis on radical relations and on Nancy's understanding of the *in*-common points to a possible approach for rethinking our forms and practices of being-together. However, I would also argue that the solution is not to abstract such reformulations to reside either in the realm of abstract theory nor to be sought in entirely technological and disembodied solutions. Such a politics of abstraction could be seen more as a symptom of our current social organization and practices than is currently recognized. Abstract processes require integration into more concrete and embodied practices for them to address such integrative/differentiating dilemmas in an ethically adequate manner.

As the previous chapters have demonstrated, there is a strong social and theoretical impetus to turn to technological developments to provide new social formations that will be better than those currently experienced (even if as lost) in the real world. Kevin Robins notes that

> [t]hese virtual ideologies are perpetuating the age-old ideal of a communications utopia. Immediacy of communication is associated with the achievement of shared consciousness and mutual understanding. The illusion of transparency and consensus sustains the communitarian myth, now imagined at the scale of global electronic *Gemeinschaft*. It is an Edenic myth. (Robins, 1995: 151)[1]

While this book does not wish to advocate abandoning technology as a way of extending social relations and social practices—that would be both unrealistic and idealistic—it does cast doubts on this solution-istic attitude toward the use of technology. It also asserts the theoretical necessity of considering the forms of relations that are evident within and between these mediated spaces.

This concluding chapter therefore attempts to tie the theoretical assertions made in Part One together with the contributions from Part Two. The aim is to turn these various elements into the beginnings of a cohesive theoretical framework for the discussion of the interplay of technology and community.

The Inter/Relation between Social and Ontological Forms

This book started out with the central supposition that using technology to extend and mediate social relations and integrative practices affects the form and experience of community. It argued that how we live together in a technologically dominated society needs to be considered when constructing accounts of community. Community describes ways of being-together. It therefore involves relations between people as well as the framing of these relations within/by integrative social practices.

The increasing societal reliance on the technological extension of social forms impacts on the forms of community enacted and on the types of community relations experienced. In Chapter One, I analytically differentiated between several forms of community, arguing that such differentiation was necessary if we are able to accommodate analysis and discussion of the changing ways in which we relate and the practices that we enact. Forms of community were differentiated according to the dominant structural framing of ontological categories. These analytical distinctions between traditional, modern, and postmodern communities were therefore set up as a way to facilitate discussion of different community forms. However, I also noted that these forms of community intersect and coexist with one another. As the *Arena* position argues, it is necessary to recognize that extended forms of social relations coexist with those that are constituted in more concrete or embodied forms. Failure to recognize this intersection or coexistence limits the possibilities for a comprehensive analysis of contemporary social life.[2]

Central to my position about the relation between technology and community forms is the argument that changing ontological forms—of time and space, knowledge, and embodiment—influence the ways in which we experience ourselves in-relation. Some of the ways in which these experiences of changing forms are brought about are through the processes involved in using communications technologies as a medium for social interaction and integration. I labeled these processes: rationalization, abstraction, and extension. These processes intersect with the ontological categories as persons in the particularities of their various practices enact patterned modes of organization, presence, and understanding. Differing modes of practice have ramifications both for the subjectivity of the individual and for her/his intersubjective relations and social forms.

I argued that as the dominant means and modes of practice become increasingly abstracted from the body, regularly traverse/compress time and space, and theoretically and phenomenally focus on the individual, social and intersubjective relations change in form. The use of communication technologies to extend social forms and integrative practices plays a central role in the increasing dominance of these abstract and extended social forms. The processes that are involved have ramifications for the types, depth, and mutuality of community forms. While technology is employed to extend and enhance relationships and integrative practices across time and space, I also argue that these same technological processes potentially provide the settings for the increased individuation and compartmentalization of the individual. Under conditions of increasingly individuated relations, social forms become thinner or more specialized, leading to increasingly one-dimensional functions and relationships. Such abstraction also increases the likelihood or tendency to treat extended relationships in a more instrumental manner—as something that fulfills a desire of the individual or subject.[3] Obviously, instrumental relationships are evident in all social forms, whether they are conducted within the face-to-face or through technological means. However, I argue that these tendencies increase when social forms are commonly extended; when such extended relations are the dominant mode through which people conduct their lives. This stance is given support by a growing field of empirical research focusing on social forms enacted within virtual communities. For example, in an article on teen chat rooms and teen online dating, Lynn Schofield Clark (1998) argues that individuals who initiate or enact relationships online frequently display individualistic characteristics that are accentuated through the focus on self-gratification—and thus on more instrumental relationships.[4] She writes,

> I think the fact that the "other" in the relationship is hardly considered, or is assumed to share one's level of commitment and self-gratification, is telling. Teens in chat rooms, after all, experience themselves as a gathering of unconnected individuals, seeking others (or usually one other) with whom to converse and thereby achieve gratification. (181–182)

While it could be argued that any dating initiative—whether conducted online or within more concretely embodied social settings—is focused on self-gratification and is individualistic in nature, this approach is more obvious or more likely in abstract or extended relationships.[5] In the example above, the relationships that are initiated or practiced are instrumental in nature. Participants frequently either understand the Other as the same as themselves or they do not consider the Other except as a self-gratification resource.

It may also be possible to argue that as participants become more intimately acquainted with the Other, this relationship may change; moving from a gratification or typified interaction to one that is more intensely personal and mutualistic. However, while these intensely personal mutualistic relationships operate entirely within a self-representational disembodied postmodern community realm, I have argued that such relationships are thinner or more specialized and focused than those that take place within embodied traditional communities. Representations of self are thinned, and lifted out of the complex embodied environments in which they are immersed. In other words (or to use earlier terms) these relationships and their participants are abstracted out of and away from their immediate surroundings. This leads to all of the characteristics asserted in previous chapters: increasingly one-dimensional relations that are practiced instrumentally.

Beth Kolko and Elizabeth Reid (1998) make a similar point. They describe the characters or subjects that participate in virtual communities as being thinner and displaying less complexity or flexibility than that which is displayed by subjects in off-line (traditional or modern) communities. They write:

> [T]hese multiple instances of the self may allow the individual projecting them to experience a greater diversity of himself or herself than would otherwise be the case, but each single instance operates on a very limited psychological and social plane. (218–219)

Consequently,

> the individual virtual persona is at once too committed to the particularity of the self it projects and too uncommitted to the continuity of that self. (220)

Thinner selves are less likely to be able to accommodate or negotiate confronting situations or exposure to difference.[6] They are also less likely to engage in depth with others in any but a compartmentalized fashion.

In previous chapters, I queried the level of commitment demonstrated within and toward postmodern communities and abstract relationships as a consequence of this focus. When any party or member of a community can simply disappear through the click of a mouse or a change of character, I questioned the level of obligation and degree of responsibility experienced by participants toward other members of that community or to the community itself. Clark makes a similar observation:

> Because the focus in the Internet date is on individual gratification, teens experience no sense of obligations to the person with whom they are ephemerally committed; …[for example], if a person fails to show up at the preappointed time, there are no consequences. (Clark, 1998: 181)[7]

I find it interesting that since the time that the writing of this book was first initiated, I have seen a gradual change from the early utopian and celebratory writings about such communities, to less sanguine analysis. Virtual communities and the Internet have been in public existence now for more than twenty years.[8] Early excitement about the possibilities offered by the technology is being tempered more and more by a critical awareness of other issues. Elizabeth Reid is an example of one author who has become increasingly critical of utopian and uncritical representations of virtual communities.[9] In an article coauthored with Beth Kolko, the inflexible and sometimes irresponsible nature of community participation is noted. The article observes that frequently within virtual communities the "virtual persona lacks social responsibility when ties to place are displaced" (222). In addition, it is noted that

> Virtual spaces more often than not are precisely this—locales where participants, those multiple and fluid selves that Turkle (1995) delineates, move through the surface of virtual worlds, unable to burrow into the layers of the community and experience the idea of action and consequences. (223)

These observations support many of the assertions that I have made as to the implications of interaction through extended and abstracted community forms.

I have also discussed both ontological and phenomenal pressures that hold consequences for the contemporary Western individual and the relations that s/he enacts. This means that the ways in which social forms were extended across time and space, thereby enhancing relationship possibilities, were examined. However, it was also noted that the form of such interaction and the subjective influences, such as surveillance and individuation pressures, served to separate or compartmentalize individuals from their perception and experience of their social environs. These seemingly paradoxical outcomes are insufficiently noted by commentators. It was remarked on in Chapter Six, for example, that while Poster celebrated the increase in interconnectivity between individuals as a consequence of the use of communication technologies, he failed to explain the (commented on) simultaneous existence of the isolated contemporary individual. I have suggested that such coexistence can be explained by the processes that I have described.

Questions Concerning Technology

As technology plays a more extensive role in our lives, these issues of individuation, compartmentalization, and the corresponding rationalization of social relations become more pressing. Technological practices are increasing daily. For example, setting up a house with wireless (WAP) technology so that it is permanently online and permanently responsive is now a real possibility. This new online house will monitor its occupants, regulate light and heating, and enable the ordering of services and supplies at the push of a button or a voice command. The practical functions and routines of everyday life are increasingly being mediated through technology. Banking, shopping, and paying bills are all possible now without dealing directly with people. Video technology can be easily incorporated into computer-Internet-mobile phone activities, and audio and visual capacities enhanced to the point that abstract but visually face-to-face interaction will soon be a generally available option. Social practices are increasingly oriented around privileging such individuated, compartmentalized processes. For example, while I live in my flat alone, it is within a group of flats occupied by other people. Yet while the telephone and my computer enable me to keep in contact with friends and family—my social network—and therefore I do not feel alone, this belief ignores consideration of the potentially communal setting within which I live. The fact that most of my neighbors do not know one another, and do not try to know one another, is indicative of the predominance of particular social understandings and practices.

These practices and understandings accentuate the importance of control over choice, and of the individual nature of such control. Exposure to the Other is filtered out except in chosen and controlled circumstances; for example, accidental meetings with my neighbors do not usually result in more than the enactment of social pleasantries or feelings of discomfort. The fact of lived physical proximity increasingly becomes a lifestyle issue. This accentuation on the individual cultivated by the intersection of the processes of abstraction, extension, and rationalization on ontological forms undermines awareness or consideration of the social except as a resource to be accessed by the individual, not as something within which the individual is already necessarily immersed. As such,

> [i]ndividuals are forced into a profound inwardness, and cling for comfort to a belief in their own uniqueness, in the process elaborating a complex inner world of self. Hence the fundamental dialectic of modern society—maximum individualization and maximum 'freedom' is developed only at the price of maximum fragmentation, maximum uncertainty, maximum estrangement of individual from fellow individual. (Rose, 1999: 66)

Technology is often linked ideologically with the achievement of freedom. The rhetoric surrounding the Internet and other communication technologies graphically demonstrates such a conceptual linkage. Yet the notion of freedom that underpins this ideology is one that ignores the importance and richness of social relations and community. This understanding of freedom is one that privileges the individual 'out of context' as if the individual is not immersed and involved in relations of social connectedness and experiences of community. It has been asserted throughout this book that the individual is only an individual among other individuals, and that this being-together cannot be dismissed or ignored. What is needed is for an understanding of freedom to be developed that is able to accommodate the importance of individual agency and self-expression while simultaneously embracing the relations that make such agency exciting and valuable. Taylor's argument for an ethic of authenticity that necessarily operates within a socially recognized framework takes us some of the way. Yet such an ethic requires further work when it is extended into a disembodied realm where embodied and disembodied social settings and social connections merge.

> An important point to remember is … that many of our on-line relationships are embedded in one's off-line. The increased use of technology in the workplace and in school means that CMC [computer-mediated communication] in many ways exists side-by-side with social relationships already formed and that relationships formed only on-line develop differently or just more slowly than others. (Jones, 1998b: 29)

Questions of authenticity also become more of an issue as these mediated functions of daily life are undertaken through technology or even through the use of simulations. Online, you could be interacting with a character presented by an individual or you could be interacting with a 'bot' that has been programmed in specific tasks and social responses. Such possibilities are leading to discussions about the development of, or possibilities for, the posthuman, and to reconceptualizing our understandings of and relationships with technology. While I have queried some of these theoretical approaches, I have also argued for more attention to be directed toward investigating technologically mediated social forms. All of these possibilities raise new questions and dilemmas for our ways of being-together.

The Integrative/Differentiating Dilemma in More Detail

The community theorists addressed in this book all attempt to provide their own solution to the integrative/differentiating dilemma—ways of being-together with difference. They try to understand how this dilemma can be accommodated within contemporary community formulations—a theme that has been recurrent throughout this book.

Taylor argues for an ethic of authenticity that recognizes and encourages individual self-realization (difference) within a socially recognized framework (integrative). Nancy locates the understanding of community at the level of the ontological. He employs the concept of singular beings to emphasize uniqueness and singularity (as always different) while simultaneously stressing the essential sociality and immersed nature (he talked of incomplete sharing) of such beings (integrative). Poster's approach is to stress the multiplicity of identity enabled through the technological and linguistic possibilities of mediated communication (differentiating), while asserting the possibilities for community within cyberspace for such multiple identities (integrative). Poster's failure to adequately address the social (apart from perceiving community as an option that can be accessed online because of the possibilities enabled by technology) is demonstrative of the concerns expressed by this book that technologically mediated social forms encourage the individuation and compartmentalization of the individual and an accompanying instrumental approach to many of such individuals' social relations.

Yet while Nancy and Taylor both recognize the importance of the social (although they situate the debates at different metaphysical levels), they were not helpful in terms of analyzing differing forms of community or the implications of technologically mediated social relations. Further consideration of the processes enacted by the use of technology and the consequences of technologically extended social forms are warranted.

What is of concern therefore is how our relations are practiced and understood within technological society. The actuality of our ontological and social embeddedness with others confers a social, political, and ethical responsibility on our relations with these others. It is this responsibility that lies behind the struggle that faces community theorists in formulating ways of understanding and negotiating the integrative/differentiating dilemma. If our relations with these others are increasingly becoming more abstract, mediated, thinner, and more instrumental than we would wish, how do we begin the processes of understanding and instituting alternate modes of practice and forms of community? Or is this the wrong question? Are we searching instead for an ideal toward which we can constantly seek to work, yet carry the implicit understanding that such modes of being-together will never, and can never, be completely achieved?

I would argue that while an ideal is admirable and indeed necessary for any social direction, there are practical and concrete situations that require more immediate and pressing solutions. The theories of community presented by Nancy and Poster reflect increasingly abstracted social processes with their removal of community from the embodied and concrete (although in distinctly different ways). For example, virtual communities are celebrated by Poster as providing a space and form for a new experience of community. This experience is depicted as multiple, liberating, equalizing, and thus providing a richer experience of togetherness. However, a critical examination of these understandings reveals, paradoxically, a thinning of the complexities of human engagement to the level of one-dimensional transactions, and a potential detachment of the user from the political and social responsibilities of the real space environment. This tendency toward a withdrawal from the active political sphere of real space, or the withdrawal from attempts to realize an embodied form of community, is mirrored in Nancy's work.

In their desire to avoid placing restrictive or totalizing tendencies on the experience or understanding of community, both of these theorists (although emphasizing either a technological and nontechnological orientation) have removed from community the grounding conditions of tangible, or embodied relations, relegating community either to the sphere of ontological, pre-political, pre-historical existence, or to an experiential existence within the nodes of a computer network system. This general movement toward a separation or abstraction of community from the political possibilities of real space has worrying implications. Both approaches, in effect, remove any necessity for direct, embodied, political action. The depth of commitment to others within a community is undermined, raising questions about the possibility of any responsibility for the Other. As Nancy emphasized, a concern or respect for the Other is vital for any valid experience of community. Through the withdrawal of community from an embodied, political, and social arena—either to lodge within a philosophical abstraction or to become a disembodied, technologically enabled interaction—an ethical or political concern for the Other is rendered impotent and unrealizable. Community is then relegated to an ideal rather than a reality, or else abandoned altogether.

Concern for and accommodation of the Other can be seen in the understanding of radical relations that was described in earlier chapters. Radical relations—when incorporating Nancy's understanding of the incomplete sharing, but mutually constituted and constituting, of the *between* of sociality—offer an interesting and potentially useful conceptual approach for reworking understandings of community. This understanding of radical relations encompasses recognition of the simultaneous separation and togetherness of being-together, thus enabling possibilities for both the ongoing negotiation of, and the ongoing resistance to, the form/experience of such relations. While Nancy's stripping back of the subject-in-relation to an ontological *compearance* of singularity (and thus to an abstract philosophical approach) raises questions on a number of levels, further work on this understanding of *in-relation* is merited.

Radical relations, because of their mutually constitutive nature, necessarily incorporate respectful reciprocity between each participant. However, egoistic or instrumental relations do not necessarily of themselves incorporate such acts or understandings. Instead, reciprocal acts within such relations are more likely to be calculated in order to achieve certain outcomes, or treated as self-gratificatory measures. As Cheris Kramarae noted with regard to abstracted or cyber-intimacy:

> These forms of intimacy [cyber-erotica] come without any necessity or even desirability of giving to another. In her fictional but serious warning of the future, Marge Piercy (1991) [*He, she, and it:* p. 382] wrote of the simulations of the 21th [sic] century: "You watch or rent a stimmie and you enter that actor or actress. You feel what they feel. They're yours. But you don't belong to them. You are freed from the demands of reciprocity." (Kramarae, 1998: 116)

The removal of reciprocal demands can be perceived as liberatory for the individual, but again, it also points to an increasingly individuated subject who engages in instrumental acts (and thus objectifies the Other, or to use a Heideggerian notion, turns the Other into "standing reserve").

Such criticisms of extended or mediated relations could attract claims that I am simply displaying nostalgia (of which I have criticized others for displaying) for earlier forms of being-together. It could be argued that earlier or more embodied relations and ways of being together can be similarly instrumental and objectifying of the Other. This latter point is an important qualification. One needs only to turn on the news—or to look through historical accounts—to realize that instrumental and objectifying ways of being-together also abound among less mediated communities. However, this book is not attempting to argue that earlier modes of being-together are *necessarily* more rewarding or more radical. What it is saying is that abstracted and individuated experiences of the self are more prone to demonstrate particular types of instrumental relationships with the Other simply through the processes instituted with the use of technology to mediate social relations. The focus therefore is to be placed on finding ways to realize more radical relations within and between our varying forms of community.

Questions Concerning Practice

In the introduction, I first presented the notion of an ethical and political responsibility toward the Other that needs to be considered within any theoretical endeavor. Stephen White's two ethics—a responsibility to act and a responsibility to Otherness—were raised as a possible way of thinking about these concerns.

It could be comfortably argued that all the community theories discussed in this book are concerned to some degree, either implicitly or explicitly, with the second responsibility—the responsibility to the

Other—although how successful such formulations are has been questioned. The first responsibility, the responsibility to act, has been less central in all of the approaches. Both responsibilities are necessarily required to work together so that totalizing practices are avoided, but also so that acts of inequity or oppression can be addressed. I will first deal with the responsibility to the Other, and then turn to the responsibility to act. This is done as part of an attempt to garner some sense of where we need to go from here.

An awareness of or concern for responsibility to the Other underlies the differentiating part of the integrative/differentiating dilemma. The concern of all contemporary community theorists is to avoid advocating or promulgating theoretical approaches that do not allow room for relations with the Other; that are able to accommodate the Other's difference. Each theorist has therefore suggested his own particular solution.[10]

As discussed above, I have some concern with the ways in which these are approached, and in particular, with the approach proposed by Poster. Understood in isolation, as disconnected from embodied and concrete realms (if this is in fact possible), the solution of virtual communities is inherently problematic. Apart from the tendencies toward instrumentality and a lack of responsibility for one's own actions that are suggested within such social forms, virtual communities accentuate the egoistic understanding of the Other as the Same. The technological format within which such communities reside removes embodied and cultural difference (except in terms of textual content) and homogenizes members through this process.

What is required, if we are to accommodate an awareness of and concern for the Other, is the development of understandings and practices that foster radical relations both within and between communities. Radical relations necessarily require recognition of the Other as worthy of respect, as equally participatory, and therefore as equally contributing to, and being constitutive of, the communicative/ social space. This understanding can be realized within relations between similar forms of community, and across the spectrum of community forms; from the most abstract to the most concrete. Radical relations allow for community without communion, and through such an allowance can accommodate the tensions that are evident within attempts to reconcile the integrative/differentiating dilemma. This tension embraces the enactment and importance of the *in-common* without negating singularity. How these relations can be fostered is a question for continuing discussion. However, recognition of its possibilities is a valuable point from which to begin this conversation.

This book has argued that the recognition of commonality and the practices of exclusion are, of themselves, not problematic. Indeed, it has been suggested here that these may be necessary social practices if community is to be experienced at all. However, what can be problematic is the manner in which such commonalities and exclusions are embraced and enacted. This concern brings us to the second responsibility: the responsibility to act.

The emphasis on a responsibility to act is made by White (1991) in reaction to criticisms directed at the poststructuralist and some postmodern theoretical positions, as to their apolitical or nihilistic tendencies. The debate is by now common knowledge and does not require further development here. However, White and others make an important point. It is one thing to draw attention to acts of oppression, but unless that awareness is expected to *do* anything, to result in any particular action or alteration in practice, then a moral deficit could be argued. Alternately, it could be suggested that action is implicitly expected as a consequence of such theoretical activity and that theorizing is a practice that has specific consequences. Yet recognition of this implicit assumption does not generally appear to take place.

There needs also to be theoretical recognition of the importance of physical bodies and the impact on these bodies as a consequence of our ways of being-together, of the ways in which we understand such being-together. As Nancy (1992) wrote:

> And still: a body dying of hunger; a tortured body; a broken will; an emptied look; a mass war grave; a ridiculous, frustrated, condition; and also the dereliction of the suburbs, the wandering of migrants; and even a confusion of youth or of old age; an insidious deprivation of being, a wasting (*bousillage*); a stupid scrawling: *all this exists*. It exists as a denial of existence. And there is nothing beyond existing (*l'exister*), and the existence to which one denies a sharing is itself a denied existence. This denial wherever it appears, reaches all existence, for it touches the *in* of the in-common. And thus we compear and respond to it, that is, to ourselves. (392)

The impact on physical bodies cannot be removed by simply relocating social forms into an abstract realm. Such a conceptual maneuver is a denial of existence. In practical terms, it is also an impossibility, except at one level; Recognition of these bodies, and of their shared finitude, could allow some room for the fostering of radical relations. The interconnection and relations between the extended and the immediate need to be acknowledged and theorized more adequately.

There is a growing recognition of this fact—that cyberspace and real space are not bounded and impermeable—among cybertheorists. Yet though the acknowledgment increasingly exists, it also frequently gets lost in the excitement fostered by technological possibilities. Poster, for example, recognizes the bringing of modern sensibilities into the virtual realm (and thus recognizes that the cultural and social encoding that is enacted outside the virtual bleeds into the virtual), and he also argues for new possibilities. But the question that must be asked is: How does he theorize or understand this essential physicality—despite the ways in which it is inscribed and understood—of lived existence and the importance therefore of bodies (of selves and of others) within any conceptualizing of community? The answer is far from obvious.

The merger or crossover between the *real* (concrete and embodied) and the *virtual* (whether extended in cyberspace, across geographical space, or indeed through its theoretical abstraction) becomes an important site for considering such relations and their interconnections. Despite the potential dangers, we must incorporate recognition of the impact on bodies of our ways of being-together and attempt practical measures to address such impacts. A growing amount of research is compiling a (sometimes contradictory) picture of the ways in which the virtual and the real are synthesized; and of the ways in which people employ technology to supplement, enhance, and strengthen their embodied social practices.

A Cautionary Tale

> The importance of the disappointment engineered communities have brought cannot be understated. We can no more "build" communities than we can "make" friends; or, at least, as David Harvey (1989) pointed out, "the potential connection between projects to shape space and encourage spatial practices … and political projects … can be at best conserving and at worst downright reactionary in their implications"(p. 277). (Jones, 1998b: 14–15)

While these words from Jones overstate the divide between the community-as-project and the community-as-accident-of-history, the translation of theory into practice—or a move from the abstract to the concrete—is a difficult process to undertake. Many people point to the disastrous application of Marxism, where the outcome was far removed from the egalitarian and emancipatory intentions contained within the theory. The vision did not translate straightforwardly into reality, and in many cases totalizing practices and repression resulted.

A similar concern can be reasonably expressed about the translation of contemporary community theory into political practice. The example of the Communitarian Network (introduced briefly in Chapter Four) provides a cautionary tale that is worthy of brief digression here.

The Communitarian Network is a sociopolitical group. Headed by sociologist Amitai Etzioni, this group accentuates the point made that *communitarian* does not refer to a specific theory, but to an orientation, for its members can be described as having widely differing political backgrounds.[11] They describe themselves as communitarians on the basis of being "people committed to creating a new moral, social, and public order based on restored communities, without allowing puritanism or oppression" (Etzioni, 1993: 2). In other words, they are interested in creating or restoring communities that are able to effectively and practically negotiate the integrative/differentiating dilemma. The Communitarian Network approaches this dilemma by arguing for a synthesis of liberal and communitarian ideals. Of primary concern for these communitarians is what they describe as rampant individualism, with its emphasis on self-advancement and individual rights. According to their writings, society is full of self-interested, self-motivated individuals who only want to take from society; they do not wish to contribute. For example, they point out that people expect to be tried by a jury of their peers but that they are not willing to serve as jurors themselves (Etzioni, 1993: 3). This individual-oriented behavior has detrimental implications for the health and functioning of the community. The picture painted by the Communitarian Network fits in many ways with the understanding Taylor has of contemporary Western society suffering from the three malaises of modernity.

In 1993 Etzioni published an outline of the group's communitarian agenda in his book *The Spirit of Community: Rights, Responsibilities, and the Communitarian Agenda.*[12] He argued that both the individual and the community hold equal moral significance; both should therefore be accorded the same attention and consideration.[13] Yet the ways in which the group has applied this understanding to concrete practical situations belies such equal standing.

The Communitarian Network does not have a detailed program for reform. Instead it functions in an ad hoc manner, with members speaking publicly on issues where they feel they have an interest, and more specifically, in contesting legal cases where they feel the issue of individual rights has exceeded the boundaries of the good of the community.[14] Emphasis is placed on implementing communitarian goals through institutional means: through the family, schooling, and state and community organizations. The practical policy translation of these goals, however, becomes one that is problematic for effectively reconciling the integrative/differentiating dilemma: The approach becomes predominantly one of asserting commonality, and the dominance of one particular version of this commonality. For example,

Etzioni and Galston advocate the following: compulsory national service; schools teaching morality and common values; divorce made more difficult to obtain; and a strong community emphasis on the desirability of two-parent families. The group does not outline how these community values should be decided on, or what happens when values within a community to which one belongs conflict with values of another community to which one may also belong. Etzioni writes that the values of the larger community—American society—should be taught but does not outline what these are. Such statements provoke the criticisms of class and race bias, with one commentator wondering "if the communitarians aren't really complaining about the declining power of the white middle and upper classes" (D'Antonio, 1992: 32).

Looking from outside the movement, it seems as if such comments are accurate. The proposals initiated by this group appear largely conservative, and morally authoritarian. The recognition and consideration of the Other is assimilated into a more homogeneous understanding of community where all must follow/fit into certain normative understandings contained within a larger community. Similar criticisms are also being directed toward advocates of the so-called 'third way.'[15] As this brief excursion into examining one particular attempt at translating theory into practice demonstrates, the translation is neither unproblematic nor straightforward. However, it is not sufficient to argue that because of such problems, any translation is not possible nor desirable. What is required is an awareness of and willingness to continually examine, contest, and negotiate any formulations or practices.

Where to From Here?

While I am certainly not going to propose a definitive solution to these dilemmas—that is left as a task for later ongoing studies—some exploratory ideas are worth raising for further discussion. Obviously, the development of ways for integrating theory with practice are an ethical and political requirement for the health and viability of our current and future communities. Keeping in mind Nancy's warning that community cannot be a project, and that it cannot be made, is an important prerequisite for any such proposal. But it is also important to note Nancy's statement that community—a concept and practice of community/ies—is a task that cannot be abandoned.

A possible beginning can be found in reformulations of community theory. However, as this book has consistently argued, it must be a reformulation that is able to accommodate and work with recognition of the implications of using communication technologies. The processes of abstraction, rationalization, and the extension and compression of time and space that are instituted through the ways in which techno-society uses these technologies potentially lead to the increased individuation and compartmentalization of the individual from her/his immediate social surroundings, and also to changes in the nature and form of many relationships. Changes in the form and experience of various integrative practices are also relevant. Yet, as has been argued, focus cannot be located entirely within the realm of disembodied (or postmodern) communities. Any analysis must also be able to accommodate recognition of the coexistence and intersection of the varying and multiple forms of community that exist. And it is not viable or even desirable to advocate the complete abandonment of such technologies and processes in favor of pre-technological social forms.

One approach would be to use the *Arena* argument as a way to understand the layered social forms and the increasing abstraction of social life. As has been explained, the *Arena* thesis argues that any social analysis necessarily needs to recognize and consider the coexistence and intersection of varying 'levels' of social forms. Such an approach partly underlies the impetus for my analytical recognition and differentiation among traditional, modern, and postmodern forms of community. This differentiation provides both a means of and a language for the discussion of these community forms as constituted within/through different constitutive modes of practice.

There are a number of dimensions to the *Arena* argument. One dimension asserts that while these varying social forms intersect with one another, they are also influenced by the dominant constitutive mode of social practice that is being enacted within any one particular historical period. This would suggest that the current historical period's focus on increasingly abstracted and mediated social relations and integrative practices has wider ramifications for less abstract forms of community. To incorporate my arguments, then, this would be to claim that these less abstracted forms are influenced by the increasing individuation and the enhanced tendencies toward instrumental relations evident within these abstracted, interconnected forms.

Another dimension of the *Arena* thesis states that these varying levels of social form are brought about in part by the increasing application and appropriation of social practices by the use of technology. While I have argued that I do not concur (with the *Arena* assertion) that there is necessarily a loss of cultural meaning as a consequence of the technological extension and appropriation of social forms,[16] I do understand that the use of technology to extend and enact social practices deserves more serious consideration than granted by many community theorists. I agree with the depiction of an expanding societal abstraction of social forms and integrative practices that can be explained (in part) by the growing utilization of technological means to extend and mediate social relations across time and space.

However, I also argue for the importance of recognizing and understanding changes in ontological forms and the consequences of the intersection of these various experiences within the social. We need to look for an understanding of the overlay and interplay of varying forms of community that allows for the intersection of the phenomenal and the ontological. This understanding would be one that recognizes commonality without enforcing a common essence, and that incorporates an ethics open to the ongoing negotiation toward radical relations with the Other. While this book is not able to suggest a solution or formula for this understanding, it has opened up a number of previously unconsidered areas for analysis that may help move us closer in this direction.

Conclusion

> I operate as a man-machine interface—i.e. as a technological form of natural life—because I must necessarily navigate through technological forms of social life. As technological nature, I must navigate through technological culture. And technological culture is constitutively culture *at a distance*. Forms of life become forms of life-at-a-distance. Because my forms of social life are so normally and chronically at-a-distance, I cannot navigate these distances, I cannot achieve sociality apart from my machine interface. I cannot achieve sociality in the absence of technological systems, apart from my interface with communication and transportation machines. (Lash, 2001: 107–108)

Like many technology commentators, Scott Lash overemphasizes the impact of technology on social relations. His grand overarching pronouncements about the contemporary world overlook the fact of a technologically lived coexistence with earlier or less abstract social forms or indeed with varying but simultaneous forms of community. Instead, technology itself is credited with bringing about dramatic and all-encompassing transformations in culture, social relations, and ways of being-together. While this seemingly technologically determinist approach fails to adequately acknowledge the intertwining of the social with the technological or to separate processes from outcomes, the importance of technology for the realization of particular forms of social relations also cannot be denied. For while it is not true that contemporary sociality cannot be achieved without the use of technological systems, it is true that such technological mediation is becoming increasingly central to the ways in which we live together. This technological mediation has implications for our ontological experiences and understandings of time, space, knowledge, and the body. It in turn leads to changing subjectivities and changing experiences and understandings of being-together. These changing experiences and understandings need to be able to be acknowledged and accommodated within contemporary theories of community.

I began exploring some of these implications in this book. Early on, I proposed the analytical recognition of differing forms of community as one way in which the discussion of changing social forms could be accommodated. Indeed I suggested that this recognition was the only way that a nostalgic *Gemeinschaft/Gesellschaft* division could be avoided. Community describes ways of being-together. It is not a static social form—it changes over time according to the ways in which it is understood and experienced across space and time, and through bodies. To argue otherwise runs the risk of privileging a particularly romantic, static, and outdated understanding that is inadequate for addressing social forms in contemporary life. A more productive approach is to engage with differing forms of community according to the manner in which they are structured through and across the various ontological categories of time and space, embodiment, and knowledge. Such recognition enables the discussion of varying ways of being-together that may exist in-simultaneity. It also provides the conceptual tools to begin addressing the paradoxes of being-together through technological extension and mediation.

People are not givens inasmuch as they are not ahistorical entities: They change and practice life according to their experiences, social relations, and the understandings through which they filter such experiences. Such an understanding of intersubjectivity still seems to me to be so obvious as to be commonsensical (although this could well be because of the current filters and frameworks through which I understand and act in the world). Changes in the ways in which life is organized and practiced across differing conceptions of time and space, for example, denote different understandings of the world and the ways in which such a world is to be negotiated. We no longer believe that the world is flat—our ability to travel across space and into space has reinforced earlier scientific propositions that once seemed ludicrous and indeed blasphemous. Likewise we now think of and practice our relations with Others, and experience our sense of belonging to communities, differently from when technologically enabled time-compression was not possible.

In this book, I have not attempted to prescribe a particular or alternative understanding of community. Such a task—to use Nancy's term—is one that would require much more time, attention, and dialogue than has been possible here. It also would be an ongoing task inasmuch as it is one that I understand as being necessarily and continually negotiated, contested, and evolving.

Instead, the aim has simply been to highlight some of the contradictions, omissions, and questions that become evident when bringing together the seemingly disparate but practically entwined and lived concepts of technology and community. The book has highlighted some of the positive contributions brought by theorists of varying orientations to understandings of community, as well as noting areas that require more sustained consideration. For example, through the course of writing the second part of the book, it became very obvious that the recognition and analysis of the social individual—if I can use such a term—was an important consideration that is often overlooked. To try to understand and formulate enriching ways of being-together without taking into account such recognition cannot achieve anything more than linking a series of individuals together. As cited earlier, Morris (1996) commented, "[o]ne plus one plus one plus one plus one just never seem to add up to more than a number!" (226). There are very obviously connections or bonds between individuals that cannot be accounted for simply by aggregation. Understanding the importance of integrative practices and structural considerations advances our understanding to some extent. Yet further consideration of the intersection of the structural and subjective influences or factors that make communities remains as a necessary pursuit. When the integrative and interactive practices of community are stretched across time and space, they change in terms of their degree of abstraction and of depth. This is one of the reasons why consideration of the technologically social remains an imperative.

Moreover, it is apparent that negotiation of togetherness with difference is a continuing and central focus of contemporary considerations of community. However, as noted, it is also increasingly apparent that attempts to address such concerns often lead theorists to move to an abstract realm that is disconnected from considering the very real and concrete implications for such relations upon the bodies of others. I have tried to negotiate this integrative/differentiating dilemma through introducing the notion of radical relations—relations that, as Nancy explained, are incompletely shared. Such relations cannot ignore the Other, nor can they obliterate the Other. Such relations, I have argued, are not fostered by the ways in which we currently utilize technology in Western techno-society.

The use of technology to enable our being-together to take place across increasingly vast temporal and spatial expanses is achieved through the instigation and operation of certain processes. These processes are particularly interesting. The processes of abstraction, extension/compression, and rationalization, as the book has made clear, are not unique processes linked inextricably to the use of technology—they are enacted throughout all areas of contemporary Western life. However, I argued that technology epitomizes and accentuates such processes—being both an outcome of and an instrument for their enactment.

Technology in and of itself does not predetermine social direction or the predominance of particular social forms. However, the manner in which technology is utilized, the purposes to which it is applied, and the processes that are enacted through such utilization do have consequences for our social relations. This book has attempted to unpack some of these consequences to discern aspects and areas that arise out of the intersection of the technological and the social (while still recognizing that the technological is inherently social) that warrant further academic analysis. While I have tried to focus in particular on examining technological processes, I have not completely ignored the fact that the possibilities that technology offers for extended social practice have enabled many activities that would not have been as easily or as broadly possible as those currently experienced in contemporary society. I argued that while interconnective ability is heightened by these technological possibilities, it is also important to recognize that the processes through which extended social relations are enacted also heighten the compartmentalization of and focus on the individual. Such an individual is not understood as and increasingly does not experience her/himself as embedded within an ontologically important sociality. To diminish the importance of the social seems to me to also diminish the importance of the Other—except perhaps in the sense of being a useful resource.

I have suggested as a consequence that the current dominant modes of understanding, of organization, and of presence favor an instrumental approach to the Other. The increasing absorption or appropriation of social activity into the technological realm is therefore not unproblematic. The manner in which such absorption is managed is not inevitable or predetermined. With knowledge and reflection about the implications of such processes, we have the capacity to direct, manage, and alter the ways in which technologically mediated social relations are experienced and the priority that they are accorded in our lives.

This book has been many more years in the making than originally planned. The delay in completion has meant that the fields of research across which the book straddles have advanced considerably. In particular, academic works on cyberculture, on the various social configurations enabled or enacted through technologically mediated communications, and on the impact of new technologies have increased exponentially. Some of these works have (rewardingly) validated many of my suppositions through empirical and ethnographic studies. When I first began writing, most of the material available detailed utopian claims as being realized or yet potentially realizable within virtual communities and technologically mediated social relations.[17] This material has now been enriched considerably by a wide diversity of views and of research around the issue and practice of technologically mediated social forms. However, I have not yet seen anything that addresses in the same way the concerns raised in this book as to the necessity of considering the implications of technology when formulating new understandings of community. Most of the work on technology and community still carries an inherent 'boundedness' through its isolation within technological confines, despite an increasing academic awareness of the importance of conceptualizing cross-boundary practices.

The only possible exception to this claim might be pointed toward the growing body of work on the network society. This literature is interested in exploring the social practices that are enacted across technological/nontechnological boundaries. While there is certainly important work taking place in this area, again, I have yet to see any larger work (i.e., larger than chapters or articles) that explores many of the questions and suppositions presented in this book.

Despite my assertions as to the importance of practical and concrete action in the renegotiation of community and of our relations with the Other, I am acutely aware that this book has primarily been situated within the realm of the abstract. While this has been partly explainable by my own time and space constraints, I would also argue that to stress the importance of merging theory and practice or of merging the concrete and the disembodied is more than that asserted by the community theorists examined herein. It is acknowledged that it is the nature of intellectual activity to abstract from the concrete and the particular. However, it is vital that any discussion of community recognizes that ultimately it is the concrete realization and practice of our relations with Others that form the motivating impetus for such examinations. And it is an ethical imperative that such recognition is re-embedded within the concrete and political of the everyday. One of the tasks that lies ahead is therefore to begin discussions as to how such re-embedding can be brought about.

Notes

[1] He goes on to argue that "[t]echno-community is fundamentally an anti-political ideal" (Robins, 1995: 151). As the rest of this chapter will make apparent, this is an argument with which I largely agree.

[2] The *Arena* argument asserts that the failure to recognize the coexistence of various levels of social practice or the coexistence of various forms of extended relationships with those of a basic sociality leads to an inadequate one-dimensional analysis. Such one-dimensional analysis is therefore unable to accommodate consideration or discussion of the various complexities arising from the intersection of contradictory elements.

[3] While the participants in extended relationships may not be seeking to explicitly control the other, they may be approaching the relationship in a more utilitarian or instrumental manner—as something that is accessed in the most efficient and self-gratificatory manner possible for that individual.

[4] "The participants in the relations experience a satisfaction in relationships that have no reference to their peer group or social status and may be considered more individualistic as a result. Moreover, it is not a complete lack of commitment but a tenuous and ephemeral commitment that links participants" (Clark, 1998: 180).

[5] For example, Clark refers to Giddens's understanding of a "pure relationship" where "Persons are no longer constrained in their selection of romantic partners by the social mores of their families or communities. Instead, relationships are sought out and maintained solely for the gratifications they provide to the persons involved. Therefore, these relationships of modernity, Giddens argued, are always organized in relation to the reflexive self who asks, 'how is this relationship fulfilling to *me*?'" (Clark, 1998: 176). The question therefore is whether such relationships are more consistently individualistic and instrumental in online settings, or when mediated social forms are the dominant mode of practice?

[6] "Interpersonal problems require flexibility for resolution. Compromise, change, empathy and negotiability are qualities vital to the continuance of relationships…. Virtual presence often can preclude change or only allow it at the expense of continuity" (Kolko & Reid, 1998: 219).

[7] While the assertion as to "no consequences" is an exaggeration inasmuch as the continuity of the relationship is placed into jeopardy, or the neglected party may well feel rejected or disappointed, the depth or complexity of such relationships is indeed drawn into question. Clark does add the qualification that in this arena, a lack of seriousness is assumed to be one of the rules of participation (181).

[8] The introduction of the World Wide Web as a user-friendly interface facilitated this rapid adoption.

[9] Earlier work was less critical and more utopian about the possibilities enabled by technology. For example, see Reid (1991).

[10] I use the term solution here advisedly, since Nancy and Taylor, for example, may well argue that their understandings simply represent certain givens that are inadequately understood or represented in other theoretical understandings or other practices. As such, they are not advocating solutions. Solution also seems to contain a finality that I think Nancy would be likely to reject.

[11] For example, within the political parties themselves, two Democrats: Al Gore and Daniel Patrick Moynihan; and two Republicans: Dave Durenberger and Alan Simpson. And on the editorial board there is Nathan Glazer, who is described as a right neoconservative with Martha Nussbaum a left-liberal (Magner, 1991: A3).

[12] This book caught the attention of the media as being only one of two books lying on former President Clinton's desk.

[13] He asserts that liberals and communitarians give primary importance to their one particular orientation. In many ways he misinterprets the theoretical approaches of those communitarians previously described. For the communitarians are not collectivists and do recognize the significance of individual agency. However, there is the recognition that this agency is affected by the mores and interests of others and by the situation in which the individual is embedded.

[14] I have been using the term community singularly here; however, the communitarians actually see there being many communities within the greater community of the United States. The issue of the negotiation of differing values between and across these communities is, however, not addressed.

[15] See Scanlon (2000) for discussion of these issues.

[16] See my argument as to why in Chapter Two.

[17] Of course there were also valuable and now classic texts such as Allucquere Roseanne Stone's work that carried more complex and nuanced analyses. These early texts are noteworthy both for their awareness of the issues raised by the intersection of the technological and the social and for this awareness at early stages of the public adoption of these technological forms.

Bibliography

Abbey, Ruth. (1996/97). Communitarianism? Community without society. *Arena Magazine*, no. 26 (Dec/Jan.), 38–39.

Abbey, Ruth, & Taylor, Charles. (1996). Communitarianism, Taylor-made: An interview with Charles Taylor. *Australian Quarterly*, vol. 68, no. 1, 1–10.

Adams, David. (2000). SMS speaks to deaf needs. *The Age*, 1 August, p. 3.

Agamben, Georgio. (1993). *The coming community* (M. Hardt, Trans.). Minneapolis: University of Minnesota Press.

Anderson, Benedict. (1991). *Imagined communities: Reflections on the origin and spread of nationalism* (Rev. ed.). London: Verso.

Balsamo, Anne. (1996). *Technologies of the gendered body: Reading cyborg women*. Durham, NC: Duke University Press.

Barnes, Susan. (2003). *Computer-mediated communication: Human-to-human communication across the Internet*. Boston: Allyn and Bacon.

Barney, Darin. (2000). *Prometheus wired: The hope for democracy in the age of networked technology*. Sydney: UNSW Press.

Barrett, William. (1978). *The illusion of technique: A search for meaning in a technological civilization*. New York: Anchor Press/Doubleday.

Bauman, Zygmunt. (1996). Morality in the age of contingency. In P. Heelas, S. Lash, & P. Morris (Eds.), *Detraditionalization: Critical reflections on authority and identity* (pp. 49–58). Cambridge, UK: Blackwell Publishers.

_____. (1997). *Postmodernity and its discontents*. Cambridge, UK: Polity Press.

_____. (2001). *The individualized society*. Cambridge, UK: Polity Press.

Beck, Ulrich, & Beck-Gernsheim, Elisabeth. (1996). Individualization and "precious freedoms": Perspectives and controversies of a subject-orientated sociology. In P. Heelas, S. Lash, & P. Morris (Eds.),

Detraditionalization: Critical reflections on authority and identity (pp. 23–48). Cambridge, UK: Blackwell Publishers.

Bell, Colin, & Newby, H. (1979). *Community studies: An introduction to the sociology of the local community.* New York: Praeger.

Bell, Daniel. (2001). Communitarianism. *The Stanford Encyclopedia of Philosophy (Winter Edition),* Edward N. Zalta (ed.). http:// plato.stanford.edu/archives/win2001/entries/communitarianism/ (accessed 10/22/04).

Bell, David, & Kennedy, Barbara M. (Eds.). (2000). *The cybercultures reader.* London: Routledge.

Bellah, R. N., Madison, R., Sullivan, W. M., Swidler, A., & Tipton, S. M. (1991). *The good society.* New York: Alfred A. Knopf.

Benedikt, Michael. (Ed.). (1992). *Cyberspace: First steps.* Cambridge: MIT Press.

Benhabib, Seyla, & Dallmayr, Fred. (Eds.). (1990). *The communicative ethics controversy.* Cambridge: MIT Press.

Bernasconi, Richard. (1993). On deconstructing nostalgia for community within the west: The debate between Nancy and Blanchot. *Research in Phenomenology,* vol. 23, 3–21.

Bernstein, Richard J. (1991). *The new constellation: The ethical-political horizons of modernity/postmodernity.* Cambridge, UK: Polity Press.

Bhabagrahi, Misra, & Preston, James. (Eds.). (1978). *Community, self and identity.* The Hague: Mouton Publications.

Blanchot, Maurice. (1988). *The unavowable community* (Pierre Joris, Trans.). New York: Station Hill Press.

_____. (1993). *The infinite conversation* (Susan Hanson, Trans.). Minneapolis: University of Minnesota Press.

Boden, Deirdre, & Molotch, Harvey L. (1994). The compulsion of proximity. In Roger Friedland and Deirdre Boden (Eds.), *NowHere: Space, time and modernity* (pp. 257–286). Berkeley: University of California Press.

Bogard, William. (1996). *The simulation of surveillance: Hypercontrol in telematic societies.* Cambridge, NY: Cambridge University Press.

Borgmann, Albert. (1984). *Technology and the character of contemporary life.* Chicago: University of Chicago Press.

Bourdieu, Pierre. (1977). *Outline of a theory of practice* (Richard Nice, Trans.). Cambridge, NY: Cambridge University Press.

Bourdieu, Pierre, & Coleman, James C. (Eds.). (1991). *Social theory for a changing society.* Boulder, CO: Westview Press.

Bowers, John, Pycock, James, & O'Brien, Jon. Talk and embodiment in collaborative virtual environments. CHI 96 Electronic

Proceedings [online] www.acm.org/sigchi/chi96/proceedings/papers/Bowers/jb_txt.htm (accessed 11/10/00).

Buber, Martin. (1958). *Paths in utopia* (R. F. C. Hull, Trans.). Boston: Beacon Press.

Buttimer, Anne, & Seamon, David. (Eds.). (1980). *The human experience of space and place*. London: Croom Helm.

Cahnman, Werner J. (Ed.). (1973). *Ferdinand Tönnies: A new evaluation, essays and documents*. Leiden, The Netherlands: E. J. Brill.

Calhoun, Craig. (1986). Computer technology, large-scale social integration, and the local community. *Urban Affairs Quarterly*, vol. 22, no. 2, 329–349.

_____. (1991). Indirect relationships and imagined communities: Large-scale social integration and the transformation of everyday life. In Pierre Bourdieu & James S. Coleman (Eds.), *Social theory for a changing society* (pp. 95–130). Comments by Gudmund Hernes and Edward Shils. Boulder, CO: Westview Press.

_____. (1998). Community without propinquity revisited: Communications technology and the transformation of the urban public sphere. *Sociological Inquiry*, vol. 68, no. 3, 373–397.

Cascardi, Anthony J. (1992). *The subject of modernity*. Cambridge: Cambridge University Press.

Castells, Manuel. (2001). *The Internet galaxy: Reflections on the Internet, business, and society*. Oxford, UK: Oxford University Press.

Clark, Lynn Schofield. (1998). Dating on the net: Teens and the rise of "pure" relationships. In Steven G. Jones (Ed.), *Cybersociety 2.0: Revisiting computer-mediated communication and community* (pp. 159–183). Thousand Oaks, CA: Sage Publications.

Cohen, Anthony P. (1985). *The symbolic construction of community*. London: Ellis Horwood Ltd. and Tavistock Publications.

Conley, Verena Andermatt. (Ed.) on behalf of the Miami Theory Collective (1993). *Rethinking technologies*. Minneapolis: University of Minnesota Press.

Connery, Brian A. (1997). IMHO: Authority and egalitarian rhetoric in the virtual coffeehouse. In David Porter (Ed.), *Internet culture* (pp. 161–180). New York: Routledge.

Connolly, William E. (1991). *Identity/difference: Democratic negotiations of political paradox*. Ithaca, NY: Cornell University Press.

Corlett, William. (1989). *Community without unity: A politics of Derridian extravagance*. Durham, NC: Duke University Press.

Crary, Jonathon, & Kwinter, Sanford. (Eds.). (1992). *Incorporations: Zone 6*. New York: Urzone.

Crossley, Nick. (1994). *The politics of subjectivity: Between Foucault and Merleau-Ponty.* Avebury: Ashgate.

—————. (1996). *Intersubjectivity: The fabric of social becoming.* London: Sage Publications.

D'Antonio, Michael. (1992). Tough medicine for a sick America. *Los Angeles Times,* 22 March, p. 32.

Dallmayr, Fred (Ed.). (1978). *From contract to community: Political theory at a crossroads.* New York: Marcel Dekker.

Dean, Mitchell. (1995). For a political ontology of ourselves. *Political Expressions,* vol. 1, no. 1, 17–30.

Derrida, Jacques. (1992). *Given time: I. Counterfeit money* (Peggy Kamuf, trans.). Chicago: University of Chicago Press.

—————. (1995). *The gift of death.* (David Willis, Trans.). Chicago: University of Chicago Press.

Dery, Mark. (1996). *Escape velocity: Cyberculture at the end of the century.* Chatham: Hodder & Stoughton.

Dibbell, Julian. (1998). A rape in cyberspace, or how an evil clown, a Haitian trickster spirit, two wizards, and a cast of dozens turned a database into a society. In Richard Holeton (Ed.), *Composing cyberspace: Identity, community, and knowledge in the electronic age* (pp. 83–98). Boston: McGraw-Hill.

DiMaggio, Paul, Hargitti, Eszter, Neuman, W. Russell, & Robinson, John P. (2001). Social implications of the Internet. *Annual Review of Sociology,* 27, 307–36.

Dreyfus, Hubert L. (1996). The current relevance of Merleau-Ponty's phenomenology of embodiment. *The Electronic Journal of Analytic Philosophy,* no. 4 [online] www.phil.indiana.edu/ejap/1996.spring/dreyfus.1996.spring.html (accessed 7/14/00).

Dreyfus, Hubert L., & Rabinow, Paul. (1982). *Michel Foucault: Beyond structuralism and hermeneutics.* Afterword by Michel Foucault. Chicago: University of Chicago Press.

Ellul, Jacques. (1964). *The technological society* (John Wilkinson, Trans.). New York: Vintage Books.

Etzioni, Amitai. (1990). Liberals and communitarians. *Partisan Review,* vol. 57, no. 2, 215–227.

—————. (1993). *The spirit of community: Rights, responsibilities, and the communitarian agenda.* New York: Crown Publishers.

—————. (Ed.). (1995). *New communitarian thinking: Persons, virtues, institutions, and communities.* Charlottesville: University Press of Virginia.

_____. The community of communities: A communitarian position paper. *The Communitarian Network* [online] www.hfnl.gsehd.gwu.edu/~ccps/ Comofcom.html (accessed 1/15/00).

Featherstone, Mike. (2000). Post-bodies, aging and virtual reality. In David Bell & Barbara M. Kennedy (Eds.), *The cybercultures reader* (pp. 609–618). London: Routledge.

Featherstone, Mike, & Burrows, Roger (Eds.). (1995). *Cyberspace/ cyberbodies/cyberpunk: Cultures of technological embodiment.* London: Sage Publications.

Feenberg, Andrew. (1995). Subversive rationalization: Technology, power, and democracy. In Andrew Feenberg & Alastair Hannay (Eds.), *Technology and the politics of knowledge* (pp. 3–22). Bloomington: Indiana University Press.

Feenberg, Andrew, & Hannay, Alastair (Eds.). (1995). *Technology and the politics of knowledge.* Bloomington: Indiana University Press.

Fernback, Jan, & Thompson, Brad. Virtual communities: Abort, retry, failure? [online] www.well.com/user/hlr/texts/VCcivil.html (accessed 12/02/00).

Fischer, Claude S. (1992). *America calling: A social history of the telephone to 1940.* Berkeley: University of California Press.

Fischer, Francis. (1997). The place of a thinking. In Darren Sheppard, Simon Sparks, & Colin Thomas (Eds.), *On Jean-Luc Nancy: The sense of philosophy* (pp. 32–37). London: Routledge.

Flax, Jane. (1993). Multiples: On the contemporary politics of subjectivity. *Human Studies*, no. 16, 33–49.

Foucault, Michel. (1977). *Discipline and punish: The birth of the prison* (A. Sheridan, Trans.). London: Allen Lane Penguin Books.

_____. (1988). The ethics of care for the self as a practice of freedom. In James Bernauer & David Rasmussen (Eds.), *The final Foucault* (pp. 1–20). Cambridge, MA: MIT Press.

Frazer, Elizabeth, & Lacey, Nicola. (1993). *The politics of community: A feminist critique of the liberal-communitarian debate.* Hempstead: Harvester Wheatsheaf.

Friedland, Roger, & Boden, Deirdre. (1994a). NowHere: An introduction to space, time and modernity. In Roger Friedland & Deirdre Boden (Eds.), *NowHere: Space, time and modernity* (pp. 1–60). Berkeley: University of California Press.

Friedland, Roger, & Boden, Deirdre (Eds.). (1994b). *NowHere: Space, time and modernity.* Berkeley: University of California Press.

Fynsk, Christopher. (1991). Foreword: Experiences of Finitude. In Jean-Luc Nancy, *The inoperative community* (pp. vii–xxxv). Minneapolis: University of Minnesota Press.

Gallaher Jr., Art, & Padfield, Harland. (Eds.). (1980). *The dying community*. Albuquerque: University of New Mexico Press.

Gibson, William. (1984). *Neuromancer*. New York: Ace.

Giddens, Anthony. (1984). *The constitution of society: Outline of the theory of structuration*. Cambridge, UK: Polity Press.

_____. (1987a). *Social theory and modern sociology*. Cambridge, UK: Polity Press.

_____. (1987b). *The nation-state and violence: Volume two of a contemporary critique of historical materialism*. Berkeley: University of California Press.

_____. (1991). *Modernity and self identity: Self and society in the late modern age*. Stanford, CA: Stanford University Press.

_____. (1994a). *Beyond left and right: The future of radical politics*. Cambridge, UK: Polity Press.

_____. (1994b). Foreword. In Roger Friedland & Deirdre Boden (Eds.), *NowHere: Space, time and modernity* (pp xi–xiii). Berkeley: University of California Press.

Gill, Gerry. (1984). Post-structuralism as ideology. *Arena* 69, 60–96.

Gilligan, Carol. (1982). *In a different voice: psychological theory and women's development*. Cambridge, Mass.: Harvard University Press.

Glendon, Mary Ann. (1991). *Rights talk: The impoverishment of political discourse*. New York: The Free Press.

Goldberg, David Theo. (Ed.). (1990). *Anatomy of racism*. Minneapolis: University of Minnesota Press.

Goody, Jack. (1986). *The logic of writing and the organization of society*. Cambridge, UK: Cambridge University Press.

Guignon, Charles B. (Ed.). (1993). *The Cambridge companion to Heidegger*. Cambridge, UK: Cambridge University Press.

Habermas, Jürgen. (1979). *Communication and the evolution of society* (T. McCarthy, Trans.). Boston: Beacon Press.

_____. (1981). *The theory of communicative action, volume 1: Reason and the rationality of society* (T. McCarthy, Trans.). Boston: Beacon Press.

Haraway, Donna. (1991). A cyborg manifesto: Science, technology, and socialist-feminism in the late twentieth century. In *Simians, Cyborgs, and Women: The Reinvention of Nature* (pp. 149–181). New York: Routledge.

Hård, Mikael, & Jamison, Andrew. (Eds.). (1998). *The intellectual appropriation of technology: Discourses on modernity*. Cambridge, MA: MIT Press.

Harvey, David. (1990). *The condition of postmodernity: An enquiry into the origins of cultural change*. Oxford, UK: Blackwell Publishers.

Hayles, N. Katherine. (1993). The seduction of cyberspace. In Verena Andermatt Conley (Ed.), *Rethinking technologies* (pp. 173–190). Minneapolis: University of Minnesota Press.

Heelas, P., Lash, S., & Morris, P. (Eds.). (1996). *Detraditionalization: Critical reflections on authority and identity.* Cambridge, UK: Blackwell Publishers.

Heidegger, Martin. (1977). *The question concerning technology and other essays* (William Lovitt. Trans.). New York: Garland Publishing.

Heim, Michael. (1994). Heidegger and computers. In Timothy Stapleton (Ed.), *The question of hermeneutics: Essays in honor of Joseph J. Kockelmans* (pp. 397–426). Dordrecht, Netherlands: Kluwer Academic Publications.

Hekman, Susan. (1991). Reconstituting the subject: Feminism, modernism and postmodernism. *Hypatia,* vol. 6, no. 2, 44–63.

Heroux, Erick. Interview with Mark Poster: Community, new media, post-humanism [online] www.uoregon.edu/~ucurrent/2-Poster.html (accessed 6/8/00).

Herring, Susan C. (Ed.). (1996). *Computer-mediated communication: Linguistic, social and cross-cultural perspectives.* Amsterdam: John Benjamins.

Hiskes, Richard P. (1982). *Community without coercion: Getting along in the minimal state.* London: Associated University Presses.

Holeton, Richard. (Ed.). (1997). *Composing cyberspace: Identity, community, and knowledge in the electronic age.* Boston: McGraw-Hill.

Holmes, David. (1997a). Identity and community in cyberspace. In David Holmes (Ed.), *Virtual politics: Identity and community in cyberspace* (pp. 1–25). London: Sage Publications.

_____. (1997b). Virtual identity: Communities of broadcast, communities of interactivity. In David Holmes (Ed.), *Virtual politics: Identity and community in cyberspace* (pp. 26–45). London: Sage Publications.

_____. (Ed.). (1997c). *Virtual politics: Identity and community in cyberspace.* London: Sage Publications.

_____. (2002). Transformations in the mediation of publicness: Communicative interaction in the network society. In *Journal of Computer Mediated Communication,* vol. 7, no. 2, Jan., 1–14 [online] www.ascusc.org/jcmc/vol7/issue2/holmes.html (accessed 7/16/04).

Honneth, Axel. (1995). *The fragmented world of the social: Essays in social and political philosophy.* Charles W. Wright (Ed.). Albany: State University of New York Press.

Ihde, Don. (2002). *Bodies in technology*. Electronic Mediations, Vol. 5. Minneapolis: University of Minnesota Press.

Ingram, David. (1998). The retreat of the political in the modern age: Jean-Luc Nancy on totalitarianism and community. *Research in Phenomenology*, no. 18, 93–124.

James, Paul. (1992). Forms of abstract "community": From tribe and kingdom to nation and state. *Philosophy of the Social Sciences*, vol. 22, no. 3, 313–336.

_____. (1993). What is life like on planet nescafe? *Arena Magazine*, no. 5, 30–34.

_____. (1996). *Nation formation: Towards a theory of abstract community*. London: Sage Publications.

Jameson, Frederic. (1991). *Postmodernism, or, the cultural logic of late capitalism*. London: Verso.

Jones, Steven G. (Ed.). (1995). *Cybersociety: Computer-mediated communication and community*. Thousand Oaks, CA: Sage Publications.

_____. (Ed.). (1998a). *Cybersociety 2.0: Revisiting computer-mediated communication and community*. Thousand Oaks, CA: Sage Publications.

_____. (1998b). Information, internet, and community: Notes towards an understanding of community in the information age. In Steven G. Jones (Ed.), *Cybersociety 2.0: Revisiting computer-mediated communication and community* (pp. 1–34). Thousand Oaks, CA: Sage Publications.

Jordan, Tim. (1999). *Cyberpower: The culture and politics of cyberspace and the Internet*. London: Routledge.

Kamenka, Eugene. (Ed.). (1982). *Community as a social ideal*. London: Edward Arnold.

Kanter, Rosabeth Moss. (1972). *Commitment and community: Communes and utopias in sociological perspective*. Cambridge, MA: Harvard University Press.

Kaplan, Morris B. (1991). Autonomy, equality, community: The question of lesbian and gay rights. *Praxis International*, no. 11, July, 195–213.

Keegan, Victor. (2000). The buzz: When your mobile knows your voice. *The Age*, 1 August, 1–2.

Kennedy, Barbara M. (2000). Introduction II: The virtual machine and new becomings in pre-millennial culture. In David Bell and Barbara M. Kennedy (Eds.), *The cybercultures reader* (pp. 13–24). London: Routledge.

Kiesler, Sara B., & Hinds, Pamela. (1993). Technology, information, and social behaviour. In *The knowledge economy: The nature of information in the twenty-first century*. Nashville, TN: Institute for Information Studies, Northern Telecom Inc., & the Aspen Institute.

Kirkpatrick, Frank G. (1986). *Community: A trinity of models*. Washington, DC: Georgetown University Press.

Kitchin, Rob. (1998). *Cyberspace: The world in the wires*. Chichester, UK: John Wiley & Sons.

Kolko, Beth, Nakamura, Lisa, & Rodman, Gilbert B. (2000). *Race in cyberspace*. New York: Routledge.

Kolko, Beth, & Reid, Elizabeth. (1998). Dissolution and fragmentation: Problems in on-line communities. In Steven G. Jones (Ed.), *Cybersociety 2.0: Revisiting computer-mediated communication and community* (pp. 212–229). Thousand Oaks, CA: Sage Publications.

Kollock, Peter. (1999). The economies of online cooperation: Gifts and public goods in cyberspace. In Marc Smith & Peter Kollock (Eds.), *Communities in cyberspace* (pp. 220–239). London: Routledge.

Kramarae, Cheris. (1998). Feminist fictions of future technology. In Steven G. Jones (Ed.), *Cybersociety 2.0: Revisiting computer-mediated communication and community* (pp. 100–128). Thousand Oaks, CA: Sage Publications.

Kraut, R., Lundmark, V., Patterson, M., Kiesler, S., Mukopadhyay, T., & Scherlis, W. (1998). Internet paradox: A social technology that reduces social involvement and psychological well-being? *American Psychologist*, vol. 53, no. 9, 1017–1031 [online] www.apa.org/journals/amp/amp5391017.html (accessed 7/19/01).

Kristeva, Julia. (1993). *Nations without nationalism*. New York: Columbia University Press.

Kuzweil, Edith. (1980). *The age of structuralism: Levi-Strauss to Foucault*. New York: Columbia University Press.

Lash, Scott. (2001). Technological forms of life. *Theory, Culture & Society*, vol. 18, no. 1, 105–120.

Lenk, Klaus. (1982). Information technology and society. In Adam Schaff & Gunter Friedrichs (Eds.), *Microelectronics and society: For better or for worse* (pp. 273–310). Oxford, UK: Pergamon Press.

Lessig, Lawrence. (1999). *Code and other laws of cyberspace*. New York: Basic Books.

Levin, Hannah. (1980). The struggle for community can create community. In Art Gallaher Jr. & Harland Padfield (Eds.), *The dying community* (pp. 257–277). Albuquerque: University of New Mexico Press.

Liebersohn, Harry. (1988). *Fate and utopia in German sociology, 1870–1923*. Cambridge, MA: MIT Press.

Ling, Rich. (2000). Direct and mediated interaction in the maintenance of social relationships. In A. Sloane and F. van Rijn (Eds.), *Home informatics and telematics: Information, technology and society* (pp. 61–86). Boston: Kluwer.

Lingis, Alphonso. (1994). *The community of those who have nothing in common*. Bloomington: Indiana University Press.

————. (1997). Anger. In Darren Sheppard, Simon Sparks, and Colin Thomas (Eds.), *On Jean-Luc Nancy: The sense of philosophy* (pp. 197–215). London: Routledge.

Loomis, Charles P. (1955). Translator's Introduction. In Ferdinand Tönnies, *Community and Association (Gemeinschaft und Gesellschaft)*, pp. ix–xxvii. Trans. and supplemented by Charles P. Loomis. London: Routledge and Kegan Paul.

Luke, Timothy. (1996). Identity, meaning and globalization: Detraditionalization in postmodern space-time compression. In Paul Heelas, Scott Lash, & Paul Morris (Eds.), *Detraditionalization: Critical reflections on authority and identity* (pp. 109–133). Cambridge, UK: Blackwell Publishers.

Lyon, David. (1994). From big brother to electronic panopticon. From *The electronic eye: The rise of surveillance society*. Minneapolis: University of Minnesota Press [online] www.rochester.edu/College/FS/Publications/Lyon.htm (accessed 7/13/01).

Lyotard, Jean-François. (1989). *The postmodern condition: A report on knowledge* (G. Bennington and B. Massumi, Trans.). Minneapolis: University of Minnesota Press.

MacIntyre, Alistair. (1981). *After virtue: A study in moral theory*. London: Duckworth.

Magner, Denise K. (1991). Probing the imbalance between individual rights, community needs. *Chronicle of Higher Education*, 13 February, A3.

Mansfield, Nick. (2000). *Subjectivity: Theories of the self from Freud to Haraway*. St. Leonards, NSW: Allen & Unwin.

Marcuse, Herbert. (1968). *One Dimensional Man*. London: Sphere Books.

Mauss, Marcel. (1990). *The gift: The form and reason for exchange in archaic societies* (W. D. Hall, Trans.). London: Routledge. [*Essai sur le Don* first published by Presses Universitaires de France in *Sociologies et Anthropologie*, 1950.]

May, Todd. (1993). The community's absence in Lyotard, Nancy and Lacoue-Labarthe, *Philosophy Today*, vol. 37, no. 3, 275–284.

McCoy, Thomas S. (1993). *Voices of difference: Studies in critical philosophy and mass communication*. Creskill, NJ: Hampton Press.

McLuhan, Marshall. (1962). *The Gutenberg galaxy: The making of typographic man*. Toronto: University of Toronto Press.

McLuhan, Marshall, & Fiore, Quentin. (1967). *The medium is the massage*. Harmondsworth, UK: Penguin Books.

McLuhan, Marshall, & Powers, Bruce. (1989). *The global village: Transformations in world life and media in the 21st century*. Oxford, UK: Oxford University Press.

Meyrowitz, Joshua. (1985). *No sense of place*. New York: Oxford University Press.

Morris, Paul. (1996). Community beyond tradition. In Paul Heelas, Scott Lash, & Paul Morris (Eds.), *Detraditionalization: Critical reflections on authority and identity* (pp. 223–249). Cambridge, UK: Blackwell Publishers.

Mulhall, Stephen, & Swift, Adam. (1992). *Liberals and communitarians*. Oxford, UK: Blackwell Publishers.

Mumford, Lewis. (1952). *Art and technics*. London: Oxford University Press.

Myers, Fred. R. (1986). *Pintupi country, Pintupi self: Sentiment, place and politics among Western Desert Aborigines*. Canberra: Australian Institute of Aboriginal Studies.

Nancy, Jean-Luc. (1990). Sharing voices. In Gayle L. Ormiston & Alan D. Schrift (Eds.), *Transforming the hermeneutic context: From Nietzsche to Nancy* (orig. published as *Partage des Voix*). Albany: State University of New York Press.

_____. (1991a). Of being-in-common. In Miami Theory Collective (Eds.), *Community at loose ends* (pp. 1–12). Minneapolis: University of Minnesota Press.

_____. (1991b). *The inoperative community* (P. Connor, Ed.; P. Connor, W. Garbus, M. Holland, S. Sawhney, Trans.). Minneapolis: University of Minnesota Press.

_____. (1992). *La comparution*/The compearance: From the existence of "communism" to the community of "existence" (T. Strong, trans.). *Political Theory*, vol. 20, no. 3, 371–398.

_____. (1993). War, law, sovereignty–*techné* (Jeffrey S. Librett, Trans.). In Verena Andermatt Conley (Ed.), *Rethinking Technologies* (pp. 28–58). Minneapolis: University of Minnesota Press.

_____. (1997). *The sense of the world* (J. Librett, Trans.). Minneapolis: University of Minnesota Press.

_____. (2000). *Being singular plural* (Robert D. Richardson & Anne E. O'Byrne, Trans.). Stanford, CA: Stanford University Press.

Nisbett, Robert A. (1962). *Community and power* (formerly *The quest for community*). New York: Galaxy Books.

Nunes, Mark. (1997). What space is cyberspace? The Internet and virtuality. In David Holmes (Ed.), *Virtual politics: Identity and community in cyberspace* (pp. 163–178). London: Sage Publications.

Ong, Walter J. (1977). *Interfaces of the word: Studies in the evolution of consciousness and culture*. Ithaca, NY: Cornell University Press.

_____. (1982). *Orality and literacy: The technologizing of the word*. London: Methuen & Co.

Ostwald, Michael. (1997). Virtual urban futures. In David Holmes (Ed.), *Virtual politics: Identity and community in cyberspace* (pp. 125–144). London: Sage Publications.

Parsons, Talcott. (1973). Some afterthoughts on *Gemeinschaft* and *Gesellschaft*. In Werner J. Cahnman (Ed.), *Ferdinand Tönnies: A New Evaluation, Essays and Documents* (pp. 151–159). Leiden: E. J. Brill.

Peck, M. Scott. (1987). *The different drum: Community-making and peace*. New York: Simon & Schuster.

Porter, David. (1997). *Internet culture*. New York: Routledge.

Poster, Mark. (1984). *Foucault, Marxism, and history: Mode of production versus mode of information*. Cambridge, UK: Polity Press.

_____. (1989). *Critical theory and poststructuralism: In search of a context*. Ithaca, NY: Cornell University Press.

_____. *Seulemonde*: Conversation with Professor Mark Poster. [online] http://nosferatu.cas.usf.edu/journal/poster/mposter.html (accessed 8/20/01).

_____. (1990). *The mode of information: Poststructuralism and social context*. Oxford: Polity Press.

_____. (1995). *The second media age*. Cambridge: Polity Press.

_____. (1997). Cyberdemocracy: The Internet and the public sphere. In David Holmes (Ed.), *Virtual politics: Identity and community in cyberspace* (pp. 212–228). London: Sage Publications [online] www.humanities.uci.edu/~human/history/faculty/poster_mark/writings/democ.html (accessed 7/15/01).

_____. (2001a). The information subject. *Critical voices in art: Theory and culture*. Commentary by Stanley Aronwitz. Amsteldijk, Netherlands: G+B Arts International.

_____. (2001b). *What's the matter with the Internet?* Minneapolis: University of Minnesota Press.

_____. (2002). Everyday (virtual) life. *New Literary History*, 33(4), 743–760.

Putman, Robert D. (2000). *Bowling Alone: the collapse and revival of American community*. New York: Simon & Schuster.

Rabinow, Paul. (Ed.). (1984). *The Foucault reader*. Harmondsworth, UK: Penguin Books.

Rapp, Friedrich. (1981). *Analytical philosophy of technology* (S. R. Carpenter & T. Langenbruch, Trans). Dordrecht, Netherlands: D. Riedel Publishing,.

Reid, Elizabeth M. (1991). Electropolis: Communication and community on Internet relay chat. Honours Thesis [online] www.aluluei.com (accessed 8/26/01).

Renninger, K. Ann, & Shumar, Wesley. (Eds.). (2002). *Building virtual communities: Learning and change in cyberspace*. Cambridge, UK: Cambridge University Press.

Rheingold, Howard. (1993). *The virtual community: Homesteading on the electronic frontier*. Reading, MA: Addison-Wesley.

Rice, Ronald E. (2002). Artifacts and paradoxes in new media. In D. McQuail (Ed.), *McQuail's reader in mass communication theory* (pp. 125–133). London: Sage.

Rich, Spencer. (1990). Balancing community and individual rights: New journal to examine ethical issues. *Washington Post*, 25 December, A17.

Robins, Kevin. (1995). Cyberspace and the world we live in. In Mike Featherstone & Roger Burrows (Eds.), *Cyberspace/cyberbodies/cyberpunk: Cultures of technological embodiment* (pp. 135–156). London: Sage Publications.

Rose, Nikolas. (1996). Authority and the genealogy of subjectivity. In Paul Heelas, Scott Lash, & Paul Morris (Eds.), *Detraditionalization: Critical reflections on authority and identity* (pp. 294–327). Oxford, UK: Blackwell Publishers.

_____. (1999). *Powers of freedom: Reframing political thought*. Cambridge, UK: Cambridge University Press.

Rosenblum, Nancy L. (Ed.). (1989). *Liberalism and the moral life*. Cambridge, MA: Harvard University Press.

Sandel, Michael. (Ed.). (1984). *Liberalism and its critics*. Oxford, UK: Blackwell Publishers.

Scanlon, Chris. (2000). The network of moral sentiments: The third way and community. *Arena Journal*, New Series, no. 15, 57–80.

Schaff, Adam, & Freidrichs, Gunter. (Eds.). (1982). *Microelectronics and society: For better or for worse*. Oxford, UK: Pergamon Press.

Schutz, Alfred. (1971). *Collected papers II: Studies in social theory* (Arvid Brodersen, Ed.). The Hague: Martinus Nijhoff.

_____. (1972). *The phenomenology of the social world* (G. Walsh & F. Lehnert, Trans.). London: Heinemann Educational Books.

_____. (1973). *Collected papers I: The problem of social reality* (Maurice Natanson, Ed.). The Hague: Martinus Nijhoff.

Selznick, Philip. (1994). Foundations of communitarian liberalism. *The Responsive Community*, vol. 4, no. 4, 16–28.

Shapiro, Andrew L. (1997). Privacy for sale: Peddling data on the Internet. *The Nation* [online] http://past.thenation.com/issue/970623/0623shap.htm (accessed 6/12/01).

Sharp, Geoff. (1985). Constitutive abstraction and social practice. *Arena Journal*, no. 70, 48–82.

————. (1993). Extended forms of the social: Technological mediation and self-formation. *Arena Journal*, New Series, no. 1, 221–237.

————. (2000). Globalization now: Outstripping critical analysis. *Arena Journal*, New Series, no. 15, 101–116.

Sheppard, Darren, Sparks, Simon, & Thomas, Colin. (Eds.). (1997). *On Jean-Luc Nancy: The sense of philosophy*. London: Routledge.

Smith, Marc. (1992). Voices from the WELL: The logic of virtual commons. [online] www.usyd.edu.au/su/social/papers/virtcomm.htm (accessed 8/27/01).

Smith, Marc, & Kollock, Peter. (Eds.). (1999). *Communities in cyberspace*. London: Routledge.

Stapleton, Timothy J. (Ed.). (1994). *The question of hermeneutics: Essays in honor of Joseph J. Kockelmans*. Dordrecht, Netherlands: Kluwer Academic Publications.

Stevenson, Nick. (1995). *Understanding media cultures: Social theory and mass communication*. London: Sage Publications.

Stever, James. (1993). Technology, organization, freedom: The organizational theory of John Dewey. *Administration and Society*, vol. 24, no. 4, 419–443.

Stone, Allucquere Rosanne. (1992). Virtual systems. In Jonathon Crary & Sanford Kwinter (Eds.), *Incorporations: Zone 6* (pp. 609–621). New York: Urzone.

————. (2000). Will the real body please stand up? Boundary stories about virtual cultures. In David Bell & Barbara M. Kennedy (Eds.), *The cybercultures reader* (pp. 504–528). London: Routledge.

Taylor, Charles. (1983). *Social theory as practice*. Oxford: Oxford University Press.

————. (1984). Hegel: History and politics. In Michael Sandel (Ed.), *Liberalism and its critics* (pp. 177–199). Oxford, UK: Blackwell Publishers.

————. (1985a). Atomism. In *Philosophy and the human sciences: Philosophical papers, vol . 2* (pp. 187–210). Cambridge, UK: Cambridge University Press.

————. (1985b). *Human agency and language: Philosophical Papers 1*. Cambridge, UK: Cambridge University Press.

_____. (1989a). Cross purposes: The liberal-communitarian debate. In Nancy Rosenblum (Ed.), *Liberalism and the moral life* (pp. 159–182). Cambridge, MA: Harvard University Press.

_____. (1989b). *Sources of the self: The making of modern identity.* Cambridge, UK: Cambridge University Press.

_____. (1991). *Ethics of authenticity.* Cambridge, MA: Harvard University Press.

_____. (1995). *Philosophical arguments.* Cambridge, MA: Harvard University Press.

_____. (2004). *Modern social imaginaries.* Durham, NC: Duke University Press.

Thompson, John B. (1995). *The media and modernity: A social theory of the media.* Cambridge, UK: Polity Press.

Tirrell, Lynne. (1993). Definition and power: Toward authority without privilege. *Hypatia*, vol. 8, no. 4, 1–34.

Tönnies, Ferdinand. (1955). *Community and association (Gemeinschaft und Gesellschaft).* Trans. and supplemented by Charles P. Loomis. London: Routledge and Kegan Paul.

Turkle, Sherry. (1995). *Life on the screen: Identity in the age of the Internet.* New York: Simon & Schuster.

University of Chicago Press. An interview/dialogue with Albert Borgmann and N. Katherine Hayles on humans and machines [online] www.press.uchicago.edu/Misc/Chicago/borghayl.html (accessed 8/13/01).

Van Den Abbeele, Georges. (1997). Lost horizons and uncommon grounds: For a poetics of finitude in the work of Jean-Luc Nancy. In Darren Sheppard, Simon Sparks, and Colin Thomas (Eds.), *On Jean-Luc Nancy: The sense of philosophy* (pp. 12–18). London: Routledge.

Vidich, Arthur. (1980). Revolutions in community structure. In Art Gallaher Jr. & Harland Padfield (Eds.), *The dying community* (pp. 109–132). Albuquerque: University of New Mexico Press.

Virilio, Paul. (1993). The third interval: A critical transition (Tom Conley, Trans.). In Verena Andermatt (Ed.), *Rethinking technologies* (pp. 3–12). Minneapolis: University of Minnesota Press.

Walker, Michael, Wasserman, Stanley, & Wellman, Barry. (1993). Statistical models for social support networks. *Sociological Methods and Research*, vol. 22, no. 1, 71–97.

Walzer, Michael. (1983). *Spheres of justice: A defense of pluralism and equality.* New York: Basic Books.

Weiss, Gail. (1999). *Body images: Embodiment as intercorporeality.* New York: Routledge.

Wellman, Barry. (2001). Physical place and cyberplace: The rise of personalized networking. *International Journal of Urban and Regional Research*, vol. 25, no. 2, June, 227–252.

Wellman, Barry, & Haythornthwaite, Caroline. (2002). *The Internet in everyday life*. Oxford, UK: Blackwell.

Wellman, B., Quan-Haase, A., Boase, J., Wenhong, C., Hampton, K., Isla de Diaz, I., & Miyata, K. (2003). The social affordances of the Internet for networked individualism. *Journal of Computer Mediated Communication*, Vol. 18 (3). Available: www.ascusc.org/jcmc/vol18/issue3/wellman.html (accessed 9/9/03).

Werry, Christopher C. (1996). Linguistic and interactional features of Internet relay chat. In S. C. Herring (Ed.), *Computer-mediated communication: Linguistic, social and cross-cultural perspectives* (pp. 47–63). Amsterdam: John Benjamins.

White, Stephen. (1991). *Political theory and postmodernism*. Cambridge, UK: Cambridge University Press.

Whitley, Edgar A. (1997). In cyberspace all they see is your words: A review of the relationship between body, behaviour and identity drawn from the sociology of knowledge. *Information Technology and People*, vol. 10, no. 2, 147–163.

Willson, Michele. (1995). Community: Compelling solution? *Arena Magazine*, no. 15, Feb/Mar., 25–27.

_____. (1997). Community in the abstract: A political and ethical dilemma? In David Holmes (Ed.), *Virtual politics: Identity and community in cyberspace* (pp. 145–162). London: Sage Publications.

_____. (2001). Community with(out) others. *Mots Pluriel*, no. 18, August [online] www.arts.uwa.edu.au/MotsPluriels (accessed 9/20/01).

Wittel, Andreas. (2001). Toward a network sociality. *Theory, Culture and Society*, vol. 18, no. 6, 51–76.

Woolley, Benjamin. (1992). *Virtual worlds: A journey in hype and hyperreality*. Oxford, UK: Blackwell Publishers.

Young, Iris Marion. (1990). *Justice and the politics of difference*. Princeton, NJ: Princeton University Press.

_____. (1992). Together in difference: Transforming the logic of group political conflict. *Political Theory Newsletter*, no. 4, 11–126.

Index

General Editor: Steve Jones

Digital Formations is an essential source for critical, high-quality books on digital technologies and modern life. Volumes in the series break new ground by emphasizing multiple methodological and theoretical approaches to deeply probe the formation and reformation of lived experience as it is refracted through digital interaction. **Digital Formations** pushes forward our understanding of the intersections—and corresponding implications—between the digital technologies and everyday life. The series emphasizes critical studies in the context of emergent and existing digital technologies.

Other recent titles include:

Leslie Shade
 Gender and Community in the Social Construction of the Internet

John T. Waisanen
 Thinking Geometrically

Mia Consalvo & Susanna Paasonen
 Women and Everyday Uses of the Internet

Dennis Waskul
 Self-Games and Body-Play

David Myers
 The Nature of Computer Games

Robert Hassan
 The Chronoscopic Society

M. Johns, S. Chen, & G. Hall
 Online Social Research

C. Kaha Waite
 Mediation and the Communication Matrix

Jenny Sunden
 Material Virtualities

Helen Nissenbaum & Monroe Price
 Academy and the Internet

To order other books in this series please contact our Customer Service Department:
 (800) 770-LANG (within the US)
 (212) 647-7706 (outside the US)
 (212) 647-7707 FAX
To find out more about the series or browse a full list of titles, please visit our website:
 WWW.PETERLANGUSA.COM